D0719014

ACHIEVERS

Also by Ivor Kenny

Industrial Democracy
The Atlantic Management Study
Government & Enterprise in Ireland
*In Good Company**
*Out On Their Own**
Boardroom Practice
*Talking to Ourselves**
The Death of Shibboleths
Freedom & Order
*Leaders**
Can You Manage?

* Books in this series

ACHIEVERS

VISIONARY IRISH LEADERS
WHO ACHIEVED THEIR DREAM

With best wishes

Ivor Kenny

Ivor Kenny

Published by
OAK TREE PRESS
19 Rutland Street, Cork, Ireland
www.oaktreepress.com

© 2005 Ivor Kenny

A catalogue record of this book is
available from the British Library.

ISBN 1 904887 03 1

Printed in Ireland by ColourBooks.

As always for
Maureen
and the family,
with a special welcome for
Christopher John (2005).

Contents

Acknowledgements

My warm thanks to:

- The leaders who wrote this book with me;
- An old friend, Tony Barry, who wrote the introduction for the Tom Roche chapter;
- Joe Gilmartin, a friend since college days, who unerringly spots flaws in logic or English;
- Gillian Acton, my friend and colleague in UCD for 18 years;
- My respected publisher, Brian O'Kane of Oak Tree Press, supportive and understanding.

We have tomorrow
Bright before us
Like a flame

Yesterday
A night-gone thing,
A sun-down name,

And dawn today.

*

LANGSTON HUGHES
The Dream Keeper
1932

INTRODUCTION

With the exception of the three academics and Ken Whitaker, the participants in the book have ended up rich, some seriously rich. That was not the criterion by which they were chosen. They were chosen (a) because they had a dream, or purpose, or vision and (b) because they had achieved it.

On November 15, 1987, following the publication of the first book in this series, I was invited on to one of the first *Sunday Shows* on RTÉ Radio. In charge was a young Richard Crowley, recently our man in Israel, calm and intelligent (unlike some of his prolix colleagues). When I entered the studio, I was convinced I was being set up. There was the gossip columnist, Terry Keane, and Eamonn McCann from the far left. I thought Keane might be helpful. I braced myself for McCann.

Crowley began with a smart question: "Would you say this was a *nice* book?" I countered with a smart reply, "Why? Did you want me to write a nasty one?"

Keane pounced: "Why are your questions not in the text? Why do you hide them?"

I said, "I gave a couple of chapters to my family to read – one with questions, one without. They were unanimous that questions were interruptions, that the chapters read better without them. The reader would be focused only on the subject. The interviewer was unimportant."

Keane said, "Well, you should not have listened to your family." The relationship deteriorated. McCann intervened, "This is a great book! Now we see how the minds of fellows like Smurfit work – that's invaluable."

There is a distinct change from the spoken to the written word, more so when the questions or interjections (which, in any event, are few and far between) are eliminated as superfluous. Some participants are embarrassed at what they feel reads like an ego trip. People can't tell their stories without liberal use of the first person singular and, anyway, you, the reader will form your own judgment. This was a particular phenomenon with the four preceding volumes, where every reader I met had a different "favourite" chapter – and where those who knew well the participants had their likes and, particularly, dislikes reinforced with even-handed prejudice. Books like this do not change embedded views.

There cannot be achievement without its shadow, failure. Winston Churchill said that success was the ability to go from one failure to another with no loss of enthusiasm.

To the participants, laying blame for failure would be a waste of time. Brody Sweeney says company reports can blame external forces for a bad year, instead of the fact that "the management had made a dog's dinner of the business". Dogs' dinners, outrageous fortune, a thousand natural shocks were obstacles to be removed in pursuit of a clear objective. They may have shaken the men and women in the book but they did not knock them off course.

Business strategy has accumulated a number of old saws such as, "If you don't know where you're going, any road will get you there" or the oft-quoted *Proverbs 29,18*: "Where there is no vision, the people perish". When I had the temerity to "teach" strategy (you can't *teach* strategy), I would define it as the step-by-step removal of constraints set against a vision of some ultimate objective. It was not a bad definition to be getting on with and, since we're on a biblical roll, the participants in this book possessed the "faith that could remove mountains." Obstacles can look like mountains when you face them. When you've overcome them, they shrink. The worst, the panic-stricken, moment in implementing strategy is when you don't know what to do next, but it was the basic faith in themselves that brought these men and women through dark nights of the soul, a faith that removed the mountains. Philip Lynch says, "The lesson all of this taught me was to hang in there, to have faith. I suppose I had confidence in an ability to see beyond the crisis."

The book celebrates success and I hope adds a little to our understanding of why some people are successful.

In the dark days of 1984, I wrote: "We Irish find it hard to stomach success. We rejoice in failure. Our never speaking well of one another may be near the truth. Our disagreements are rarely *ad rem* but mostly *ad hominem*. There is an unwillingness to concede the good faith of the other person. Our society is not one which rewards what is new and different."[1]

That has changed but it has not changed utterly. Dermot Desmond still talks about the "valley of the squinting windows".

Our growing self-confidence has been paralleled by a universal dumbing-down. My father, a journalist, worked under C.P. Scott, editor of the *Manchester Guardian*. Scott famously said, "Comment is free, but facts are sacred". There was a time when you could assume that an intelligent person looking for truth would find obvious the fallaciousness of the *ad hominem* argument. The embarrassment you would feel if you invoked such arguments was sufficient to stop you doing so. We can no longer make this assumption. Even if we continue to assume that we are dealing with intelligent people, we cannot believe that they are acting on an impulse to find the truth. The purpose of their "truth" is to satisfy psychological and ideological needs, not its concordance with reality. Whether incompetence or deceitfulness is to blame is neither here nor there – we end up with, if not misinformation and fallacy, a pottage of overwritten nonsense that is a restatement of the trivial and the obvious.

Aquinas's definition of truth was *adequatio intellectus et rei*, i.e. an exact correspondence between perception and reality. However, we only know something within given horizons. Hence all human knowledge of truth is one-sided. No human statement can be taken as definitive. The disclosure of truth is a process of dialogue.

This liberating definition is from Karl Rahner and others in *Sacramentum Mundi*.[2] (It was, at least to me, a far cry from the more pontifical statements with which we are familiar.)

How could we ever do justice to the words used in court: "The truth, the whole truth and nothing but the truth"? They mock our clumsy efforts even to remember and convey our experiences, never mind the barriers created by our many social dependencies. We like to please, to be thought well of, to avoid hurt, to have a quiet life, to stay inside our intellectual comfort zones. We are not Yeats's swift indifferent men. Add to that the fact that much of what is inside our heads is *mediated*.

---

[1]   *Government & Enterprise in Ireland*, pp. 17/18.
[2]   (1970), New York: Herder & Herder, Vol. 6.

Janus-like the media face two ways: telling the truth and pleasing their market. There is no getting away from that latter dependency. It will not be denied by lofty arguments about journalistic standards, or taste, or vulgarity or dumbing-down. That is simply to shift the argument onto other ground and, in any event, my standards may not be yours. The whole truth is out of reach in the media, in work organisations, even in the family.

Contemporary social critics too often speak from their own despair or a kind of cynical chic that betrays their sense of impotence. Optimism is in poor taste. What seems to be concern is frequently self-indulgence.

We should never believe our own propaganda. It might help to apply to our own lapidary words the same astringent eye we apply to the pomposities of others. Since none of us can ever possess the whole truth, it might help to listen a little more carefully and to commit occasionally the indiscretion of changing our minds.

Can we get the "whole truth" about the people in this book, can we know *all* about them? As well ask them to confess their sins publicly. Nobody has the right to prise open people's lives. It was Asmodeus, the King of Demons, who went about lifting the roofs of people's houses. Which of us has never told a lie or cut a corner? To quote *Proverbs 29,11*: "A fool uttereth all his mind".

They are all different. It would hardly be possibly to put between the covers a wider variety of businesses, backgrounds and personalities.

All of them work hard, continuously. And they don't want to stop. The grail beckons, leading them on because, as in the fable of the frog and the scorpion, it's in their nature.

Unlike St. Paul's vision on the road to Damascus, for some "the heavens never opened for the spirit to descend on me".[3] For several the vision came clearer as the journey progressed and the lights on the car picked out the road ahead. Pádraig Ó Céidigh, after his Christmas dinner, "stepped into a dream" on a half-finished air-strip in Connemara (now a relaxed Carnmore Regional Airport).

---

[3]   Michael Smurfit, *In Good Company* (1987), p. 200.

From recent international studies, we have the chilling fact that two-thirds of the people in leadership positions in the Western world will fail.[4] They will then be fired, demoted or kicked upstairs.

The most common reason for their failure is their inability to build or maintain a team.

Everyone in the book built enduring teams. Most also had a small number of trusted advisers – but made up their own minds. Some had a capacity for many friendships, reflected in the team sports they chose. Others were a bit solitary with just a few intimate friends.

They were never all over the place. They never made promises they could not keep. Their distinguishing characteristic was not an approach or reaction to the world. It was how they perceived the world. Visionary leaders see things differently from the rest of us.

The thing they had in common was the ability to focus exclusively and unremittingly on their ultimate objective. Time for me to get out of the way and let them talk.

Ivor Kenny
University College Dublin
August 2005

---

4   Enoch Powell is often misquoted as saying "All politics end in failure". What he actually said was, "All political lives, unless they are cut off in midstream at a happy juncture, end in failure, because that is the nature of politics and of human affairs". Effective leaders don't hang around. They know when to let go.

1

LORD BALLYEDMOND
EDDIE HAUGHEY

NORBROOK

*If you don't have a vision, it's very difficult to have a
starting point. A vision is a dream. If you don't bring a
dream to realisation, then it's an hallucination.*

LORD BALLYEDMOND, EDWARD HAUGHEY, is Chairman and Managing Director of Norbrook Laboratories Limited and Norbrook Holdings. There are 11 companies in the Group.

He was born in Co. Louth on January 5, 1944. His father was Edward Haughey, a company director. His mother was Rose Traynor, a housewife. He was the youngest in a family of three: one boy and two girls.

He is married to Mary Gordon-Young, a solicitor. They have three children: Caroline, Edward and James.

He is also Chairman/Managing Director of Ballyedmond Research Farm, Corby Castle Estate, Haughey Air, Haughey Airports Limited and is a director of Bombardier Shorts plc.

A Peer of the Realm, he sits on the cross benches in the House of Lords, London.

He is a member of the Inter-Parliamentary Union – British Group, Palace of Westminster.

He was a member of the Irish Senate from 1994 to 2002, where he was a front bench spokesman on Northern Ireland.

He was a member of the Forum for Peace & Reconciliation and is a member of the Parliamentary Committee on Foreign Affairs and of the British Irish Inter-Parliamentary Body.

He was Chairman of the Irish Aviation Authority from 1993 to 1994.

He has a number of honorary doctorates and is an Honorary Fellow of the Royal College of Surgeons in Ireland. He is a Fellow of the International Academy of Management.

Among his *pro bono* appointments are trustee of the Royal College of Veterinary Surgeons, London, trustee of Dublin City University, member of the Board of the Institute for British-Irish Studies, a director of Armagh Observatory, member of the Board of University College Dublin Foundation, member of the International Development Board of the RCSI, and chairman of the Pharmacy Development Board of the RCSI.

Among previous appointments, he was a director of Bank of Ireland, Northern Advisory Board, 1986 to 1999.

Apart from the peerage, his honours include an OBE for services to industry, Honorary Consul for Chile, *Gran Oficial* of the Order of

Bernardo O'Higgins (Chile) and Permanent Vice-President of the Anglo Chilean Society. He is a Justice of the Peace.

*I*n Out On Their Own *(1991), Lord Ballyedmond, Eddie Haughey, said, "The end is never near. If you get to the end, you've had it". Yet, in this short chapter, he says publicly (for the first time that I know of) that he intends to retire in four years. With the greatest respect to an old friend, I find that hard to believe. Eddie Haughey is Norbrook. He built it from nothing to its present eminence. He may retire physically but hardly mentally.*

In 1967, he set up his company, bought some veterinary products from friends in Holland, put his own label on them and sold them locally. He had also decided to go into the medical field, but found you could "use a hell of a sight more penicillin on animals than you would on humans". Now Norbrook has a turnover in excess of £150m sterling, employs 1,100 people and has expanded across the globe. The company has won four Queen's Awards for Export.

Lord Ballyedmond is unique in being appointed to the upper houses of both parliaments on these islands – as a senator in the Republic and as a peer in the House of Lords.[5] His maiden speech in the Lords was acclaimed. He rejoices in his honours and, because he lives in Northern Ireland, has avoided sneers at his ennoblement from the usual begrudgers in the Republic.

He is tough and shrewd, a generous friend and an hilarious story-teller. For this conversation, I sat back and listened, because, as you will see, he asked and answered his own questions.

He lives with Mary, his wife, a practising solicitor, in Ballyedmond Castle on the shores of Carlingford Lough at the foothills of the Mourne mountains. He designed and completely rebuilt Ballyedmond "with more taste than economy", having read and studied and seen the models. He has another castle in Cumbria and a house on Fitzwilliam Square, Dublin.

---

[5] A note for purists: The Sixth Marquis of Lansdowne in 1927 had a right to sit in the House of Lords as an Hereditary Peer, while a senator in the Irish Free State.

The conversation was recorded in Lord Ballyedmond's office at Norbrook Laboratories, Station Works, Newry, Co. Down, on February 10, 2005.

Lord Ballyedmond's biography is in *Out On Their Own* (1991).

Lord Ballyedmond
Eddie Haughey

In every company, there's a gestation period from the time it began until it really takes off. Norbrook, as it is today, really took off in the 1980s. If you don't have a vision, it's very difficult to have a starting point. A vision is a dream. If you don't bring a dream to fruition, to realisation, then it's an hallucination. You must always sit down and come to terms with yourself and ask yourself the question, "Can I deliver?" If you can convince yourself that you can deliver, then you start out to do so.

We all approach it in different ways. Some of us start at the end and work in a sequence. Some of us may start at the beginning, work to a point and then jump almost to the end. We all have these different approaches, different personalities, and different techniques.

My technique is to think laterally, with a focus on the issue. When you solve the issue, then you add the detail. The issue could be that I want to turn over £100m. The reason I arrive at £100m is because the total market is £250m.

I have enormous respect for my late mother. She always said to me, "You will hear a lot of bees in your lifetime but you may not see a lot of honey."

If you're going to succeed, you have to be good enough to judge those who can deliver, either deliver for you or with you.

I have heard many different definitions of a manager and a leader. I believe you have to be both. You have to bring people along with you, on the one hand, but, on the other, you must see and achieve the goal. They are synergistic. It takes a special person to surmount the many obstacles you meet.

I meet some pleasant people and some not so pleasant. A key to success is that I do not dwell on either. I adopt the policy of forgive your enemies but never forget their names. I then continue on, focused, to achieve the goal. When you adopt a focused approach, some will say it's uncaring; others will interpret it as ruthless. Others will call you a fool who ignores the risks.

When people ask me if I am an entrepreneur, I ask them what they mean. For me, to deserve the title entrepreneur, you must have succeeded. I have never yet met an entrepreneur who failed. A failed entrepreneur is an oxymoron.

I came, not from humble, but from modest beginnings. I like to say that I am a modest man but that I was never humble. At this time when I'm talking to you, I am deemed by others to have risen to the heights in business. They measure that by my ennoblement. I have to tell them that they are wrong. There are many broken lords around. I met a man recently who told me that he was an OAFNB. When I asked what that meant, he said, "An old aristocratic family nouveau broke". I don't believe that, if you go around carrying a title, it gives you immunity from the vigour of the bank manager or those who want to take away from you what you have. It's the opposite of armour plating.

Norbrook is now on the crest of a wave. This is for two reasons. One, good luck on my part. Two, I made some good decisions. I won't say good judgment – I can't say whether I made those decisions from judgment or whether they just evolved in my mind in the prevailing circumstances. We are now the largest in the world at what we do, the manufacture of veterinary pharmaceuticals and the chemical synthesis of the raw materials that produces these pharmaceuticals.

Our conversation for the first, 1991, book acted as a catalyst for me. I had to ask myself if I could really achieve what I was saying to Ivor Kenny. It gave me great pleasure when you took just now from your briefcase a copy of the book and told me that much of what I had said had come to pass. What I said to you in those days flowed naturally and without a great deal of deep thought. Since then, those recorded thoughts of mine have caused me to ponder and to analyse and it's good to be sitting here today and saying yes, a lot of them did come to pass.

Norbrook is in a very competitive market. A lot of people tell me that the competition in the future will come from Asia. That may well be so but I consider it good. We have here the knowledge, the expertise and the head-start. If we work just that little bit harder, and we can lobby governments to give us sensible fiscal systems, then I feel we can compete easily with our Asian counterparts.

I intend to continue with Norbrook as it is now on the path that I began. I shall continue for at least three years. I have proved that we can grow indigenously at 20% per annum. However, on this very day I have completed an acquisition in the Czech Republic. That will give me entry into an exclusive market for anaesthetic for veterinary, medical and dental use. Our product is the only one that is licensed by the European Community and the FDA in the United States. Those markets represent 80% of the commercially desirable world market. It's not easy to find niches that give you exclusivity. All the legislation is against that. I hope to be able to continue with this product for from three to five years, and then enhance a molecule to give it additional value.

As you sat down, my secretary handed me a press release quoting the Taoiseach, Bertie Ahern, who had just spoken of a company in the Republic of Ireland which has announced a specific advance on an AIDS drug. Norbrook is the sole supplier of an active ingredient for that project. Let's hope it will be successful – it's a long way off and we have to wait and evaluate it.

I have to look to the future and judge where Norbrook and I are going. A lot of the wealth in the world is controlled from the Middle East. Now, a lot of wealth in the world is controlled by the population of India. How many multinationals are controlled by these two cultures? Very few. Why? In both cultures, they tend not to trust the outsider and to use their own families. The Americans tend to use everybody else – but they put the systems in to try to ensure that those who are working for them are transparently accountable.

There are difficulties with the American system. It is bureaucratic and pyramidal. It inhibits the individual from making a decision. It discourages initiative. But you must balance that against the possibility of making a foolish and costly decision. For the next two years, I'd like to focus on a programme that accommodates both, with new technology, new means of communication, a new attitude, and with better education.

I read a lot about training programmes. I listen to lectures from gifted individuals. I attend lectures by skilled advocates. But I have yet to meet anybody who can create the entrepreneur or the manager if the basic material is not there. I see those seminars as a useful aid, cream on the cake, but the cake must be there in the first instance.

I often wonder where that cake comes from. Is it baked through birth and rearing? Is it environmental or genetic? These are old questions. I believe it's a combination of all these, with a large input from people who mould, control and develop our personalities.

The veterinary pharmaceutical industry – and indeed the medical pharmaceutical industry – will change dramatically over the next five years. Development will become more difficult. The authentication of efficacy and safety will become more onerous. The goal posts will move. Legislation will make it more difficult to generate innovative data without validation and revalidation. We could get into a regulated situation where negligence in not evaluating correctly the data that have been generated could become a criminal offence. What do I mean by that? The law might very well say you are qualified in the subject, you are deemed to be skilled in the art, because we have licensed you. Now, the obligation on you is to get it right. You are not legally entitled to make a mistake. That is the worry.

Where is the licensing system throughout Europe going? We know that Europe is never very far behind the United States in licensing and regulation. One thing is sure. Environmental is going to be a serious issue.

Let's move on to Norbrook in the future. I am now 61 years old. I have three children: two lawyers and a medic. They are at a crossroads in their lives. One son is 26, the other is 24. They have to decide whether to enter the business with me or pursue their own careers. Even at this juncture, all three of them – including my daughter, who is a barrister in London – have been successful.

Of course, I would like the boys to join me in the business. Let me tell you why. First, I would like to perpetuate the business. Secondly, in your life you create a certain amount of assets. It takes a lot of money to maintain these assets. I don't think any profession nowadays would generate enough money to maintain them – there has to be another source of income. Therefore, I would encourage them either to come right into the business or to be involved in it in some way to further the business and protect the assets acquired in my lifetime.

What have I achieved in my lifetime? It's there in my CV. And I'll let you into a secret. I intend to retire from Norbrook at age 65. I always got great joy from writing. People have asked me, "Eddie, if you write, what would you write about?" I avoid answering, simply because I don't think you can say what kind of writing you would enjoy until you start into it.

I was asked, "What kind of person are you, Eddie? Could you describe yourself?". That's not an easy question. I responded by saying that I was elated by success and educated by failure. I have had failures and I have had many successes. I hope that, in the next phase of my life, I will derive as much joy from writing as I have got from my business life.

I was asked what the key to my success is. The true answer is that I don't know. What I *can* say is this: to succeed, you need stability. Stability starts with your parents, with your wife, with your family. Stability continues in your everyday business. I need many advisers. Business these days calls on the law, on the accountants, on the scientists, on the administrators. And, if you were to ask me again, what the key to success is, I would say that it is to use everybody's expertise and collate it, focused on what you wish to achieve.

I have been asked how my subordinates see me as a manager. There is no clear, definitive answer. Some of them enjoy me, some of them resent me, indeed one or two of them loathe me. If you were to measure my management style on a scale of aggression from 1 to 10, I'd say that today I could be 1 and tomorrow 9. I have a very good team of people that I have developed over the years. But loyalty lasts only as long as there is respect. From day one, you must earn the respect of your subordinates. How do you get that respect if you can't match them in your knowledge of their specific expertise? That's not necessary, if you analyse what they have to offer, and they can see that you are going to apply *their* knowledge to what *you* want to achieve. That will command respect. That's what management is all about: the application of expertise, all brought together and focused on achieving the objective.

Northern Ireland has had a long sad history of violence, of lack of understanding and of hatred. A lot of the hatred has come from lack of understanding or indeed from invincible ignorance, not *wanting* to understand. We can all become tranquillised, intoxicated, in our own little cocoons and not wish to understand another's position.

Where do we go now? Northern Ireland has come a long way. Nine years ago, any outsider would say Northern Ireland had the franchise on terrorism. That is no more. Terrorism is now a universally dirty word. I'm sad to have to say that the dreadful events of 9/11 had, on Northern Ireland, a beneficial effect. It brought home to people the scourge of terrorism. There is little organised violence at present. What violence we do have is related largely to criminal, rather than political, activity. I believe this will continue for the next five years.

But I see, out of all this, the evolution of democratic, inclusive government. It will evolve from the middle-of-the-road parties. The far right and the far left will have to learn that they must move closer to the centre.

Northern Ireland is a small province, 1.5m people. The Republic can no longer be regarded as a subject of ridicule, as not being a suitable partner. The far-sighted governance of Ireland for the past 20 years has been an example to the rest of the world. I believe the Irish Government, and the UK Government, will together play a crucial part in making Northern Ireland a harmonious State. A devolved government in Northern Ireland is the irrefutable solution. The question of a united Ireland has become less important. What we need are a united people. Paramilitarism hurts many people. We don't have to be very bright to know that it can't be sustained. It will no longer be tolerated. Our younger people are increasingly better educated and will not be persuaded by old, emotive arguments. In 10 years' time, we shall have a united people in Northern Ireland, competing commercially in a healthy, civilised manner with the Republic. They will be partners where necessary.

Northern Ireland is now an integral part of Europe. Europe replaces the British Empire. Business in Northern Ireland is now widely spread. In the past, there was only one major customer, the UK mainland. Now the customer is global. Does business follow the flag? I don't think the flag is relevant any more in business. Business will follow where the money is available. The money will be available where the economy is right. The economy will come right, when all the segments are coming together. Competition in the future will be transatlantic and/or from across the Indian Ocean and China. There will be three major players in the world: Europe with Russia, the United States, and Asia.

2

DENIS BROSNAN

KERRY GROUP

There's a difference between believing in yourself and being dictatorial. If you don't absolutely believe in the ability of yourself with your colleagues to achieve a vision, then it can't happen. The day you stop believing is the day you no longer climb the mountain

DENIS BROSNAN was the founder and head of the Kerry Group plc. He resigned as Managing Director in December 2000 and continued as Chairman of the company until August 2003.

He was born in Tralee, Co. Kerry, on November 19, 1944, the youngest in a family of two boys and one girl.

His father was Daniel Brosnan, a farmer; his mother, Mary Breen, a primary school teacher in London, prior to her marriage.

He was educated at St. Brendan's College, Killarney, and at University College, Cork, where he completed a Master's Degree in Dairy Science.

He was married in 1970 to Joan McNamara. They have two sons and two daughters: Cathal, Aimée, Paul and Mary.

He has long been associated with racing. He runs a stud farm in Croom, Co. Limerick. He was appointed by the Government as Chairman of the Racing Board in 1990 to help plan the future for Irish racing. He played a key role in the establishment of the Irish Horseracing Authority in 1994 and has been its Chairman since that time. He has played a key role also in the establishment of Horseracing Ireland, which will take over the activities of the Irish Horseracing Authority and also certain duties now carried out by the Irish Turf Club.

He is Chairman of Leisure Holdings plc and its associate companies, which has investments in bloodstock, leisure and the healthcare sector (Barchester Healthcare), both in Ireland and in the UK.

He is Chairman of Friends First, part of Eureko NV Group, which is developing a major pan-European financial services group.

He is Chairman of the Board of Management of the Conway Institute of Biomolecular & Biomedical Research.

He is keenly interested in all sport, including gaelic football, soccer and golf.

I first met Denis Brosnan in Parknasilla following the 1985 IMI National Conference in Killarney. He asked me if I'd left the IMI. I said, "Four years ago". He said, "We'll have dinner in the Park Hotel in Kenmare tomorrow night". He drove us at a hair-raising pace on the twisty road in a worn BMW.

A few months later, I found myself addressing the Kerry Annual Management Conference. Kerry conferences are very hard work. It must have been a relief to see a slot marked, "Talk. Ivor Kenny.", during which the troops could have a quiet doze. Denis's introduction was, "This is Ivor Kenny. I suppose ye know him. He'll be working with us for the next year." The audience woke up.

That was the beginning of a happy and productive relationship – I conducted three major studies of the Kerry Group, in 1985, 1988/89, and in 2000 when the Group had greatly expanded. In 1998, two independent directors were appointed to the Board: Michael Dowling, a former Secretary General of the Department of Agriculture, and myself.

When I first went to work with Kerry, a very senior banker said to me, "That's a one-man band, isn't it?". A moment's thought would have stopped him fantasising that an organisation which even then was big, complex and political could be run like a village shop, never mind the leading multinational it is today. Denis Brosnan cast a long shadow, but Kerry was not a monolith. The major divisions have a high degree of autonomy. It is the key ingredient in their energy and enthusiasm. There is a corps of over 80 senior managers. They come in all shapes, sizes and nationalities. To a greater or lesser extent, they share the predominant Kerry characteristic: the will to win.

Denis Brosnan said, "It never struck me that something could not be done". (Martin Rafferty[6] said of him, "There was Denis Brosnan with his back to the sea".)

---

[6] *Out On Their Own* (1991).

This chapter illustrates an abiding characteristic of visionary entrepreneurial leaders. They never stop. Denis Brosnan mentions the milestones on Kerry's path but you can sense the impatience as he wants to get on to what he's doing now.

The old story, Kerry, and the new story, Barchester Healthcare, are interwoven in the chapter: "What's my target today? We have a healthcare company which is worth £1bn sterling. Our five-year target is to get it up to about twice that size. At that point, I hope I can say we have built two Kerrys in 35 years – 30 years for one and five years the other."

The conversation was recorded in the author's office in UCD, on March 8, 2005.

Denis Brosnan's biography is in *In Good Company* (1987). For a comprehensive history of the Kerry Group, 1972-2000, see James J. Kennelly (2001), *The Kerry Way*, Dublin: Oak Tree Press.

DENIS BROSNAN

Kerry did two things in 1982. We bought into consumer foods, non-milk – Denny's and Duffy's. That same year, we set up overseas offices to start maximising our raw material, milk, trying to add value to it. Finbarr O'Driscoll was sent to Chicago and Michael Griffin to London. They were the big changes in the early 80s. The need for the plc arose out of these developments. We needed money to buy, and equal, the companies we saw out there. We needed a structure beyond a co-operative. The plc emerged. The first eight years or so from 1972 were the hardest slog. In those years, we thought we might be just another co-operative like Dairygold, Mitchelstown, Golden Vale, Avonmore. Our ambition was to be as good as them.

With disease eradication in 1979, we got hit with 20% of our milk supply disappearing. We had to do something. That something brought us new geography and new products. Consumer foods did not need milk as a raw material. The geography took us to America and all the places that followed. Each step took five to seven years and led logically to the next.

So on from 1981/82 and the purchase of Beatrice in 1988. We had seen the opportunity in the US market – a future in food ingredients as distinct from dairy products. Instead of trying to track the smallest player around, we decided we'd focus on who was the biggest player. Beatrice was the number one supplier of ingredients into the food industry. It was more or less in play. A New York venture capitalist company bought the Beatrice organisation to break it up. They took the view that the value of the parts would be far greater than Beatrice as a whole. This was music to our ears. We had a chance to buy the piece that we wanted. That moved us into the plc in 1986 and we were keeping our eye on the ball of Beatrice. It moved through various hands. We kept ourselves focused on buying the right company in the right marketplace. That was a huge milestone for Kerry. That brought us not only to the USA but also to other parts of the world, as Beatrice had agents and sales-forces in many countries – in South America and eastwards in Taiwan and the whole Asian region. Beatrice had a presence in the Middle East and in Australia. It was not a huge presence everywhere but it gave us a very good knowledge of the markets. It's now 17 years and they are still the markets that are being developed today. That had its own momentum.

At that time, Kerry was valued on the Irish market at about £120m. We bought Beatrice for $135m with a conversion rate of 1.20. We bought something our own size. Kerry has a market cap of €3.6bn today. Buying Beatrice would be like Kerry buying something today at €3.6bn value. It was a big step but it worked out and we never looked back. Then there were other big steps along the way. To gain a significant presence in consumer foods, we bought Mattessons Wall's from Unilever in 1992. We bought DCA for almost £300m in 1994. We bought Dalgetty for about £400m in 1998. In between were lots of small acquisitions. There was plenty to be bought and Kerry was always there to buy them. Kerry would still be buying two or three acquisitions a month. The world is now the marketplace. You have to be there for the big ones as well.

By December 2001, I had given 30 years to Kerry. For a lot of reasons, it was enough. One reason was that I did not want to travel the world any more every month. I came to the view that I could not drive the Kerry organisation as hard as I would like. The footprint was created – Kerry was on all the continents. Kerry had one of the best executive teams of any company we were competing with. They were well ready to carry it on. I had started at 27 and finished at 57.

There was another reason at the back of my mind – in 1993, a group of friends had come together to invest in whatever areas we saw worthwhile in that year. One area was nursing care, Barchester Healthcare. There were about 200 shareholders involved, some large and some small. Even though it had its own management structure in the UK, I could never give the project enough of my time.

I often wondered if the skills I had learned in Kerry – strategy, capability, clarity – could be transferred into another business. In January 2002, Barchester Healthcare had 1,200 operating beds in the UK – a small company with about 20 nursing homes. We had a vision that, within a five-year timeframe, we could turn it into an enterprise that was as big as the Kerry Group, say €3.5bn to €4bn turnover. Three years on and we're now the most significant operator in the UK in care beds. We care for everybody from the three-month-old going to the crèche to the 103-years-old suffering from Alzheimer's, and everybody in between.

What has been proven is that the same drivers are needed for success. It's true for that business and for any other business. What do you need? A vision, a strategy and how to get there. You need capital, capability, clarity and responsibility.

I have said to senior management, "Just write down the six key things you are responsible for in 2005 and concentrate on them". We agree on the targets and then everyone must stay absolutely focused on them. If you have people all focused in the same direction, then you'll have an organisation that will succeed.

It just shows that whether you're in the food sector or in the care sector or wherever you are, you just practise the same disciplines.

The old definition of the difference between leadership and management is that leadership is doing the right things and management is doing them right. If you start off doing the wrong things, it doesn't matter how good your management is because they can never correct it. You have to start with a vision and then develop a strategy of how you're going to get there. Care is a major growth area. There are a whole lot of segments we haven't entered at all as yet. With life-spans increasing, it means people are working longer. It was traditional in Ireland that you retired at 65, though in the USA you work until you are much older. When everybody is at work, you *need* a culture of care. People will pay for care so long as it doesn't interfere with their work routine.

Back in the '70s and '80s, young people would give their right arm to join Kerry. If you worked hard, you'd progress hugely and see the world. It got very different as we moved into the '90s. Those coming from the third-level colleges wanted to see what the career opportunities were. They had several different options and they were weighing them up. They also felt that Ireland was now such an exciting place that they didn't want to see the world any more. They would not be particularly attracted to being sent off to Asia. Everything changed in that period. Graduates knew themselves and the opportunities and were far more assertive.

I still believe that a charismatic leader will get the maximum from these people. In Kerry, we got the maximum out of people at every point in time. We got them to buy into the dream. When Kerry went plc in 1986, we pioneered things like share ownership and options. But it was still very small compared with what's there today. In today's world, there is a far greater demand for ownership.

I still think you could build a Kerry today but you would have to do it in today's environment and not the environment where we succeeded in in the '70s and '80s.

How many people go to work thinking how dull and boring their job is? They don't realise they're part of a vision. In Kerry, in 1986, there was share ownership for all employees. It then accounted for 3% of the company. Today, the norm is about 15%. Wherever the person was – they all had some shares. It was very new then. Now it has been perfected and moved on.

I suppose I had a big following in my time and we all lived and practised the dream. Everybody in the organisation must believe in and understand that vision and understand their part in achieving it. What's different today is that there must be a financial reward as well – it's not simply a matter of getting to the end of the road.

There is, of course, no end to the road. When we bought what then was our biggest purchase, Beatrice, I saw it as just one more step. Two or three years afterwards, we were back on the acquisition trail again. Our heads were over water so we could add another piece to the jigsaw.

The farmers were not only shareholders in Kerry, they were suppliers and they had to be rewarded for their efforts. They took pride in the fact that they got more than they would get in all the competing enterprises in Ireland – they always got the few extra pence on the gallon of milk or the few extra pounds for their pigs. And they felt good because they were shareholders. In the first instance, it was the recognition that they were owners of the company and, second, that they had something monetary to go with it. For employees, it is somewhat the same. Those who contribute, who are part of the dream, must be recognised and acknowledged.

Very few farmers sold their shares. Those who did sell, had to sell, and they spent the money wisely – build a house, buy a car, send the kids to college. But for the most part, they liked the idea of the share going up and up in value.

Way back in the early '70s when we wanted to buy the Dairy Disposal Company, one of the original four was Tim Lyons, who died when he was 49 in June 1984. In 1973, Tim looked at me and said, "It will never happen". One year later, it had been done.

By achieving those goals and, meeting all those milestones along the road, everyone began to believe that "it would happen". The danger always was that people might over-believe. Some people might believe you could walk on water. You had to be careful and choose something that was always achievable, not fiction.

You have to know the capability of the total team and at every point in time. You have to know that everybody is stretched, playing to their full potential, but never over-stretched to the stage where they are not thinking rationally and, as a result, not contributing as much as they are capable of contributing.

All organisations are absolutely dependent on their people, but success is dependent on those in the organisation who can maximise the talents of those for whom they're responsible, whether they are responsible for a team of six or a department of 100. The difference between a good, a mediocre and a bad organisation is not the people who work in it. As in all organisations, if you take a cross-section, you can be sure the amount of talent is probably about the same. In the successful organisation, the chief executive and key people are maximising the talents of the total workforce.

When I was leaving Kerry, I used the phrase *veni, vidi, vici*. Chapter closed. You don't go back – you have to move on. I wanted to move on.

I have been chairman of the Irish Racing Authority for 15 years. That came fast after Kerry being a plc and the major acquisitions of Beatrice and the others. We have seen dramatic changes in the Irish racing industry. Ireland is now number three in the world in the production of thoroughbred horses. It's behind only the USA and Australia. For a small little island, the change has been dramatic. I would hope that, for my 15 years, I helped in the thought processes that brought the industry to where it now is. I mentioned healthcare but, in addition, I was chairman of a major leisure company. Kerry had got 30 years and I wanted to see if I could use the same disciplines in industries beyond the food industry. When you do that you must be absolutely focused.

What's my target today? We have a healthcare company which is worth about £1bn sterling. Our five-year target is to get it up to about twice that size. I, and everybody else involved, need to stay focused. And at that point, I hope I can say we have built two Kerrys in 35 years – 30 years for one and five years for the other.

Let's go back to the art of good, maybe great, management – disciplining oneself into what's important and seeing that everybody around is disciplined in the same way. It's no different now than it was in the last 30 years – I know what I must get done this year. We're now at review time and the people who are being reviewed have between five and 10 key issues. They know what they must absolutely concentrate on. I am totally disciplined – no side-show will divert me, so I must try and ensure that no side-show will divert the others. Every now and then, I would call on them and ask them if they have read their key issues for this year and have they read them recently. I usually get the answer, "Yes, I looked at them last week". They realise that, by the end of the year, they must have the five to 10 issues (there are never more than 10) absolutely under control. You build the house a brick at a time.

When it comes to focus in business, there is no room for being partially focused. We had a great dinner last night and absolutely enjoyed ourselves but today we're totally focused on what needs to be done. The camaraderie of the day before can never be allowed to seep into the absolute focus.

I hope that people don't fear me. If people feel they really can't get things done, they can ask for help. The wrong way is to let things go half-done or undone until they are found out.

Some time ago, in an organisation to which I have not referred, I put in a person who turned out to be more interested in solving today's problem than looking at the bigger, long-term picture. Today's problem was not the issue – we had far bigger problems to solve. He went to a friend of mine, who told him "to remember that Denis is about six months ahead of you in that job". The man took the lesson to heart and we had a great relationship ever after when he realised that Denis Brosnan was way beyond where his thinking was. For those who know me, it was easy.

Years ago, I used be way too far ahead of the team. I had to learn that there wasn't any good in being out there on your own. You had to be near to the team, making sure they were being pulled along.

Of course, I took an awful lot of advice. That was easy. I had a plc in my head from about 1983. As I told you, in 1982 we started developing around the world. We took various stages in moving the Co-Op to a plc. For a year or so, it was knocking around in my own head, then moving it on to Hugh Friel and some of the others and getting lots of external advice. We could not have gone international with the Co-Op as the holding company.

Let me go back to the very beginning, with Tim Lyons telling me I was mad buying the Dairy Disposal Company – but for me that *had* to happen, and it did. The question was how to make it happen rather than saying that it could not happen.

There's a difference between believing in yourself and being dictatorial. If you don't absolutely believe in the ability of yourself with your colleagues to achieve a vision, then it can't happen. Your colleagues are not going to deliver that vision unless they know you're going to take them there. Think of the explorers in the Antarctic. There always had to be a leader. Somebody had to say, "We can get there". Everybody else had to believe in the leader of the expedition. You had to be able to see over the next mountain and be prepared for the unpredictable if you got over it. It's no different in business. You have to know that, even if you get over the mountain and meet disaster, the leader will take you through it. The day you stop believing is the day you no longer climb the mountain.

3

DERMOT DESMOND

INTERNATIONAL FINANCIAL SERVICES CENTRE

When I believe in something, I give myself totally to it.
When I commit, I have nothing left in the reservoir.
Everything mentally goes into accomplishing.

DERMOT DESMOND is Chairman of International Investment & Underwriting (IIU), which he founded in 1995. IIU is a private company, operating from the International Financial Services Centre in Dublin, specialising in direct equity investment and underwriting, funds management and capital markets trading.

He was born in Cork on August 14, 1950, the eldest of four children: three boys and one girl.

His father was Andrew Desmond, a Collector of Customs and Excise. His mother is Sheila Twomey.

He was educated at Marino National School and Good Counsel College, New Ross.

He is married to Patricia Brett. They have three sons and one daughter: Brett, Zoe, Ross and Derry.

In 1981, he founded National City Brokers (NCB). In 1994, he sold his stake to National Westminster Bank (now part of Royal Bank of Scotland).

In 1984, he founded Quay Financial Software. He sold his 80% shareholding in 1995 to CSK Japan.

In 1985, he established Financial Courseware Limited, now known as Intuition.

Through his private investment vehicle (IIU), he has a substantial number of investments in a variety of businesses worldwide. The main investments include: London City Airport, Sandy Lane Hotel, Barbados, and Celtic Football Club plc. He also owns BETDAQ, a global player in the rapidly emerging betting exchange sector. In 2000, he established Daon, identity software technology systems.

He is Chairman of Respect, the fundraising arm of the Daughters of Charity who are committed to improving the lives of people with intellectual disabilities.

He is an honorary fellow of the Royal College of Surgeons in Ireland.

He is a board member of several companies, charities and educational bodies, in addition to being a sporting enthusiast. He is a keen golfer and plays annually in the AT&T at Pebble Beach and in the Dunhill Pro-Am in Scotland. His handicap is 9.

I n Out On Their Own, *Dermot Desmond says, "There is a piece in the Sail Ireland song about the narrowest line between the hero and the fool. I'd prefer to walk that line than to be a nonentity. A nonentity to me is somebody who does not do his best. I think life is about doing one's best".*

One of the great rowing coaches, Steve Fairbairn, of Jesus College, Cambridge, said, "If you can't do it easy, you can't do it at all".

Doing it easy does not mean not doing one's best. Doing one's best implies a capacity for total focus. Denis Brosnan, in the previous chapter, said, "You must be absolutely focused". Dermot Desmond says, "When I believe in something I give myself totally to it".

Denis Brosnan said, "What has been proven is that there are all the same drivers for good management". Dermot Desmond said, "I had a deep belief that skills are transportable".

If Dermot Desmond did not have the vision, what Michael Buckley called a "a big hairy idea", and if he did not apply his transportable skills, there would be no International Financial Services Centre in Dublin, employing over 17,000 people, paying €663m in Corporation Tax in 2004.[7] He kept focus, even when powerful constituencies were ranged against him.

The IFSC is an outstanding, perhaps sadly the only, example of the public and private sectors genuinely collaborating as a team. I was at a conference in London which was to sell the IFSC. It was addressed by Pádraig Ó hUigínn. An English banker turned to me and said, "Your Sir Humphrey is bloody marvellous".

---

[7]   I am indebted to Ken O'Brien for these figures from his excellent *Finance Dublin Yearbook* (www.financedublin.com/yearbook). In a May 2003 interview with Ken O'Brien, Dermot Desmond estimated the historic contribution at that time was €7 to €10 billion, which, he said, "paid for a lot of hospital beds and education".

Like all visionary entrepreneurs, Dermot Desmond's abiding value is his personal freedom. He eventually found that Ireland's "valley of the squinting windows" was not to his taste: "I did not want to be owned and controlled by a begrudging mentality".

In my erstwhile youth, there was a hoary old joke. A man was trying to climb a greasy pole. A German came along and gave him explicit technical instructions. An Englishman said, "Hold on, old boy, let me give you a hand". An Irishman waited until he was half-way up the pole and then pulled him down.

Our talent for begrudgery is lessening only now, as we become accustomed to unwonted prosperity – but there is still a piquancy in failure.

I had my conversation for Out On Their Own *with Dermot Desmond in NCB in Mount Street. His office was a glass box in the dealing room. That same year, 1991, I ran into him at an Institute of Public Administration conference in Dublin. He was then Chairman of Aer Rianta, the State-owned Irish airports authority. He worked well with a strong and clear-headed chief executive, Derek Keogh, who resigned not long after Dermot left. When they both left, Dublin airport spiralled into the abyss, while the Government, with its chronic strategic incompetence and in thrall to the trade unions, stood idly by. As he passed me at the IPA conference, he said, "I want you to do a study of the Aer Rianta Board". I said, "I don't do boards". He said, "You will", and I did. It was a productive study and led to a Board Charter signed up to by all the directors, including the worker directors. (I had worked in another State company where the worker directors phoned their union reps at the coffee break.)*

He has boundless energy. The only difference I could detect after 14 years was that his moustache, by which he is known as "the Kaiser", had changed from black to white. ("Kaiser" is from the wrong country. Its origins were, I believe, in Afghanistan, where Dermot once worked and where, if you did not wear a moustache, you might be regarded as less than manly.)

Dermot left Merrion Square that day to visit his mother in Donabate. As he stepped into an uncompromising Bentley coupé, I could not resist asking, "How is the Bentley?". He grinned broadly, waved goodbye and said, "It's only a symbol".

The conversation was recorded in Dermot Desmond's house on Merrion Square, Dublin 2, on April 17, 2005.

Dermot Desmond's biography is in *Out On Their Own* (1991).

DERMOT DESMOND

The International Financial Services Centre ultimately came about by my establishing NCB as a moneybroking/stockbroking firm in 1981. It was apparent at that time that technology would be the driving force in the way people sold financial services. I became involved in establishing Intuition, a computer-based training company and also Quay Financial Software, which integrated information services. I was looking at the impact technology would have on businesses domestically and globally. That gave me a view of where the financial services market was going. I saw what we needed to do to compete. While NCB got off the blocks pretty quickly, we were still competing with Davy's, who dominated the market. We believed we had two advantages: one was that we had superb people and secondly, we had a broader view of the potential for financial services in Ireland.

In NCB, we needed a sound economy to give us a sound basis for financial services. Our gross domestic borrowing was huge from 1985 to 1987. Unemployment was running at 18% to 19%. We had got to the stage where, if we could not raise funds externally, the IMF was going to be called in.

In the mid-1980s, I was invited by Greg Sparks to a dinner in the Shelbourne Hotel. He was a partner in Farrell Grant Sparks, the firm that audited our accounts. The dinner was hosted by Ruairí Quinn, who had just been appointed Minister for Labour. It was his first ministry and Greg was one of his advisers. Ten or 12 businessmen were invited. Ruairí told us he was honoured to be made a Minister. He wanted to have an enlightened approach to his role in Government. He said he realised that we could not increase taxes any more. He went round the table for any ideas – telling us there was no such thing as a free dinner. When it came to me, I said, "The only things I know a little about are technology and finance. There is a great opportunity for Ireland to be a leader in global financial services. We're in the age of technology, of change, and the first movers will have a major advantage. With technology, financial services can be located anywhere – they do not need to be in the traditional centres. In telecommunications, Ireland has skipped a few analogue generations and we're now straight into digital – the future for telecommunications. We have a highly-educated workforce, talented people, and we can compete with anybody in the world. We're not afraid. In technology, we have the ability to be lateral thinkers. That's what you need to be good software developers and writers. We need legislation to cover funds management, treasury activity, insurance, so that an international bank could locate in one place. Financial services are dominated by English and American firms – they have the leading centres. We have an opportunity to become that neutral centre to manage finance for these multinational financial institutions or even the several corporations who are larger than banks".

We all adjourned to Kitty O'Shea's. When I was driving home about one o'clock in the morning up the Stilorgan Road, I was thinking did everyone give their two ounces of bullshit or do I really believe what I said. I wrote a paper outlining the concept of an IFSC and got Peter Kelly of PriceWaterhouse to look at it. Peter came back to me and told me there was merit in it. I then submitted the paper to Ruairí Quinn, who agreed we should pursue it.

Niall Greene was in charge of the Youth Employment Agency. They, with NCB, funded the study. It was 1985 and the study cost £375,000. NCB paid for half, which, in that year, was half our profits. Some people said I was mad. The study went into a drawer in the Department of Labour. The mandarins had no enthusiasm for it.

In late 1986, P.J. Mara invited me to a Fianna Fáil dinner in New York. My background was not Fianna Fáil – I was not that interested in politics. One side of my family came from Fine Gael. P.J. Mara had told Charlie Haughey of the success we enjoyed in NCB and suggested I have lunch with him in New York.

I had a really honest and open lunch with Charlie, where we talked about the economy and I told him the mistakes I thought were made by Fianna Fáil. I said there had to be radical change in the management of the economy if we were to pull out of our difficulties. I told him about the financial services idea and my frustration, having put a significant amount of money into proving the concept and the mandarins having no interest. There was no direct benefit to me. I did a 360 degree turn from my more remote perceptions of Charlie

Haughey. He was charismatic. He knew the issues and he was very bright.

I was invited out to Kinsealy. Conor McCarthy was there and a number of other businessmen. Charlie said, "We are going to have an election. I want to devise an economic policy". This was a whole new world to me. All I was was one of these upstart stockbroking guys, trying to hustle and get market share. I was pretty nervous and Charlie asked around the table. Everybody to a person, male and female, said, "Cut taxes". Charlie replied, "I agree absolutely". He went on, "However, I could not cut taxes at the higher end and forget about the people in Ballymun and Ballyfermot". That was one of the sea-change moments of my life. What Charlie wanted to do was take care of the weak and to be just. What the businessmen (including me) around the table wanted first, of course, was a cut in their own high tax payments. Charlie's point was that taxes had to be cut on an equal basis. You had to motivate the people on the lower incomes as well as those on the high incomes. He explained that the lower levels were contributing more than the higher levels. He said, "I want to get to a position of cutting taxes but to do that we've got to raise revenues and we must cut down on costs". He felt the majority views around the table were unfair, unjust and not politically acceptable – I then became a real fan.

He came to lunch in the NCB office in Mount Street where we had a brilliant economic team, people like Pat McArdle, Kevin Barry, Dermot O'Brien, Michael Buckley and Michael Walsh, all around the table with Charlie Haughey, giving him their views on the economy.

Later, he called me out to Kinsealy and told me he was going to run with the financial services centre. He asked me to write a manifesto. Michael Buckley and I wrote it for Fianna Fáil. Then, in 1987, when they were elected, I suggested to Charlie that he get the heads of all the Government departments together with the heads of the banks and have everybody really participate in the whole design. We needed to move quickly, because what we did not want was conflict between the different departments and between the financial services organisations. We wanted them all to come together in the national interest. We had to focus on the mission and take self-interest out of it. He got all the people around the table, Mark Hely-Hutchinson from Bank of Ireland, Gerry Scanlan from AIB, insurance people, Seán Cromien was head of the Department of Finance.

I said the first thing we needed was a chairman to pull it all together. Charlie said he would put Pádraig Ó hUigínn in as chairman. AIB said they did not want to go down to the Docks. The Docks were part of the IFSC manifesto. You had to give the Centre an identity and that's where I picked. There would be no point in having "Dublin" as the centre. What we were striving for was architectural excellence. My office was in Mount Street, a Georgian street destroyed by developers. The Centre had to be part of a new Dublin, of creating new standards. The Docklands were owned by the Government so there was no conflict of interest. There were tax breaks down there which could fast-track investment.

The Finance Bill was coming out in March and we needed to have the financial services regulations passed.

At the first meeting, the banks had their own vested interests in having all their activities in Bankcentre for AIB or in Baggot Street for Bank of Ireland. They did not want a foreign exchange operation down in the Docks. They wanted to take all the benefits and not make the investment. The mandarins were asking what about the Data Protection Act, they were afraid so much of our taxes would slip out of the economy. They were not thinking about the influx of funds and encouraging tax-paying banks to increase their operations here. The mandarins believed we would have dilution in our tax-take.

The meeting went on for about two-and-a-half hours. I thought the IFSC would never happen. Charlie wasn't there. Pádraig Ó hUigínn chaired the meeting. We were in grave danger of not thinking about the national interest and of losing to self-interest the big picture.

I went to Charlie. I was practically in tears. I told him it was not going to work, that everybody had their own agenda and that those agendas were not in the national interest. Their agenda was to take whatever benefits might come from an International Financial Services Act but not to make an investment. I told him the mandarins were singing off the same hymn sheet as the banks and wanted to prevent it.

Charlie looked at me and smiled. He said, "Didn't I give you all the players? Didn't I give you Ó hUigínn?" I told him I did not know they were going to act as they did, that I did not realise that the vested interests could be so divisive. I told him I was not a politician, that I did not have the experience, that I did not understand it. Charlie said, "I'll attend the next meeting".

When he came to the meeting, he looked around the table and said, "We are going to implement everything in the manifesto. There will be no dilution. The Financial Services Bill is going to be enacted by March 17. Desmond and Buckley will draft it. The only changes we will countenance are improvements. You can contribute to it in a positive way but you will not prevent it. We have taken a Government decision. You are going to encourage approval of this Bill". Charlie demonstrated both charisma and power. It was that meeting that made the Financial Services Centre.

Then the people became a team and took ownership of the Centre. We brought in people with international credibility, people like Séamus Paircéir, Tomás Ó Cofaigh and Maurice Horgan. We called them "the three wise men" and they went around the world marketing the centre. They did an unbelievable job. A lot of people contributed their wisdom and knowledge into building the Centre.

It all began with that dinner with Ruairí Quinn. If he had never asked my opinion, I would never have had the chance to give it. Everything is about knowing where the opportunities are and how you can capitalise on them.

That's the story of how the Financial Services Centre came about.

It caused me more grief and more pain and more joy than any other business. Very few believed it would be successful. The media certainly did not believe it. The financial services people were Doubting Thomases – they believed it would be short-term, just a couple of years.

When I believe in something, I give myself totally to it. A lot of people think that's great and a lot think it's a big mistake. When I commit, I have nothing left in the reservoir. Everything mentally goes into accomplishing.

We had plans drawn up to build new offices for NCB in Percy Place, the old British Leyland site. When the Centre came along, our commitment was to it. We'd buy a building in the Centre and move NCB into it. I didn't want anybody to say that it was all right for me – still operating from Mount Street.

I bought a building, same as everybody else, gave a hefty margin to the developer and to the Docklands. When I moved in in 1994, the building, including fit-out, was standing me £57m. It had practically bankrupted me. It was largely borrowed from people who trusted and believed in me. I had some bankers who believed in me beyond justification. I spent many a night and week worried about it. When you're really worried, you have to keep on smiling, assuring everybody that everything is all right and under control. You tell me that there is an Irish saying, "When things are bad, you paint the hall door." I was doing a lot of painting!

I had 60% of NCB and I decided to sell out entirely to Ulster Bank, to pay all my debts, to realise assets and to go into cash. Then I was going to use my own knowledge and whatever talents I had to build new businesses.

I set up my own investment office with Michael Walsh, Chris McHugh, Gina Markey and a few others. Michael Buckley had gone to AIB a few years previously.

We got a good price for NCB and I was now in the process of reinventing myself. Stockbroking was enjoyable – it was a challenge. I liked it but decided to move a lot of my activities abroad. I did not want to be in a valley of squinting windows – who was the biggest, who had the best connections, a very negative community. I had a deep belief that skills are transportable, that, if people do well in one area, there is a good chance they will do well in many others.

In a small society, there is a tendency to put scurrilous rumours around the place and some of them catch fire. I became close to Charlie Haughey and I still have huge admiration for what he achieved in the national interest. I am not his keeper but I believe he was a wonderful statesman for Ireland. But Ireland being what it is, half the population will be against him and Fianna Fáil, and half may be for him.

I put a lot of funds into technology companies and built assets and businesses. I like to think I took a long-term view. I still have Intuition 20 years later. It was the first computer-based training company in the world. We started with floppy disks and now we're providing training over the Internet to a diverse range of companies from Citybank to the pharmaceutical sector. It's been quite an excursion.

Leaving Ireland in 1994 to become a more global player gave me freedom of mind – financially, it opened up opportunities to develop businesses whether it was City Airport, new technology businesses, investing in various companies, generally having a reasonable time as investors. For the last 10 years, I have been without shareholders or creditors. I don't have to write please-love-me letters – I will repay you, give me the money. I've had a great time – I had the opportunity to invest in Celtic and work with Martin O'Neill. I have had a lot of opportunity to express my eclectic passions. I am fortunate in having good friends in John Magnier and J.P. McManus. We have done a lot of things together, had great fun socially and in being mentors to each other. They have skills and talents that I don't have. We have a forum and we throw knowledge into the middle and we each pick out the pieces that improve our level of decision-making. It's great to have people that recognise that you have something to contribute and who bring a different shade to the argument. Out of that, for example, came our building of the Sandy Lane Hotel in Barbados, knocking down the old hotel, rebuilding it and building a few golf courses which I got deeply involved in together with the support of Derrick Smith and Michael Tabor. We have created this unique property. It's changed from a business to pure pleasure that we can enjoy with our friends. You meet a lot of global people – from America, Europe, and the Far East – people you don't normally get an opportunity of meeting in one place.

Celtic Football Club is an investment in sporting heritage. I encouraged Martin O'Neill to join Celtic and I enjoy his passion for managing the players and me. I enjoy the Board who are committed to bringing Celtic forward as one of the major global clubs and I've enjoyed our success in the last four or five years winning championships and cups and reaching a UEFA final. And, of course, I've enjoyed the Irishness of Celtic. I have enjoyed working with Rangers, trying to get away from sectarianism and bigotry and trying to get Celtic and Rangers into the Premiership, one of my major career ambitions. I think the Premiership will be the better for it and so will Scottish football. There will be greater bonding and no dilution of the passion of each of our teams.

I forget about a lot of things I've done but I did enjoy investing in Baltimore[8]. I had a company, Quay Financial Software, headed by Gerry Giblin, who is a brilliant technologist. Gerry came to me from Telerate in the mid-80s. Gerry had recruited Fran Rooney to work with him in QFS. I had dinner with Michael Smurfit[9] in the States and he

---

8   See *Leaders* (2001) – Fran Rooney.
9   **Chapter 15**.

asked me what I was involved in. I told him I was in technology, looking particularly at middleware in the financial services sector. I was looking at authentication and encryption. Michael told me he had just invested in a company and thought this was a growth area. I had recently sold QFS and Fran Rooney had transferred to IIU. I asked him to look into encryption to see if there was anybody active in the business or should we set up a company. He found a professor in Trinity, Michael Purser, who had a company that was into encryption but was not well-run. It was called Baltimore. I met the professor and I liked him. I had lived in Baltimore as a kid. I felt this was an omen. We took an option for six months in the company to see what we could do with it. We felt it was something we could develop. We did a BES scheme for it. I took 60%. I put Fran in to run it. There was another, much larger company, Zergo, a public company in the UK with which we decided to merge. 1+1 we were getting 5. That was the makings of Baltimore. I had invested £1m and was quite happy the way things were going. Then the bubble started to burst and I started selling some shares. They went to £15 and I sold some more. Then £30 and I sold some more. They went to £60 and I couldn't understand it. I was told I was the biggest single investor in Ireland in technology in the previous 20 years. I had all the stripes of experience on my back. It looked as if Baltimore was going to take over the world but I wouldn't believe that until it had done so. Anyway, I sold some more shares and the price went up again. I sold five times and each time the price went up. The papers, of course, got a hold of this and the consensus was that Desmond knows zilch and everybody else knows the right thing. I began to think that maybe I had lost it.

Then I said to myself, what is the biggest threat to encryption, to Baltimore Technologies? I felt the biggest threat would be if you could encrypt by biometrics, using your face, your finger, your iris, your DNA. That was the perfect encryption. Your biometric is unique to you. You could go along to a finger-print reader and get your driving licence, buy clothes, get your passport, hire a car – then you are an independent person. You could be naked and yet you're fully covered. Nobody could steal your identity from you. I got McKinsey Consultants to do a review to see if they agreed with my idea. They said yes. It cost me a fortune. When you make money, you pay a lot of it back on consultants, simply to confirm something that you already believe in. When you have no money, you just believe in it and get it done. Then I sold more shares in Baltimore at £150. The highest was £156. They went down to 14p. I was fortunate that I was wrong – I like that kind of being wrong.

Having seen the threat, I started a company called Daon and we built a biometric company. It's one of the best companies I've ever been involved with. It's private. We've invested tens of millions of dollars in it. Now we can safely say we are number one in the world in biometric middleware. We've partnered IBM, Unisys and Accenture. The company is based in Washington and in Dublin. With recent contracts, we are at the forefront. We've sold product three times to the US Department of Homeland Security. They are the biggest buyers of biometric middleware authentication in the world. Nobody can get into America without being biometrically passed. They now have biometric driving licences in Bahrain, in some countries in Europe, in Malaysia, in Japan. We're working on social welfare products in South America. With biometric, you remove social welfare fraud. Instead of having swipe cards, you can now get in and out of airports biometrically. Our biometric engine is scaleable for hundreds of millions of people.

In America now, you have not only your fingerprint but your facial image as well. If you've grown a beard, you won't be recognised and it will ask you for your fingerprint. It will then say, "Please go ahead". It will automatically update your database to say that you now have a beard. Next time you come in, you'll be able to walk right through. If it didn't recognise your finger, then you're called in to give an account of yourself. It can get more complex, because you get carloads coming across the Mexican border. You couldn't have individual identification so what you have is heat-seeking technology to identify how many bodies are in the car. Now they're looking at electronic tags for each person crossing the border and that goes into the database. That's what Daon is about and it's growing. We have a very good team of people. It's nice to be told that you are the leader. I asked myself what the threat to Baltimore was and out of that this company came. Looking for the threat created the opportunity.

The last 10 years for me has been about freedom, for Ireland it has been about unparalleled success. The IFSC has hopefully played a part.

4

MOYA DOHERTY

RIVERDANCE

*Never, never take no for an answer. Go back into the
corner and find another route. Whatever you do, get
where you want to get.*

Born in 1958, **MOYA DOHERTY** is one of five children. Both her parents were teachers in Co Donegal.

She is married to John McColgan. They have two boys: Mark and Danny.

She attended Belgrove National School and Manor House Secondary School, Dublin.

She spent a year touring with Team Educational Theatre Company and began her television production career as a Production Assistant in RTÉ.

By 1984, she was presenting *The Live Arts*, an arts television programme, and she also presented RTÉ's first breakfast television output on *Daybreak LA*, the early morning coverage of the Los Angeles Olympics. She moved to London and worked with the breakfast television station TVAM.

She returned to RTÉ for a producer training course. She produced The People in Need Telethon and an award-winning documentary *A Silent Scream*. In 1994, she produced the Eurovision Song Contest and the interval act, *Riverdance*.

She went on to produce *Riverdance, the Show*, which opened in Dublin's Point Theatre in February 1995.

She is a director of an independent television company, Tyrone Productions, a founding Director of Today FM and a member of the Board of the Dublin Theatre Festival.

She has won several awards, including the Veuve Clicquot Business Woman of the Year and the Ernst & Young Entrepreneur of the Year. She has received honorary doctorates from the University of Ulster and from the National University of Ireland.

*N*o matter what you think of the Eurovision Song Contest, which is uniquely awful, none of us who watched the show compulsively on April 30, 1994 will forget the interval act – the music, the dancers and "the enormous swell of applause as 4,000 people rose to their feet, a sea of joyous approval", all of which led to Riverdance. A terrible cliché, but it did take the world by storm and continues today in different variants.

Moya Doherty says modestly, "Sure I had the vision to unlock the door but many others pushed it open".

In this chapter, she sets out with clarity the influences that brought her step-by-step to the pinnacle. Her loving parents – her father saying, "Never be late and always do an honest day's work"; the leadership she got from people like Liam Miller and others in RTÉ, who allowed her creative freedom and gave her support against what could have been strong public opinion.

In the first book in this series, Michael Dargan was strongly influenced by the calm of his father who said, "Never go till you're ready".[10] Moya Doherty says, "You need an accumulation of experience to take on the mantle of being in charge. I was 29 when I became a producer. It was absolutely the right age. I was ready".

The conversation was recorded in Moya Doherty's office in Abhann Productions Ltd, 23 Mary Street Little, Dublin 7, on March 3, 2005.

---

[10]   *In Good Company* (1987).

MOYA DOHERTY

I was born in Pettigo on the Donegal-Fermanagh border. I was actually born in the Erne Hospital in Fermanagh on the shores of the Lough. I was smuggled across the Border like a pound of butter. The village of Pettigo is divided by the Border. We ended up there by default, because both my parents are from Dungloe. My father was from the Gaeltacht area in Gweedore and my mother from The Rosses. They were the first of their generation to get a third-level education. Both sets of grandfathers ended up going to North America, building the tunnels on my father's side of the family, his wife in service. On my mother's side, her father was a labourer in New York. They all made their money, saved it and made the unusual journey back to Donegal and bought small businesses. There is a particular work ethic in Donegal. Maybe it is something to do with the rough Donegal terrain. When I'm driving through Donegal, I always say that the journey only begins at Lifford – it's the toughest county to get through to the north-west.

My mother and father were both national school teachers. As was the practice, my mother was put straight into teacher-training in Falcarragh at age 14. My father went a different route, ending up in St. Pat's in Dublin. They got teaching jobs in Pettigo and all five of us were born there.

There's a story – one day, walking out the Tamlach Road, they were talking about trying to buy the house they rented but they were gazumped. My father said that they were not going to live for the rest of their lives in rented accommodation. With five children coming up and teachers' salaries being pretty meagre, they had to struggle because there was a ban on married women working. Looking ahead, they could foresee their inability to send us to boarding school – there was no option locally. We moved to Dublin. I was seven, just after my Communion. I left a county before I became part of it. You end up in another county and you're never part of it. It was almost an emigrant thing. Friends I have in Australia and America are, in truth, dispossessed. They have memories of something that no longer exists.

Even though we spent the teachers' long summer holidays going back to Donegal, it was never the same. We were always the Dublin Dohertys.

I went to Belgrove School in Clontarf and ultimately settled there. I have two older sisters, Niamh and Nuala, and two younger brothers, Pádraig and Seán. I was sandwiched in the middle. I was probably the black sheep of the family. I was a little more assertive, eccentric and demanding. Niamh and Nuala seemed to do things as they should. They were very young, only 16, when they finished their secondary education. They had their degrees by 19. I suppose I was awkward – I kind of felt out of step. The two older girls were together and the two younger boys were together and I was part of neither camp. I had long conversations with the black cat in Pettigo or with a Crolly Doll. Looking back now, I see it that way. But, if you were to ask my brothers and sisters, they would probably have a completely different take on it.

From an early age, I was interested in theatre. It was instilled in me by a teacher I encountered in Belgrove, Miss O'Regan. She was from Galway – she died sadly from cancer, a young woman. She loved theatre and English. She'd have us up on our desks reciting *The Fiddler of Dooney*. She was ahead of her time in a way because, in those days, teachers would not have dressed up for the classroom. She used to come in wearing the most gorgeous suits – not only was she interested in the theatre, she was also glamorous. To me as a nine-year-old, this was extraordinary. I really felt at home in that environment of poetry and theatre. Something lit up inside me.

That was further enforced when I moved to Manor House Secondary School in Raheny and was fortunate to have again two wonderful teachers: Mrs. Walsh – she was always called Mrs. Walsh – for English, and a drama teacher, Una Parker, now well in her 80s. They were the only two things that interested me, drama and English. Niamh and Nuala had gone ahead of me in the same school so I had something to live up to. Much to my mother's dismay, they were put into the B class while I was put into the A. She had it the other way round in her head. Perhaps I was miscast.

I then got myself a place in UCD to study Irish, French and English. This was 1975 and I just did not have the interest. At that time, you could not study theatre or drama in Ireland. The course in Trinity was not until a decade later.

I had my eye on getting into the RTÉ Rep. I used dream about getting into the very famous school in New York, the Juilliard. I'd send away for brochures year-in, year-out, with not a hope in heaven of being able to afford it! I had then won several prizes at the different *feiseanna* for poetry, drama and recitation. But that was solitary stuff. All that was absolutely single focus – it was all I wanted. I think the greatest disappointment for anyone in life is not to have a passion. If you don't have a passion, your life is thin and angular. That passion carried me through those tricky years of adolescence and it helped me develop. When I look at my own children, I'm delighted when they develop a passion, even if they change that passion. I found my passion early and young and found it so enjoyable and so all-consuming.

I got a job as a broadcasting assistant in RTÉ, which certainly brought me close to drama but, after a year, I took leave-of-absence because I felt it was the theatre I wanted to be in. What helped me greatly was a one-year contract with the Team Educational Theatre Company. They were Arts Council-sponsored and they took contemporary drama to primary and secondary schools around the country. We did everything – travelling around in an old white van. We set up the stage, operated the sound, we had one roadie. The plays were about alcoholism, drugs, bullying – all issue-related.

I loved it – it was a great company: Donal O'Kelly, since gone on to write his own plays, Mary Costello from the north of Ireland, a Catholic from the Belfast's Andersonstown Road. She gave me an insight into what it was like growing up there. She subsequently went off to Australia and wrote a book, *Titanic Town*. Gina Moxley was another – she's gone on to write her own plays. She is now a well-respected playwright and actor.

It was a great year, but, six months into it, I thought this was not for me. It was very tough. We did not get paid well. I began to feel I did not have the constitution for acting. It requires great stamina to be able to cope with constant rejection in auditions. If there's one profession I admire, it's actors. The working theatre actor in this country is not recognised at all as he/she should be. In most cases, they're badly paid and, a lot of the time, they're out of work. Then they have to cope with how they look when they are getting old. It's a tough, tough business.

Having observed the directors', the writers' and the producers' work a little more closely, I thought production was where I wanted to be. The all-consuming passion for acting that I had for a decade-and-a-half suddenly dissipated, but I knew I was still in the right area. There was nothing else I wanted to do.

And so I went back into RTÉ, delighted with my new-found knowledge and became a production assistant. I had been trained as a broadcasting assistant in radio and as a production assistant in television. I secured my NUJ card and got experience as a presenter/reporter in front of the camera – which, in time, I realised was not for me. I much preferred being behind the camera.

I got my NUJ card with the help of Cian Ó hEigeartaigh. I worked for a time in the newsroom as a broadcasting assistant and was friendly with many of the journalists there, Shane Kenny, Gerald Barry, Kevin Healy. That was in the early '80s and it was at that stage that I met John, whom I subsequently married. It was tricky then. John had been separated since the mid-70s in a very different Ireland. On June 26, 1986, the proposed introduction of divorce was rejected by a massive majority – 63% against, 36% for. John was then a producer/director in RTÉ and Head of Entertainment in Network Two. John had left school at 14 – he's a decade older than me – and had worked his way up in RTÉ from messenger boy to Head of Entertainment. It's not like that any more. Remember, I went in as a secretary and went through all those jobs – it was a great training ground then. If you showed an ability to do a job, you could get recognised and promoted. I believe it's not as free now because things are tighter. I was lucky to have been there in the late '70s and early '80s.

I remember my mother saying to me, "If you came in to me looking for a job and I read your CV, I would never employ you because you have moved around so much". My mother and father could not understand it when I resigned from RTÉ in the early '80s. At that point, John had done everything he could in RTÉ. Even though he was still a very young man, he had been there for quite a while. He set his sights on London. A lot of people were emigrating in the '80s, particularly in television, because we had only RTÉ and, if you didn't get on with your boss, there was nowhere else to go – one show in town, a monopoly.

Even though it was, heaven help us, in Margaret Thatcher's Britain, things were beginning to explode in broadcasting. Breakfast television had started. Noel D. Greene, who sadly is now deceased, a lovely director/producer in RTÉ, had headed off to London. Things were very controlled by the unions whom Thatcher subsequently broke. You had to get a union card to operate as a director. The cards were much coveted.

John was fortunate. He went to TVAM, encouraged by Noel Greene. He got a director's job. Once you had a job, you could then get a union card. Over a period of five years, he became Controller of Programmes of TVAM under Greg Dyke and subsequently under Bruce Gyngell. TVAM was started by the Big Five: Parkinson, Frost, Ford, Rippon and Aitken. They hired all the bright kids out of Oxbridge. And the whole thing collapsed.

At this time, with my NUJ card, I was presenting the *Arts Programme* in Ireland. John and I were walkin' out, much to my mother's disappointment. She said, "With all the men out there in RTÉ, could you not get one that hadn't been married?". I understood her concerns. Here we are still together, 23 years later.

When my contract was up in RTÉ, I too decided to try for TVAM. I got a reporting/presenting job. I used fill in for Anne Diamond and I worked with Henry Kelly. I also did a magazine programme called *After Nine*. I did some news reporting as well – all of this on and off for a period of five years.

Those five years did much to bring together elements in my character that I had learned in the past. In Ireland, in the early '80s, you'd be lucky if you met a Protestant. There was no other cultural influence. It was a mind-opening experience to work in television in Britain with a myriad of people from America, from all over the UK, from Europe and from Australia, to be aware of just how multi-cultural London was.

I was conscious of my Irishness because, unfortunately, the IRA was very active in Britain. It was an awkward consciousness – I was working in the newsroom at the time of the Harrods' bomb. It was a tough time but rarely were we made feel bad, because we were working with a bunch of intelligent, tolerant people.

Margaret Thatcher didn't help. Then there was the miners' strike. There was almost a divide. You had poverty and struggle in the north of England contrasted with enormous prosperity in London. In television, there was huge prosperity. For the first time in my life, I earned money that wasn't penalised by a punishing tax system as it would have been here in Ireland in the '80s. I bought my first car for £4,000 cash. I could not have seen the colour of that money in Ireland. We got good pay, most of which we could take home – we were *ar muin na muice*. We bought an apartment just before the property boom. None of these things mattered to us, to me. It was really about the quality of the work. But it was a joy to be living in a culturally-rich city, to have a few bob in your pocket.

London was the gateway to the best theatre in the world. We absorbed everything that London culturally had to offer. But there came a time when the treadmill of breakfast television began to wear both of us down. It was very exciting, but it was limited as well. Five years were about as much as you could do. You were packaging everything – it was, however, a great discipline. I remember a top editor we had from the north of England. He came to me one day to ask my opinion of a journalist he was thinking of hiring. I said, "He's a thug". He said, "That's just the kind of guy we want!". He also said, "If you can't tell your story in three minutes, it isn't worth telling".

They were making very good television programmes in Britain at the time, good drama, good documentaries. John and I both had our sights on getting into day- or night-time television. It was very difficult to move. You were pigeon-holed in breakfast television.

There was a change of régime in TVAM with Bruce Gyngell. Greg Dyke had exited. The managing director's office was on the corner overlooking Camden Lock and most of the MDs ended up in the lock after about three years – they just didn't survive.

John went off to Australia with Mike Murphy to make a series of documentaries. I remained in London but began to see that, if we wanted to move to the next stage in our lives and in our relationship, we probably needed a bit more space. We were thinking about children. We got married on Christmas Eve in London in 1986 with John's brother and my sister in attendance, went back to our flat and played Trivial Pursuit. It was wonderful for me because I never wanted to be a bride. I used to have nightmares about walking up the aisle in a big meringue gown. We woke up on Christmas Day and cooked a goose for dinner.

I began to realise that maybe we were tiring of London. We had a need for wide open spaces. One day, I opened *The Irish Times* and found that RTÉ were advertising for producers/directors. I thought, "That's the job I want". John, still in Australia, had gone freelance as a director. At that time too, we set up Tyrone Productions – it was the beginning, registered in London and ultimately transferred to Dublin when we both moved back. The independent sector was up and running in Britain but was only beginning in Ireland. There was not then the legislation where RTÉ had to spend a percentage of its money on commissioning independent producers.

I got the job in RTÉ. What I wanted was not so much the job as the training. They ran tremendously good training courses in RTÉ. There was nowhere else you could get it except the BBC.

I had a very intensive six-month training course run by Michael Heaney, a tough taskmaster. None of us felt very good about ourselves when that course was over. However, I knew from the word go that I had found what I wanted. It was not that I wanted to be the boss or a control freak. I wanted to be *in* control. That has been very much in my character from an early age.

On one of my trips to Australia, I got a letter from a childhood friend, a solicitor, Martha Ryan, who lived two houses down from us in Dollymount Avenue. She had heard about my appointment and thought it was so right for me. She wrote, "Do you remember our garage? You would run plays in it and you controlled everything. You cast, you wrote and you managed everything – and you were only eight or nine". But you need an accumulation of experience to take on the mantle of being in charge. I was 29 when I became a producer. It was absolutely the right age. I was ready for it. I don't think I would have been ready any earlier.

Just as I became a producer in RTÉ, suddenly I was 30 – a classic dilemma for a woman. From never wanting a child, I instantly wanted one. I had to find the balance between motherhood and a career. RTÉ was very good about it. I've had a good relationship with management in RTÉ. Liam Miller was very good about it – he was Controller of

Programmes. Adrian Moynes was another and Joe Mulholland.[11] They were people who encouraged you and gave you the space to do the job you wanted.

I never wanted to be a manager, though that opportunity arose on a number of occasions. I was never attracted to leadership in a semi-State organisation – there were so many constraints. What I wanted was independent leadership. Even though I did not admit it to myself, instinctively I did not want to remain within the confines of a large institution. I wanted freedom. I negotiated for myself a flexible contract. They were offering either two- or five-year contracts – I took a two. When I completed the two-year contract, I was offered a five-year. That was like a death sentence. Instead, I negotiated project-by-project contracts.

John was running Tyrone Productions out of a small office in town and getting just about enough to live on. I knew I could not join him in a production company because it couldn't pay two salaries and we had to pay the mortgage and the child-minder. It was a tough time.

We returned to Ireland when the Divorce Referendum had been rejected. We were almost knocked down by the hoards of emigrants going to America and England. A good priest-friend of mine rang me and asked, "What are you two coming back to this country for? You're crazy". I suppose we just wanted to get home.

It was a difficult transition. They say that, while moving to a new city is difficult, it's even harder coming back home because you know the parameters. You speak the language, you know the gestures, you know what to expect and it's always in some way shocking to witness that nothing has changed. Even though we had lived in conservative Britain, the climate in Ireland was not positive for a liberal thinker.

I was immersed in motherhood and in work. We had two babies – just two years between them. I think that it's even harder for women now because the two parents *have* to work and they can't afford a house within a reasonable radius of their work. When I look at traffic jams going up to Carlow or to Meath, I consider that I am in an incredibly privileged position. I think of all those young mothers and fathers leaving children in crèches, going to their jobs and having to travel distances. This society is not very good at all – it does not

---

[11]   *Talking to Ourselves* (1994).

support young parents as some European countries do in a much healthier way. It's worse now than it ever was. And it was tough enough when I was doing it.

The luckiest break I had was in child-minding. We lived in Howth then. We knew Gay Byrne[12] and Kathleen Watkins well – they had a house in Donegal, where I grew up. I asked Kathleen if she knew anyone who could help out with a bit of cleaning and, when the first child was born, with some child-minding. She told me she had the very woman. She introduced me to my Doreen – Doreen and Leo McGlue. I could not have done what I did in my work without the support of this woman who walked into my life. When Danny was born in 1991, she never asked questions when I went straight into producing the Telethon for RTÉ, my first chance to executive produce. Rather than being a producer on a one-to-one with a reporter, doing a documentary, this was the first management producing job that I had. There were eight or nine outside broadcasts, 20 reporters. I was managing a relationship between RTÉ and an outside charity, People In Need. It was a big team of people and a first for me. I absolutely loved it. My only regret was that I had left a four-month-old baby at home. As a result of the Telethon, I was given the Eurovision.

During that time and subsequently with Riverdance, I would ring home and tell Doreen that I would be home at 10.00, at 11.00, at 12.00 and never once did Doreen have her coat on, ready to go. On some occasions, she would say, "Look. You're very tired. I'll take the boys to my house tonight and I'll give you a rest in the morning".

I could not have done a clear-thinking, good day's work had I not known that my children were being cared for. A lot of my contemporaries who were working were changing child-minders every year. They were being let down. They were having difficulties. I was just really lucky. I was lucky in a lot of things but that is by far the biggest. Of course, she is still with us – she's like a grandmother to the boys. We have never had a cross word. As a result of it, my two boys, one 15½ and the other 13, are incredibly independent young men because of the solid and consistent upbringing they had.

Can I take one step to the left? All of us in our family got a strong work ethic from my mother and father. My father had two sayings,

---

[12]   *In Good Company* (1987).

"Never be late and always do an honest day's work". All of us in the
family put 110% of ourselves into things. Sometimes that's good and
sometimes it's not. My brothers and sisters are all high achievers in
social and caring work. The downside of that was that my parents set
high standards and we're still trying to reach them. That inheritance is
less vivid with me now but it was very much a driving force. My
mother is still alive, my father is three years dead this year. My father
was around thankfully for the good years and to see the success. But
they made us all quite driven in their own way. Their approval played
a major part in all our lives. Now, as a parent, I am trying to balance
with my own boys. I believe, the older you get, it's better to walk to the
beat of your own drum rather than constantly walk to the beat of the
drum that has been set for you by somebody else. You switch lanes
when you get older – and that's a good thing.

Following the Telethon, I produced a number of documentaries. I
got a Jacob's Award (1993) – they were around then – for a
documentary on child sexual abuse. They were good years, years you
could start off with a blank page and create something. I was asked to
do Eurovision by Liam Miller. His phone call changed my life. I started
working on the Eurovision in 1993. It was broadcast in April 1994 and
Riverdance emerged as a full show in 1995. They were whirlwind years.
It was a prestigious thing to be asked to manage the Eurovision. It was
a big budget. It had many facets to it. I toyed with it for a while
because, as a creative product, I was not all that interested in it. In
1994, we had a lot of new entries, going from 21 to 29 – 29 songs, many
of them awful. I started doing the sums on the back of an envelope, 29
multiplied by 3, how much time do we have left to do anything? You
could, however, establish something in the opening sequence and in
the interval act.

I had already seen Jean Butler and Michael Flatley dance separately
in the Concert Hall. Bill Whelan had written the music and John had
produced. I was in the audience. I was struck by both of them,
American-Irish dancers. They brought a new athleticism to Irish dance.
It had a different look and style, even though the language was the
same. The interpretation was different. I was talking to Michael
afterwards and I had in mind to do a documentary on the evolution of
Irish dance. I was in the throes of pitching that idea to RTÉ. I thought I
could park the documentary for the moment and why not test out this

notion of where Irish-American dance was going? When I had settled that in my head, it made it absolutely clear to me that I had to produce the Eurovision.

And I was free. This is where good leadership allows ideas to grow – there was good leadership in RTÉ at that time. It allowed me creative freedom and also gave me the right kind of support against what could have been quite strong public opinion. We were casting two Irish-Americans in the lead roles representing Irish culture. Every week or so, I had to report to a steering committee, effectively the bosses of radio and television. They just wanted to keep track that this major thing was being handled reasonably efficiently. Bill O'Donovan represented radio on the committee. When I mentioned the idea of an Irish dance number, Bill asked who was writing the music. When I told him that it was Bill Whelan, he said, "Well I hope he writes something you can la to". I think he did!

What I had learned from the Telethon was that forward planning was critical. I started early on, getting my ducks in a row for the Eurovision. After I spoke to Michael and Jean, I rang Bill Whelan. I vividly remember the coffee we had. I said, "What we really want to do is something extraordinary with Irish dancing. First thing is to visually strip it down completely" but Bill wanted to make it a lot more complex rhythmically. I just had this sense of the Broadway chorus line. I did not know how we would get there. I was not an expert myself but I could always find somebody who was. A lot of it is about team-building and casting the right people. It was a perfect time for Bill, because he was exploring all those mixed rhythms. Flatley had the American energy and enthusiasm and so had Jean. We brought Mavis Ascott on board as choreographer to work with them. The piece started to build, grow and shape. It really was an absolute team effort. Sure, I had the vision to unlock the door but many others pushed it open. The alchemy that happened was the marriage of a number of minds. And we had this fantastic platform, the Eurovision, with an extraordinary set designed by Paula Farrell. I wanted a set that showed some of the modernity of Ireland – things were beginning to move here. There was the Peace Process, the economic tide was just beginning to turn. We neither led nor followed but were part of an extraordinary movement at the beginning of that dreadful cliché, the Celtic Tiger.

The Point was the venue. I chose the River Liffey as the scene for the entire Eurovision, the opening with Macnas, when we sailed an old Galway Hooker up the Liffey. The set depicted a modern, Dublin with edgy neon. I didn't want the old Bord Fáilte cliché images. I recognised that we had to sell Ireland, but I wanted the image of the whole show to be coherent and have that restless modernity that we did not have in the past in similar shows.

The timing was just right for it. I got young, talented film directors – they had a different feel and a lovely energy to them. The setting was a neon river running through this modern, urban landscape. And it all gelled. It was a lovely place to be on the night. We pushed barriers technologically that night because the voting was in-vision by satellite. That was an enormous battle with the EBU but I was well supported by my colleagues in RTÉ. It wasn't my idea at all because, technologically, I would not have been at the cutting edge. Alan Burns, from Screen Scene, came to me to tell me that there was now the technology to do in-vision voting rather than just sound. He gave me the vision and I fought the fight which taught me something about tenacity. Never, ever take no for an answer. Go back into the corner and find another route. Whatever you do, get where you want to get. The show and the set were shaping up so I had time and energy to put into this battle. It was about moving forward, about new technology, about a new way of doing things.

I had a tremendous coordinator working with me, Marie Travers. She was calm, solid and clear with a lovely sense of humour. When I got a "No" from the head boy in the EU, whose name I won't mention, I decided that I was not going to let him make the decision for all these European countries. I wrote to each one of them individually. We had to meet deadlines and we had to get particularly the big countries, like France and Germany, on side, because they were the people who were bringing the money to the table. I told them that I had been rejected at the headquarters of the EBU but I was making this personal plea. If we were not at the cutting edge of technology in the television industry, we would be left behind. I asked them to give me an answer by the following Friday evening, the absolute deadline. The replies began to come through and it was like winning an election – Germany says "Yes"! France says "Yes"! Italy says "Yes"! I went back to my friend in the EBU and told him he was overruled. I got almost more of a high out of that than *Riverdance* itself.

I remember the night of the Eurovision, April 30, 1994. I knew before then that we had something extraordinary on our hands. Hard-bitten cameramen, jaded producers, people who had been a long time in the industry, were coming to me with some excitement. As soon as I heard the music, I was confirmed in my belief that we had something extraordinary but, of course, I was preoccupied with the whole show which was not over until midnight. I could not fully appreciate what an extraordinary thing happened that night. I was in a back room calling in Bosnia-Herzegovina. That robbed me of standing in the auditorium and hearing the enormous swell of applause, 4,000 people rose to their feet, a sea of joyous approval. That was just the beginning.

5

SEAN FITZPATRICK

ANGLO IRISH BANK

The only thing that has made us special is us.

In 2005, **SEAN FITZPATRICK** retired as Group Chief Executive of Anglo Irish Bank Corporation and became non-executive Chairman.

He was born in Bray, Co. Wicklow, on June 21, 1948. His father was Michael Fitzpatrick, a dairy farmer. His mother was Johanna Maher, a civil servant. He was second in a family of two. His sister is Joyce O'Connor.[13]

He is married to Caitriona O'Toole, a former secretary in a consultancy company. They have three children: Jonathan, David and Sarah.

He was educated at Presentation College, Bray and UCD (BComm).

He qualified as a chartered accountant in 1972, having served articles with Ernst & Young (1969-1972), and worked in what is now PriceWaterhouseCoopers (1973 to 1974).

He joined Irish Bank of Commerce as an accountant in 1974. It was taken over by City of Dublin Bank in 1978. City of Dublin Bank bought Anglo Irish Bank in 1980 and Sean Fitzpatrick became general manager. In 1986, he became chief executive of Anglo Irish Bank Corporation plc.

He is a non-executive director of the Dublin Docklands Development Authority, Greencore plc, Aer Lingus and of a number of UK, European and Irish companies.

He is a Council member of the Institute of Chartered Accountants in Ireland and a past President of the Irish Bankers Federation.

---

[13] **Chapter 11.**

W*hatever happened on two romantic nights in Bray, County Wicklow, between Michael Fitzpatrick and Johanna Maher, it resulted in their two offspring, Sean Fitzpatrick and Joyce O'Connor, being between the covers of this book.*

It's a short chapter. There was a comprehensive autobiographical one in Leaders *(2001). Here Sean Fitzpatrick has relinquished his chief executive role and has become chairman. This would be contrary to best practice as handed down* ex cathedra *by lofty authorities. If I have learned one lesson from years of study and starvation, it is that it all depends on the individual, particularly on individuals who have the courage and the foresight to break the so-called rules – but who also have the nous to appear respectable so as not to frighten the horses.*

In Leaders, *Sean Fitzpatrick said, "What you need are people who are absolutely focused and want to be part of a real team". There could not be a better summary for success.*

While in this racy conversation Sean Fitzpatrick downplays his vision, here is what he said in 2001: "We started off on a great voyage. This was back in 1986, when our market capitalisation was just over €1 million. Today, it's over €1 billion. We concentrated our resources on business banking. We hired people from different banks with different skills and immersed them in our culture" and, essentially, "we gave them a very clear vision of the type of special bank we wanted to be. I was determined this was never going to be just another bank".

The conversation was recorded in Sean Fitzpatrick's office in Anglo Irish Bank Corporation plc, Stephen Court, 18-21 St. Stephen's Green, Dublin 2, on February 24, 2005.

SEAN FITZPATRICK

It's all very grand to say that we set out clearly the path we were going to walk and eventually we would get to Jerusalem. I'd love to say it was all planned and that we achieved fully what we planned. In some ways, in Anglo, we could be accused of writing our strategy backwards. We look at where we've got to and then we claim that we planned it all! However, we could not have got there by accident. We had basic core values that guided us. But we didn't get there with a well-planned strategy either. Peter Murray, who I have a lot of time for, our ex-Chairman, used to frighten me by asking me for a five-year vision for the Bank. What the hell was I going to say to him? I used to reach back into my textbooks from my time in UCD, or find out what the latest management gurus were saying. Could it simply be all about hiring the best people available and then giving them the platform on which to perform? I would tell them that it was not what was happening within AIB or Bank of Ireland or Ulster Bank that worried me. What worried me was what was happening within Anglo. We have to worry about ourselves. Will we remain lean, hungry enough, focused enough to actually do it? That's the interesting future test for Anglo. It was easy in a way to build the Bank to where it is today because no one saw us coming and we had a sort of non-establishment approach. It was easy to get a bonding: "Come on lads, we can do it". At first, we couldn't get enough quality people to come to us. Now they're fighting at the gates to get in. That's going to be another challenge, to ensure that we maximise the undoubted talent we have within the Bank.

We may have achieved a lot but I am reluctant to turn round and say that it was the result of an absolutely clear vision of 10 years ago – it was down to hard work and more than our fair share of luck.

You surprised me by reading me quotes from the chapter about me in your last book. Was I that clear all along? I'm not trying to hide now under false modesty. In my heart, I don't feel it that way. I still have to pinch myself and realise that it's great. But I can't claim credit for something I know is not really true. All we were doing was just working our balls off, doing it in a way different from the other banks and concentrating our focus on niche areas of business banking. It was also because we spoke a language people understood. We were not embarrassed to speak in language of one syllable. It was either that simple or that complicated, whichever way you want to look at it.

We never tried to compete directly with the traditional banks. We said to customers, "Use us in addition to them". That was the real secret. No one has actually twigged that about Anglo Irish Bank. We never said, "Use us instead of AIB". Anyway, the customer could not use us solely, because we did not want to, nor could we give them, a complete banking service. We did not want to do their current accounts or their money transactions. We were after the other end of the market, the cream. We only wanted to play at the sexy end. We told people, "If we can do the business with you, we'll do it. And, if we can't, we'll give you a quick No!". We were the first people to cut the rubbish out of it and to speak the language of the people we were dealing with. They were the entrepreneurs who went to work at six o'clock in the morning to run their own businesses. They were the people who opened the offices and shops and turned on the central heating. They spent the whole day ensuring that their staff were looking after their customer base. They wanted to deal with a bank who would tell them straight whether or not they were going to get the money. That was the only thing they wanted to know and we recognised that. They'd come into the car-park, come up here and be told, "We're going to give you the money" or "We're not going to give you the money". That was it and it was hugely different from their experience with other banks.

I'm not just saying it, both AIB and BOI are great banks, but we were a different type of Bank and yet people still compare us with them. It is like comparing an apple and an orange. We were part of the fruit bowl but we were not the same fruit.

The other banks used to knock us a lot. That was great – instead of stopping their customers using Anglo, it had the opposite effect, and created a certain mystique about our Bank. The customers we were dealing with knew that we were good and understood fully their banking needs. Other bankers would mutter about us, "Of course, Anglo take a lot of risk". I never saw us taking a big risk at all. Of course there was risk in lending but never huge risk. Some people in the early days saw Dermot Desmond as a risk[14] – I didn't see him as a risk at all. What other people saw as risk, I didn't. It was all a question of trust and knowing your customer.

Bernard Somers at one stage was acting for the Goodman Group. It was in examinership and he came to me for a loan of €40m, a significant part of our loan book then. Bernard had originally tried to borrow this money from other banks but they took to the hills. But, when they saw that we had done it, they quickly came down from the hills.

After the Beef Tribunal Report came out, our Board felt they should do no more business with the Goodman Group. I remember looking Larry Goodman in the eye and could see that he was saying inside, "How can they do this to me?". Anyway, we withdrew and, to my eternal shame, we were wrong. The Bank, I suppose, wanted to get closer to the establishment. But we'll never let something like that happen again.

Back in the '70s and '80s, I used talk a lot about the culture within the Bank. I do not mean at all the way people talk about the banking culture nowadays. Our culture was proprietorial. You travelled in the back of the plane when you were on Bank business, which is what you would have done if you were paying for it yourself. You'd buy your car second-hand. Can we maintain that culture especially going international? We can, if we sit around a room and look at each other straight in the eye and realise why we became successful. What has made us special? The only thing that has made us special is us. If we hold true to that, of course we can grow. Our culture is not a unique Irish thing. It's global. I've spoken to our people in the UK, in the US, in Austria and Switzerland and the same things turn them on. It's about relationships, about dealing with, and getting on with, people. The great attraction to investors in Anglo Irish Bank is that it is transportable – to the UK, for example, where we can make huge inroads over the next 20 years. In Ireland, we have about 13% of the business market and, in addition, we have now moved to the high net worth end in private banking. We will succeed, simply because people

---

[14] **Chapter 3.**

at that end of the spectrum want the quality of service at which we excel.

The last thing I wanted was a grey-headed customer coming in with a notepad and a pencil and asking how much we would charge to do such-and-such. He was not interested in what we had to offer. He was interested only in getting it cheaply. He was comparing us with five other banks but he was never a mover or shaker. We simply wanted to deal with people who wanted to deal.

I had a brother-in-law in the UK and he wanted to buy some house property. We did not do mortgages. I asked a chap I knew in a building society if they would like to do it and he readily agreed. He asked me how much my brother-in-law wanted to borrow. I told him £120,000, which was not an insignificant amount of money but it was a good deal. He called me the next day and asked was I free that afternoon. When I told him I was, he said "Well, perhaps you'd like to drop down". Bloody hell, I thought, he should have dropped up to see me as I was the customer. I did go down and I was kept waiting.

Eventually, I sat down in front of his desk and he was taking down the details. My brother-in-law did not fit conveniently into his loan form. I didn't know his address or his salary. Your man was rapidly losing interest in the deal. Eventually, I asked if he was going to give my brother-in-law the money or not, or should I get my brother-in-law to call him direct. He said "No". He wasn't a bad lender but he was not interested in giving a bespoke loan. Because the information required on the loan form was not coming easily, he lost interest.

I was delighted with the experience because it brought it home to me how easy it was for us to satisfy customers compared with our opposition.

I told that story many times to all my lending colleagues to emphasise how easy it was for us to go out there and really score. It was not because we were good, but rather because the other banks were so mediocre. I felt they just did not understand the business market and also the requirements of the typical business customer. What we have got to continue with is giving really good service. If I was asked, saving your presence,[15] to lend money to Chris Horn, I wouldn't do it, simply because I haven't a clue about the software

---

[15] The author is a director of IONA Technologies. See also **Chapter 6**.

business. Nothing personal! If, on the other hand, I was asked to back a property investment, which I fully understand, I would do so. Or I can lend to a person into whose eyes I can look deeply and who's screaming (inside) at me, "Sean, I need the money and I won't let you down". I've done that and have I been let down? Of course I have – because I did not know my customer. And that's sore. It's betrayal. I've no problem lending money to a person, knowing that there was a risk in it and, if the risk goes wrong, so be it. But where a guy screws me, I get really uptight. We have lent money to people and things have gone wrong absolutely through no fault of their own. We understand that and, on occasions, we would actually give money back to the guy. We have done that in order to drive home the culture of how we want to do business.

Years ago, Peter Killen and I went out to Lucan to chase a guy who owed us money. He had borrowed for a car. He was three payments behind and all I was concerned about was could we repossess the car. We went up and down through Lucan and eventually found him in an estate. We knocked on the door. Your man opened the door. It was late November or early December and the first thing I noticed was that he had no shoes on. He brought us into the house where he was cutting potatoes. He had a big mural on the wall – in Dublin, known as a muriel, the same as in *Coronation Street* – it was a scene in Kerry with big waves coming in. He told us he couldn't delay because his kids were coming in from school and he had to make their meal. He told us that he had a crash in the car. The wife rang the insurance assessor. When the assessor came out, the wife fell in love with him and scarpered, leaving him with the kids. They took the car and sold it. I was saying, "That's a good story but what about our money? When will you pay it back?".

Peter Killen pulled me quietly into the front room. He said, "Sean, would you ever calm down? That guy has got bigger problems than you or I have. Leave him alone". He came back here to this Bank in Stephen's Green and got €250 to give to the St. Vincent de Paul in Lucan to get things for the kids at Christmas. I would not have supported that then but I truly learned from it. That was the decency of Peter Killen, a gentle giant in this bank.

That also helped to create the culture in Anglo. Yes, we would chase after people but we also had the decency to do the right thing.

You could nearly have a tear in the eye about that but that's what made us different. It's what we try to pass around amongst the people who work here. However, at the end of the day, it's all a bit of a game – if it's only about making money, you won't make money. It's a game that you want to win.

I was sitting opposite Tony O'Reilly[16] at a dinner. At that stage, he had gone from success to success and into a stratosphere way beyond my ken. We started to talk rugby and suddenly he became real to me. He sat down opposite me and gave me the names of all the players on the Blackrock and Belvedere senior teams for the Schools Cup final over 50 years ago. I was still a bit in awe because he was my hero, not just because of his achievements but the fact that he always had a great presence, and was so Irish. Tony O'Reilly, and indeed Michael Smurfit,[17] succeeded from very small beginnings in what was a different and poorer Ireland. We were lucky in the time we were born – OK, we did not reach the same heights – but we did achieve some success.

---

[16] **Chapter 12.**
[17] **Chapter 15.**

6

CHRIS HORN

IONA Technologies

*My vision was to build a software company here in Ireland
that could compete with the best in America.*

CHRISTOPHER JOHN HORN is co-founder and non-executive Vice-Chairman of the Board of IONA Technologies plc.

He was born in Redhill, Surrey, on November 30, 1956. His father was John Horn, a tennis coach. His mother is Angela Mitson, a professional housewife. He is the eldest in a family of four. He has one brother and two sisters: Peter, Caroline and Sally-Ann. He is married to Susan Pakenham-Walsh, another professional housewife. They have four children: Stephen, Jenny, John and Linda.

He was educated at Avoca, Avoca and Kingstown, and then Newpark. And at Trinity College, Dublin where he took a BA, BAI and a PhD.

From 1984 until 1994, he was a lecturer in the Computer Science Department of Trinity College, where he was involved in many pan-European IT research projects. He worked in Brussels for the European Commission and played an integral part in the 10-year Esprit programme to improve Europe's technology industry.

He has been a non-executive director of some privately-held software companies and an adviser to venture capital companies.

He is a member of the Information & Communications Technology Working Group at the Irish Business & Employers' Confederation (IBEC). He is a former director of Science Foundation Ireland and a former and founding chairman of the Ireland China Association. He is a former member of the Board of Trinity College Dublin and of the Trinity College Dublin Foundation.

He is the current Chairman of the Irish Management Institute and also Chairman of the UNICEF Ireland Committee.

He chaired from 1998 to 1999 the Expert Group on Future Skills, part of Ireland's Educational Technology Investment Fund.

He received an honorary Doctor of Science from TCD and became an honorary Fellow of the Institution of Engineers of Ireland.

He was awarded the Gold Medal for Industry of the Royal Dublin Society.

A *short chapter. The story of Chris Horn and IONA Technologies up to 2001 is in* Leaders.[18] *This chapter deals with the profound changes in IONA and in Chris Horn's role, coming back in as CEO to manage a crisis, up to his retirement from that position and his appointment as Vice-Chairman of the Board in 2005.*

I have been a member of the small, committed IONA Board since 1999. While Chris Horn describes the recent period with restraint and objectivity, it was a painful but ultimately rewarding period. All of us, including Chris Horn himself, learned a lot. It served to make of the Board, under the leadership of an outstanding Chairman, Kevin Melia[19], a genuine team with its members bringing to the table their different experiences, skills and analyses.

Chris Horn is an iconic figure in Irish IT. His solid integrity and directness shine through. If, in the words of William of Wyckeham, "Manners maketh man", Chris Horn, in a vulgar age, is an object lesson in good, even austere, manners. I have sat with him in his modest office in the IONA building and offered my tuppence-worth of advice. He listens intently, thanks me and then does his own thing.

The conversation was recorded in Chris Horn's office in IONA Technologies, The IONA Building, Shelbourne Road, Dublin 4, on February 11, 2005.

Chris Horn's biography is in *Leaders* (2001).

---

[18] 2001.
[19] *Leaders* (2001).

CHRIS HORN

My vision was to build a software company here in Ireland that could compete with the best in America. That goes back to a combination of things: to the 1980s and the research we were doing in Trinity at the time, and to visiting Silicon Valley and seeing the level of activity there – what I saw in Dublin at the time was world-class research but not commercialisation of it. In the Valley, it was all about commercialisation, start-ups and venture capital. At the time in Trinity, we were partially-funded from Brussels and that was coming to an end. Also at the time, the European Commission was making noises about how the results of our work could be exploited in the field. The people we had and the R&D *were* world-class. Why could we not form a world-class company based out of Dublin? I could not see any structural reason why we could not do it. It was almost to prove a point!

We were not the first. There was a world-class company called Glockenspiel, formed around 1995 by John Carolan, who had worked on object technology with AT&T/Bell Labs in the States. The product was really world-beating. Their customer base was largely American but they had some operational problems in the way they commercialised their business, which ultimately led to their company being sold. John Carolan had come quite close to doing what I wanted to do but, for various reasons, it hadn't worked out. From my point of view, it was not that there was no previous attempt – they very nearly got there. They partially proved a point.

Colleagues in Trinity, Sean Baker and Annrai O'Toole, had aspirations like mine. Our attitude was why not? Why can't we do it from Dublin?

We were looking to raise some venture capital in America. We had some expressions of interest from two VCs. In both cases, they said they would not make a trans-Atlantic investment. We would have to relocate. If we relocated to Boston, they would invest. They felt our prospects and technology were good but we were physically in the wrong location. We turned that down – it was like a red rag to a bull.

By 2001 (this is well documented in your previous book, *Leaders*), I had been CEO for 10 years, starting with three part-timers and, in 1991, we had 700 or 800 people worldwide. We had revenues of approximately $180m. Profits were in the 15% to 20% range. We built that business primarily around one product, Orbix. We first shipped it in 1993. By 2001, the product was eight years old. The executive team recommended to the Board that we needed to expand our product line and look for new engines of growth. With the original product, we were in the middleware market, where our product was clearly the leader. That was in the early '90s but, by the end of the decade, that market had fragmented into about four separate sub-markets. Whereas we were the leader in one of those sub-markets, we were not even a participant in the other three. The overall market had expanded but had got more complicated. In the Spring of 2001, I relinquished the position of CEO at my own initiative and we appointed one of our internal candidates, the chief operating officer, Barry Morris.

We were at the point where our primary product was beginning to reach the end of its life. On Barry Morris's recommendation, the Board agreed with a strategy of trying to meet the four segments of the market through a series of acquisitions. We purchased our way into each of the other three segments. We closed the last and biggest of the acquisitions, Netfish, in May 2001. The acquisitions would not position us as leader in each of the four segments but by having, from one supplier, a presence in each of the segments, we would be a one-stop-shop.

The headcount went up to 1,200. The cost-base rose accordingly. In the Spring of 2001, and with September 11, the IT market went into a downturn, just at the point where IONA had completed a string of acquisitions. We had a basket of products, each of which was in different segments. For our hoped-for one-stop-shop, we had a lot of engineering work to do to get the products to work together. We had a sales organisation that was put together from the core of IONA and from the acquired companies. We were overstretched. The company was under severe pain.

Ultimately, in the Spring of 2003, at the Board's request, I came back in as CEO, having been Chairman of the Board. Barry Morris left the company in May 2003.

I saw my first job as to stabilise the company. We were burning cash rapidly. We were losing money. We had a confused go-to-market strategy, a confused product portfolio and a confused customer base. Our original core customers believed we were moving away from them and had gone from talking about our original product to a new one. They believed we were abandoning them.

When I came back, I closed down some of the ancillary product lines and closed down our offices in countries where we had a marginal presence.

When I walked in the door, we had about 750 people. Within a week or so, I had made a considerable number of those redundant. By the end of 2003, we had gone down to about 350 people and rationalised the business.

I was fortunate in having a strong Board. I have to say "Thank you" to our Chairman, Kevin Melia, who helped us through that very difficult period. Kevin has been my mentor since 1993. He gave me invaluable support.

We started to rebuild the management team. We promoted some of the people who were in a layer down from the senior management team, people like Andrew O'Sullivan, Philip Pender, Christopher Mirabile, Eric Newcomer. We hired new talent – in particular, Peter Zotto, who joined us in the Autumn of 2003 as our new chief operating officer. Peter was well known to Kevin Melia and to another member of the Board, Francesco Violante. Peter was, in fact, Francesco's boss for a time way back.

Peter has built around him a very strong team, including Bill McMurray as head of sales and Larry Alston as head of marketing. They brought a new depth of experience to the company.

In 2003, we stabilised the company. 2004 was about getting initial traction with our new product, Artix. It is not a replacement for Orbix but can be used alongside it in a new market. In 2004, we stabilised the revenues from Orbix. With Artix, the challenge was to get new, reference, customers who would verify the product worked well. We began to build a revenue pipeline around it.

2004 was a successful year although, in absolute revenue terms, we were flat. Nevertheless, we built a good base for Artix, got costs under control and were profitable for the year. We've laid a good foundation for 2005.

Going back to the vision to build a world-renowned software company, part of that vision is sustainability, being sure that we're here for the long term. We have survived very difficult times. Now we have the foundations in place to restore the company to the performance we had in earlier years.

When I came back in the Spring of 2003, I had a long discussion with my wife, Susan, about the commitment and what it meant. She had seen me work very, very hard for 10 years up to 2000. She was delighted when I stepped back. Her concern was, rightly, would this be another decade of commitment if I came back as CEO. What I wanted to do was to set the company on a sound basis and then gradually extract myself. Before coming back in 2003, I had that discussion initially with Kevin Melia and then with the full Board. I made it clear that I was absolutely committed and would try to turn the company around but did not want to do this forever. It could be as short as six months or as long as a couple of years. By late 2004, early 2005, we had our strong management team. They were committed and understood the business. Peter Zotto was running the company on a day-by-day basis as chief operating officer. I felt he would be ready for the top job by Spring 2005. Kevin Melia had been Chairman of the Board since 2003. In Spring 2005, following our first quarter results, we implemented the plan. Peter took over.

Kevin was keen to continue as Chairman. I wanted to revert to a part-time role. Kevin wanted me to become Vice-Chairman and Peter wanted me to work on an informal basis with the senior management team on areas around strategy and senior customer focus and also, of course, working as a member of the Board.

You have often said that, in the leaders you meet, one of the great learning experiences is failure. IONA did not fail, but the experiences we had when the software bubble burst were as rough as things could be. Looking back, what I learned was that we did not read rapidly enough the trends in the industry. By the Spring of 2001, what had been called the faint signals became strong enough to show that the industry was entering a downturn. Perhaps we were feeling too optimistic and too confident. We had been riding a bull market where things had gone extremely well for the industry but negative signals were coming from purchasing behaviour. One of the lessons is that I hope I am now more attuned to industry trends – industry economic trends as opposed to just technology trends, particularly in America. That would be one thing. Another thing I learned was that, having been the founder and CEO of IONA for 10 years and then suddenly there was a new CEO in place, Barry Morris, and all of the advice I had was to stand back and not micromanage the new CEO but to give him space to lead the company. The last thing he would have wanted was my looking over his shoulder, trying to outguess him and cause confusion in the ranks as to who was really running the company. I stood back a lot and gave a lot of space. Perhaps I stood back too much.

It is a difficult tiger to ride to have a former CEO as Chairman of the Board. I say that with a lot of circumspection because Peter is now the CEO and I am a member of the Board. I am aware of all the case studies where a former CEO resigns and leaves the company totally so that his or her shadow doesn't fall over the company. I have chosen to stay on in the company. It's the strong desire of the Board and of Peter, primarily because of my experience of this particular industry, so that I can use that experience to help guide strategy for the medium to long term. It's a delicate situation. This time around I'm Vice-Chairman, not Chairman. It's primarily the role of the Chairman to be working with the chief executive around verifying the implementation of strategy. That does not really apply to the vice-chairmanship. It's a more appropriate role for me than being Chairman of the Board. I hope I can continue to make a valuable contribution.

7

PHILIP LYNCH

IAWS

The lesson all of this taught me was to hang in there,
to have faith. I suppose I had confidence in an ability
to see beyond the crisis.

PHILIP LYNCH is a native of Innishannon, West Cork and was born on May 1, 1946.

He is married to Eileen Crowley. They live in County Kildare and have four adult children: Paul, Thérèse, Judith and Philippa.

He was educated at Hamilton High School, Copsewood College and Waterford Institute of Technology.

He is Chief Executive of the Irish Agricultural Wholesale Society Limited and was formerly Chief Executive and subsequently Chairman of IAWS Group plc.

He is also a non-executive Director of FBD Holdings plc, C&C Group plc, Cillryan's Bakery Ltd, Odlum Group Ltd, A. Heistand Holding AG, John Thompson & Sons Ltd and Coillte Teoranta, the State forestry company, and a former Chairman of An Bord Bia, the Irish Food Board.

*P*hilip Lynch became chairman of the board of IAWS when he retired as chief executive. Like another participant in the book, Denis Brosnan, he stayed only for a short while and then retired as chairman before he was 60, while this book was being written. He now has an array of activities.

He says, "In 1988, we could go out and convince the market to convert this old co-operative business into a public company. The real purpose of going public was to create value for our shareholders. There is no better measure of real value than the market".

The morning they were listed, he and his colleagues were heading for the Stock Exchange. He realised he did not know where it was.

He went through the necessary crucible of the bad times: "The bad press [about the R&H Hall acquisition], the fear that the media might have been right, sitting on the side of the bed at four o'clock in the morning and adding up the sum of the parts that were worth more than the total debt we had".

Philip Lynch is farsighted and shrewd – in his judgment of affairs and of individuals, but with a concealed sense of humour and a refreshing irreverence that occasionally escapes.

He has the essential attribute, "an ability to see beyond the crisis".

The conversation was recorded at the Tara Towers Hotel, Dublin, on February 7, 2005.

PHILIP LYNCH

It was always expected that I would be a farmer – not a businessman. My older brother went on to study for the priesthood in Pallaskenry, which was not unusual for a member of the family in those days.

I often wondered why I was learning algebra and geometry through Irish at the Hamilton High School in Bandon. The Irish influence came from Sean Hamilton, a wonderful teacher and an avid Irish speaker, but I could never reconcile the relevance of Irish with milking cows in the fields of West Cork. When my mother and father wanted to educate me, I did not avail of the opportunity. My brother later opted out of studying for the priesthood and returned to the family farm. Since there was not enough work for both of us, as the youngest boy, I sought work elsewhere.

My first job was with "Weeshie" Murphy, the famous Cork footballer. He gave Joe Walsh[20] and myself jobs on the same day as temporary agricultural officers working with the Department of Agriculture. We were on the minimum wage, as temporary Grade 8 employees for the summer (there is nothing below a Grade 8). We were "let off" in the winter and I lined up with everybody else in Bandon to draw the dole. It was a miserable time. But then I bought a chainsaw and cut some timber for the local shops and households, making a few bob in the process.

"Weeshie" Murphy fired me in October 1966 because I got only 1,500 miles out of the tyres on a Ford Anglia car and I had caused some grief by missing an appointment with one of his clients. There was also the issue of carrying a passenger in the car, which was against the rules (especially when the passenger happened to be female).

It was time to catch up on my education, so I went back to school – to Pallaskenry, not to study for the priesthood, but rather to study agriculture. (Pallaskenry was an agricultural college, as well as being a secondary school.) I celebrated my 21st birthday there, as a boarder, which was quite a sad occasion because I was away from my twin

---

[20] Later Minister for Agriculture, 1992-1994 and 1997-2004.

sister, Siobhán, the rest of my family and, of course, my girlfriend, Eileen Crowley, later to be my wife.

I graduated in July 1967 with a diploma in agriculture and was offered three jobs almost immediately – one with Ranks, another with Odlums and a third with the Department of Agriculture, with the prospect of becoming a permanent agricultural officer. I chose the job with Odlums. It gave me a few hundred pounds more than the Department and also provided me with a car. When I announced my choice to my mother in the milking stall, she turned around and said, "If you've taken that decision, you'll never be anything more than a jumped-up salesman". Like most mothers of that time, she regarded the passing up of an opportunity to join the Civil Service as totally irresponsible.

I began work with Odlums in 1967 as a Sales Supervisor and moved on to being a sales manager to being an assistant general manager over an eight-year period. Then, in 1975, I joined R&H Hall, part-owned by Odlums. I had a successful time there, involved in market research and business development. Meanwhile, I had gone to Waterford Regional Technical College to study accountancy and business law at night. This was time well spent and gave me a proper grasp of accounts, balance sheets and, most importantly, profit and loss statements.

In 1983, I was appointed general manager of IAWS. The recruitment process had been long and ended up with a shortlist of seven. We were interviewed extensively by Michael MacNamara, Declan Collins and others from KPMG, then Stokes Kennedy Crowley (SKC). There were also four members of the IAWS Board on the interview panel and an external advisor, Michael McStay, managing director of Philips in Ireland. Each candidate was ranked under various criteria and, when this happened, I got the votes.

I knew that the agricultural co-ops owned the IAWS and that they had a shared vision from when Horace Plunkett put them together in 1897. The UK co-ops owned 12½%, the Northern Ireland co-ops 27½%, and the balance was held by the co-ops of the South. With such a mixture, it is not an overstatement to say that there was a lot of politics involved. (In those days, you needed to be a member of Fine Gael and it did not do any harm to be from Cork – I came out pretty well on both counts.) I said to P.I. Meagher, the then Chairman, that I would accept the job as general manager of IAWS and a contract if he would manage the Board and I would manage the business. The Board accepted my proposal.

IAWS was a wonderful opportunity for me. But it also carried several risks, most of them financial. The organisation had lost £4m in the previous couple of years, most of its net worth. More particularly, it had lost sight of what it was about. It had missed out on several opportunities following accession to the European Economic Community (EEC) in the early 1970s. It was also short of vision and strategy, with no path plotted for its future, most unwise in any business. When I joined, we had David Martin on loan from SKC. The best thing I ever did was to persuade him to join the company. Declan Collins from SKC had done a good job. That formed the team that we set up.

I arrived in IAWS on a Friday and got from David Martin the debtors' balances, the list of creditors and the state of the balance sheet. I worked all day Saturday and Sunday until 6pm, when I said to Eileen, "I think we can crack this". What I had learnt over that weekend was that IAWS was not collecting its debts and was paying its creditors on time. It owed £22m to 14 banks, with huge exposure and no security. Indeed, if they had security, they would have put IAWS into receivership.

The first job was to convince the banks that we could make a success of it and the second job was to keep the company alive. We had to stop paying the creditors too quickly and get our people out on the road to collect the money owed from debtors. A number of debts were identified that could not be paid and so we had to make some write-offs. The workforce had to be reduced, from 360 to 200. These measures saved a lot of money and the result was that the following year IAWS was making money. This gave us all, including the Board, some confidence.

We had a small management team. My predecessor had had 29 people reporting to him, but I cut this number down to three. We were fortunate in making a couple of good calls. We sold our coal business in Northern Ireland for £1.75m, a very full price. We used that money to buy Boland's Mills from Ray Jackson, a receiver with SKC, and the following year the company made £1m cash. This gave the Board further confidence in what we, the management, were doing and this, in turn, led to further expansion.

Fitzwilton had a subsidiary company called Capstan Holdings in which they put Gouldings and Dublin Glass, Shanahans and Crowe Wilson, and treated them as associate companies. We bought Gouldings for £7.6m and, with it, a great can-do culture. In the following two years, we made £7m cash. Thus, the divestment in Northern Ireland together with the purchases of Bolands and Gouldings, transformed IAWS and were significant steps in building a strong, profitable business with real potential for growth. IAWS was now in great shape, had credibility with the banks and had paid off its debts.

We then convinced the Higgins family who owned the Dock Milling Company (next to Bolands), the Davis family in Enniscorthy and the Howards in Cookstown that they should create an amalgam of the flour-milling business. Overnight, four flour-milling groups came together, with IAWS having the majority shareholding. In time, there was a rationalisation. Dock Milling and Davis's closed and a good profit was made out of the properties. We brought commonsense to prevail on the market. We bought Shamrock Foods from the Duignan family in 1988. We were now well positioned to convince the market to convert the co-operative into a public company.

It proved to be a difficult period for the IAWS and its Board. There were a number of Board members who were married to Horace Plunkett's co-operative principles. They felt total commercialisation, going down the road to a public company, was not in keeping with those principles. Two members of the Board refused on principle to sit on the board of a plc. The IAWS Board and the Board of the plc were synonymous at this stage. The Board was made up of farmers who were nominated by their boards around the country. I was on the Board as general manager. We had no outside directors at that time.

The real purpose of going public was to create value for our shareholders. There is never a better measure of real value than the market. In November 1988, we were listed on the Dublin market. At 9.20 that morning, David Martin, Jim Moloney and I were running down the stairs and I had to ask Jim, "By the way, where is the Stock Exchange?". Dick Dennis was chairman and was there to welcome us. We got all the support in the world from our brokers and advisors, but once we were listed, we were left high and dry. There was no after-sales service. We now had a company that was 82% owned by the co-ops, North and South of Ireland, and the rest by the public. We had to do a presentation on the company in London and, going around the institutions, there was a real awakening. The whole episode could serve as a very good lesson for companies considering flotation.

In 1990, we made a play to buy R&H Hall. Its Board refused point blank to support our offer and so it became a hostile bid. This put me under a lot of pressure because, since it was my old employer, the view was put about, encouraged by the media, that here was a disgruntled ex-employee on an ego trip bidding for his old company. There were many people still working there who had been good colleagues of mine. The negotiations went on from April to October 1990. The Competition Authority got involved under the aegis of the Department of Industry & Commerce, where Des O'Malley was then Minister. The acquisition eventually got approval from both bodies but, in the meantime, a lot of damage had been done to R&H Hall through the hostile takeover. We were all wounded and the IAWS share price dropped from 90 pence to 34 pence over the next year. This put us to the test.

The problem was that the perception in the marketplace, including the media, was that IAWS had bought a dog. Now two dogs would make an even bigger dog. The market voted with its feet. That was a tough time, but there was tougher to come – the bad press, the fear that the media might have been right, sitting on the side of the bed at 4am adding up the sum of the parts that were worth more than the total debt we had. Going through a period like this is traumatic, but it is in these situations that management skills, loyalty, friendship and team-playing become so important. How many of these attributes are taught, or even thought about, in second and third-level business education establishments?

In 1990, we created Irish Pride Bakeries from a mixture of bakeries across Ireland, including Lydon House in Galway, Western Pride in Ballinrobe, Brennan's in Bandon, Kiely's in Tipperary, Sweeney's in Thurles, King's in Limerick, Williams in Taghmon and Brennan's of Arklow. All those bakeries had been created because of Ben Dunne, who built a bakery in Dublin and got his cousin in Macroom to start contract baking, making cheap bread. They drove the price of bread down to 17 pence a loaf and put six of our Boland's customers practically out of business. This was at the time of IAWS's peak debt.

In response, we got the six bakers together and, over the space of two or three weeks, we agreed terms with them to buy Irish Pride Bakery, all of them putting in their family businesses. IAWS put up the seed capital of £3m and that was how Irish Pride was created. The other competitors were people like Joe Brennan and Pat The Baker. The smaller bakers saw themselves being protected in the bigger scenario. The families got money and we spent some on developing the brand and rationalising the business. In November 1991, the bread business was losing £270,000 a month. All the losses were being funded by the flour supplier – i.e. us! Irish Pride now owed Bolands a considerable sum and was losing cash every month. The situation required immediate action. Harry Hunter ran Bolands. I put him in to run Irish Pride, together with Bill Minnock The two of them turned it around. Hunter was a great man: he died on the 11th fairway of the Grange Golf Club and I often wonder if the stress played a part. To give credit where credit is due, that business taught us about bread and that's where we saw the real potential of Cuisine de France – it was really at the upper end, away from the madding crowd. We now have 400 people employed in Irish Pride.

In 1991, the economy was not going well. Money was expensive. We needed a £100m loan from the banks, with Bank of Ireland and Ulster Bank heading up the syndicate. Suddenly, three of the banks pulled out of the syndicate, leaving us short of £18m. I was on my way to London when I got this news and I had to turn back to try to convince the remaining banks to stay with us and take up the £18m. That was the worst moment. Over the following weeks, we had serious discussions with the banks, with Archer Daniels Midlands (ADM), and with Greencore. We were going to give the company away if we could not raise the money. All this coincided with a difficult time in the agri-food business and the sector was seen in the eyes of the credit committees of the banks as a no-go area. That put covenants around us, which meant we couldn't buy or sell £50,000-worth of stuff. I asked the Banks if that meant I could not change my car. I had in mind a BMW 7-series for £68,000 and was told I could go ahead to keep the image right.

IAWS was very close to going under. However, we had a good business strategy, which was working, but we were running out of time. Then, within a year and a half, and despite the pressure and covenants from the banks, the business started to perform seriously well. We were growing in pure earnings-per-share terms at about 18% compound. The banks had gained confidence, as had the Board. We had doubled the size of the organisation by bringing in R&H Hall. We had grown in the Republic, in Northern Ireland and in the UK.

The lesson all of this taught me was to hang in there, to have faith. The support I got at home and from my colleagues kept me sane during this period. I suppose I had confidence in an ability to see beyond the crisis and, despite what they say about banks, I have a lot of time for those people who had faith in me and helped me. I have also forgiven those who didn't help me. I don't carry any bad feelings for them – they were under pressure themselves. Anyway, that was then and this is now.

The quest was always for earnings growth – and that was definitely there. We did not acquire anything for another four years, from 1990 to 1994. For the 16 years we were a public company, there was never a profit warning.

Although some people would say that Cuisine de France probably made us, IAWS was always in the fishmeal business in Killybegs. When the opportunity arose to buy a large co-op enterprise in the UK, with plants in Aberdeen, Grimsby and the Shetlands, we seized the moment. It's a wonderful business. You pulp commercial fish and fish trimmings and take out of them oil and protein which in turn ends up in the aquaculture industry, the fastest-growing sector in the world. Now, everybody has smoked salmon in their fridge. We called that business right.

The question the institutions always asked was what were we going to do with the free cash. David Martin, the Finance Director, would have talked up the free cash part of the business. To my mind, the question was how to spend it wisely. One course was to give it back to the shareholders, while the other was to invest it in the compound growth of the company.

In 1988, before we went public, we thought of diversifying into tanning. We set up a business, in Clondra, in Co. Longford and got £5m from a BES fund. Dr. Pat Loughrey, ex-Batchelor's, was appointed to the Board to represent the BES money involved. He was also acting as a mentor to me. The enterprise was successful for a while, but then, we had to shut the operation down – it didn't work. We were tanning sheepskins because the population of sheep was growing exponentially. We got that right but the price went west because the number of sheep all over Europe was growing at the same rate. That project taught us a lot and we scrammed. In fact, we applied that lesson in other places – when a thing doesn't work, get out quickly and move on to other things.

Meanwhile, Pat Loughrey and Ronan McNamee, also ex-Batchelor's, got together to import frozen bread from France. That was the start of Cuisine de France and it expanded rapidly, from one outlet to 1,000. Ronan was then working for IAWS, as our sales agent in Northern Ireland, selling flour to the bakeries, and he was doing very well for himself and for us, but Pat needed him full-time for their new business. I released Ronan, but kept him on commission as requested, £5 per ton of flour sold, which suited us both. Then, in 1991, Pat and Ronan offered us half of Cuisine de France for £1m. They didn't want the money – they wanted to invest in the business and build a factory. They were very grateful to me personally for the break I had given Ronan in the flour job and the commission. This made the total difference in our getting Cuisine de France eventually.

In 1995, they decided to sell Cuisine de France, which was then worth about £30m. We bid £15m for half the company – we didn't have the resources to bid for it all. Pat and Ronan did a deal with a multinational, but this went sour when that company put in their due diligence team who tried to rubbish the business and took £5m off the deal. (There's a letter on file from Pat telling us about this abortive deal and how they regretted not having done business with us, but that maybe, in the future, we could talk again.) Things came right in January 1998, when we bought the whole business. It was all done in a couple of weeks. We paid £40m for it then and £11m of an earn out, £51m in total. People were sceptical at the time, but our banks and the Board had enough faith in the deal. It transformed IAWS. In 2005, 80% of our Group plc profit will come out of that business.

People say to me if you hadn't bought Cuisine de France, where would you be now? Was it the best move? We have now spent £500m on it – we bet the farm. The jury will always be out on that because the money we spent is still there. What made the difference was that we were the only ones to run the whole operation from start to finish – sourcing the flour, making the bread, putting it in the ovens, selling it to the shops, running baking academies. We did it all and we had the logistics to support it. There are now outlets in the USA and the UK (Délice de France), as well as in Canada where an introduction to Tim Horton resulted in Cuisine de France being rolled out in 3,000 A&P stores nationwide, owned by the Tingleman family. Ronan McNamee is still associated with us. He has too fertile a mind to be stuck in one place for too long.

To make a success of your business, you've got to be lucky in the people you work with. As CEO, I had a great team around me, including the ladies on reception and probably, most importantly, the guy who opens the gate each morning. I believe the "office of the CEO" is a good system. The heads of business reported into the CEO's office. If I was not there, any one of three people had as much power as I had. My contribution to this business was as a strong manager, disciplined and demanding. I had a vision and I concentrated on it. My colleagues allowed this, but they also challenged it, as did the Board. We had many arguments about the vision and the strategy. There were never any yes-people around me.

Where does a vision come from? One, it is about earnings per share. What I learned at a young age in a public company was that it did not matter what you did in the eyes of the investing public. In the eyes of the fund managers, it was all about EPS growth. I suppose the vision was about could we find something somewhere that would deliver 18% to 20% compound growth *per annum*. That was the only thing that would give the investing public an appetite for our shares. We had to be quite choosy in the things we went into. We looked at many businesses. The criteria were common and most of the businesses we bought were on an earn-out and on a business plan. If the business plan could prove that there was 20% uplift in earnings, we would look at it very seriously. And if the owners could deliver the three-year plan, we would give them a kicker on top of that. The acquisitions had to pay for themselves and they had to enhance the IAWS Group earnings by the 20% and maintain the PE. PE is the heart and soul of the business. Most businesses have a PE of 12. The other six, to bring it to 18, is hope value.

The vision was about understanding what the investing public wanted. Maybe we went public just because Brosnan[21] and the lads in Kerry went that way. It seemed a good idea. The best part of it was that we were going to create value for our shareholders. They would have a share worth £5 rather than a co-op share worth nothing. Kerry Group created a sweeping effect, which helped us. We learned from them. Learning the mind of the institutional investor was that it was about growth, growth, growth. We had to ask ourselves if we were in that kind of business. That's why we sold businesses that were not performing. When you take a number of non-performers out of the business, the rest of the business jumps up. Then we had to concentrate on what we were going to do with the money the business was throwing off. Could we go into businesses that were unique, meaning that, from a competitive point of view, they were ahead of the posse, ahead of their time? Cuisine de France was that. We saw that early on.

The bread business taught me a lot about where to position ourselves – don't be dependent on any one big supplier or customer and try and be where the masses are not. Knowing what the market wants and timing are part of the vision. Cuisine de France was the best fit in the world for that. It's about convenience, about footfall, about impulse buying, about great products available fresh all day, just bake it when you want it – it's about today. This is also true of our operation in La Brea in the USA. It's a separate business, owned by us, and it's outstanding. Gourmet bread, expensive at about €3 or €4 for a little loaf – it's party or weekend food.

The one thing I realised early on with Cuisine was that timing was of the essence. The market won't wait, once there's an opportunity to change. If we had not done it, someone else would have.

We're now there and are not too threatened by anybody – the only threat is ourselves. We're now into food service and catering with Pierre's where, among other things, we do up-market desserts, hot food and canapés.

I was married young. I got all the business grief over at a good age and retired at 57. But I'm as busy as I ever was.

---

[21]   **Chapter 2.**

I made the decision to retire as Chairman of IAWS Group plc at the end of August 2005, but I will remain as a non-executive director where I will lend the maximum possible support to my successor and to the management team.

I have, however, continued in my role as Chief Executive of IAWS Co-Op, which is soon to be renamed. In January 2004, the board of the Society approved a growth strategy for the Society, which aims to further increase shareholder value and also liquidity for its members. Since then, significant progress has been made in repositioning the Society for future growth. The Society has built a 26% stake in NTR plc and agreed terms with the SWS Group, subject to supplementary due diligence and legalities.

In April 2005, the Board approved the process of changing the corporate status of the Co-Op to avail of opportunities in the environment, energy and services sectors. The Co-Op's other assets include full ownership of Irish Pride Bakery and Premier Proteins, as well as a 50 per cent interest in Greenore Port and a 45 per cent stake in French fertiliser company, Cedest Engrais. IAWS Co-Op has also confirmed a share exchange, allocating in the second half of 2005 11 million IAWS Group plc shares to Co-Op shareholders on a *pro rata* basis to existing shareholdings. This is a follow-on from similar exercises, which were successfully completed in 1996 and 2002, when 31.1 million IAWS Group plc shares were passed back to members.

Notwithstanding all of this, I am fortunate to be able to take more time out these days. I am able to give more attention to my family and return the support they have given to me over the years. Eileen and I have a house in Spain and both of us are keen on golf. Mind you, when you're having a bad day on the golf course, it can feel a lot more like hard work than any of the days I have put in during my business life.

We were away for a month at Christmas. We were supposed to be in Phuket. However, the Meridien Hotel could not give us a frontline beach view for those dates so we decided to go in the New Year instead. We never got there. The Tsunami hit on December 26. Maybe the old number isn't up yet.

8

MICHAEL MACCORMAC

UCD Business Schools

*I saw I couldn't get anywhere unless I engaged in the
political process in UCD. That meant I had to consider
how you get power.*

MICHAEL MacCORMAC is Emeritus Professor of Business Administration in University College Dublin and former Dean of the Faculty of Commerce.

He has retired from the directorships he held.

He was born in Ranelagh, Dublin, on May 14, 1926.

He is married to Pat Dunne, who worked in UCD. They have a daughter, Lucy, and one grandson, Matthew.

He was educated at St. Mary's College, Rathmines, and at UCD (BA, BComm, MA, MComm, DEconSc).

He is a Life Fellow of the Irish Management Institute, which he helped found, and a Fellow of the International Academy of Management.

He was Chairman of NIHE Dublin (now DCU) and of the National College of Ireland.

He served on the Board of the Higher Education Authority and on the Senate of the National University of Ireland.

He held several business appointments as director and chairman and carried out substantial research on a range of business topics and on the racing industry where he became Senior Steward of the Turf Club.

He was Chairman of St. Vincent's Hospital and of the Medico Social Research Board.

*W*hen I retired in 1982 from the IMI and settled in UCD, several of my business friends envied me. I think they had a view of academia as a place of cloistered calm. I shall always be grateful to UCD because it has given me the gift of personal freedom. But the image of cloistered calm, if it ever reflected reality, has been shattered as universities become more publicly accountable and as university heads try to push through reforms to meet the changing needs of the educational marketplace, a vulgar concept in the minds of some.

Machiavelli's oft-quoted dictum is worth repeating: "There is nothing more difficult to take in hand, more perilous to conduct, or more uncertain of success than to take a lead in the introduction of a new order of things, because the innovation has for enemies all those who have done well under the old conditions and lukewarm defenders in those who may do well under the new".

I owe Michael MacCormac several debts of gratitude. From 1977, I had been a visiting professor in Trinity College. Michael MacCormac and the President, Tom Murphy, invited me in 1982 to UCD. While I enjoyed Trinity, with Lee Lyons and Bill Watts as Provosts, the warmth of the welcome to UCD tipped the balance. And it was Michael MacCormac who gave the formal introduction when the NUI gave me an honorary doctorate that year.

I am delighted to have Michael captured between the covers, as are his former colleagues. His introduction of business studies to UCD and, by way of example, to third-level education in Ireland, could well have gone unsung. When you look at the beautiful Quinn building on the Belfield campus with 2,100 undergraduate business students, and the graduate school on its own extensive campus in Blackrock with 1,100, it's hard to think back to 1954 when the first "business subject" was put in the BComm(!).

There is nothing to add to this introduction because, as you will see, Michael, in his 79th year, tells the story of the battle for business studies with meticulous accuracy and recall.

The conversation was recorded in Michael MacCormac's home in Dublin, on February 22, 2005.

MICHAEL MACCORMAC

I am very much a Dublin man, born in Ranelagh. My parents and my two grandfathers were Ranelagh people. My grandfather on my mother's side was a builder. He built all the redbrick houses around Beechwood Avenue Church. Then he built an estate in Clonskeagh and, I gather, did not do very well out of it. He died fairly young. My paternal grandfather was a manufacturer – iron and tin. He made buckets and things in a firm in New Street. When I was small, my father owned a factory in New Street. He did not want to continue in the business and qualified as an accountant. In UCD, I found I was one of the very few people who was a Dublin man. They were all from the country. It was normal to become an academic if you were from the country, but not from Dublin.

I went to St. Mary's in Rathmines – I was there for my complete schooling after a few years in Muckross. I took the Leaving Cert. in 1944 – 18 of us in the class. We all passed bar one. He stayed on for another year, became a chartered accountant, and went to work in Zurich. He married the daughter of the American Ambassador there, who was a big machine tool manufacturer. He inherited the whole thing – she was an only daughter. He fell on his feet. He comes home now and again and has lunch with me and some others. He now dresses and behaves like an American. You'd never think he came from St. Mary's in Rathmines. More of the class emigrated: there were two doctors, two priests – one of them became the Abbot of the Cistercian Abbey in Roscrea; there were a couple of farmers; a few business people.

I suppose I was a good student, in that I passed all the exams. In my final year, there was a Holy Ghost Father who was a real producer/dramatist. He decided the school would do a play by Aodh de Blacam called *The Golden Priest*. The golden priest was Oliver Plunkett. They made me Oliver Plunkett. That was December 1943. I was on the stage for the whole period of the drama from 8.00 until 10.00. A terrible play. However, it taught me about voice delivery and how to talk. In 1947, I was auditor of the Commerce Society in UCD. A few years earlier, the auditor had been one C.J. Haughey. Charlie knew Pat and me very well. We used have the odd meal with Maureen and himself. He always said that he would never have got the BComm unless he had Pat's notes. Garret and Joan Fitzgerald were also friendly contemporaries.

I went to UCD and did a BA in History and Economics and a BComm. You could take them together in the old days. I got first in the BA. When I took my degree in History, Professor R. Dudley Edwards offered me a scholarship in Irish History, initially funded on the history of Dublin. I had to decide between History and Business. Perhaps I should have been an historian. I got third in the BComm – the first place going to my future wife, Pat. Second place went to young Paddy Byrne, the son of the legendary Lord Mayor of Dublin, Alfie Byrne. I was bitterly disappointed with my result.

I did the BComm with no difficulty at all. In those days, it was not a particularly arduous degree. After the BA and BComm, I stayed on for another year and did an MA in Economics. Pat took the MEconSc. In the course of that year, 1947/48, I sat for the Commerce Bursary. It was a travelling studentship – if you got it, you were supposed to go somewhere else and do something academic. It was worth £150, which, in those days, was enormous. The logical place to go was the London School of Economics. I found that, in the following year, they were starting for the first time in the UK a postgraduate course in business studies, a one-year diploma. I thought that would set me up in business.

There were 15 of us from all over Europe. Obviously, I was the only Irish person and there were only two English. To my astonishment, after a few weeks I got a letter saying, as a foreigner, I was entitled to a Leverhulme Scholarship. I sat for an interview and got the scholarship. That gave me nice comfortable money. So far as I remember, the Leverhulme was worth about £300.

I learned an enormous amount. There were very good people like Lionel Robbins who, amongst other things, had been director of the economic section of the War Cabinet and Basil Yamey, who taught marketing, and William Baxter, who was the leader of the accounting profession.

We met for all day, every day – it wasn't just lectures, we did projects and things. There was one very bright Englishman who got us all to read *The Times* every day before we came to college. The result was that we were completely up to date on all that was going on in the world and we had a daily competition on the news.

The fact that I did a diploma in business studies sparked me to see if I could translate that into an Irish university.

At this stage, of course, I was not employed by UCD. I came back in midsummer 1948 and started to qualify as an accountant – I thought I'd go into my father's practice. I qualified in 1951. I had a call from the Commerce Professor, Barney Shields, who told me that Dr. Beddy, who lectured on Economic Geography – one lecture during the day, one at night, everything was repeated at night – was not interested in doing the evening lecture and would I do it. Being foolish, I said "Yes". I knew no geography, never mind economic geography. I knew nothing about trade routes. Pat made up the notes for me and I dished them out.

The first lecture I had is engraved in my mind. It was to about 100 evening students in one of the theatres in Earlsfort Terrace. I was 23 and, after the lecture, three of the students who were much older than me came up to me. They were very polite, they welcomed me but told me gently I knew no geography. I told them that was a shrewd remark. They told me they had chatted after the lecture and decided I needed help. They told me they would come and talk to me after each lecture. That established my lecturing capabilities in something I knew nothing about.

That one lecture a week slightly cemented me into the university.

At the same time, 1949/50, the original committee to form the IMI was put together. George O'Brien, who was Professor of Political Economy, decided that he did not know enough about business. He looked around to see who would fill the business slot for UCD on the IMI committee – he didn't want to let it slip. He asked me and I was delighted. I was by far the youngest person on the committee. The next youngest was Michael Dargan.[22] The committee was chaired by Sir Charles Harvey of Guinness and I learned a lot in the course of a year from him about how to run committees. He started every meeting weekly at half-past two. He was a marvellous chairman because, as

---

[22]   *In Good Company* (1987).

you know, there were two separate groups.[23] When any difficult questions came up, and there were many, Charles would say, "We'll postpone that and take it at the next meeting and you can think about it in the meantime". In the meantime, you were asked to lunch in the Brewery. There, Charles and the protagonists from either side would agree on the solution to the problem. At the beginning of the next meeting, he would announce what the solution was.

One of the most important influences in my life was my serious illness, which occurred in 1959/60. I had stomach problems, which had been wrongly diagnosed overnight. Having spent five months in hospital and seven operations, I was declared cured and ready to take back my career. My surgeon was James Maher and his professionalism saved me. On the night of my final operation, I was told that it was unlikely I would survive and I had to reconcile this prospect with my state of mind. I came out of hospital with a new vision of my life and the possible contribution that I could make. I think this made me rather braver and more thoughtful.

Now, apart from the IMI, to which I was very committed, I was convinced during that period about the need for an educational foundation for people who are not skilled in business, people from other disciplines such as engineering, science and, even, medicine. I was convinced that, if I could expand my entrée to UCD as a part-timer, I could possibly influence what was going to happen there. It's not just because I'm saying it to you, I owe a lot for whatever success I attained in my thought processes to the people I worked with in IMI.

The college people were uninterested. Michael Tierney was President. He did not think much of the BComm. The Professor of Commerce did not secure from the President an extension when he reached 65. Somebody had to fill in for whatever Commerce was. They asked me to. Commerce was considerably cut down and what I had to do was two lectures a week in the third year of the BComm. One of my first lectures was on the history of trade unionism. It was to an evening class of about 25. I was talking about the Guild system. After about 15 minutes, a student stuck his hand up and said, "I think you have the wrong class. This is archaeology". In those days, Commerce was

---

[23]   See Cox, Tom (2002). *The Making of Managers: A History of the Irish Management Institute 1951 to 2002*, Oak Tree Press, Cork.

anything. One title I remember was Barney Shields's, "The Evolution of Industrial Organisation". I saw that, if I could stick with the Commerce subject, I could extend it and develop it into a proper business subject.

That didn't arise because, in 1951, they elected three people as statutory lecturers in Economics: Paddy Lynch, John O'Donovan and Jim Meenan. These were official full-time people. The only other people on the Commerce Faculty who ran the degree were George O'Brien, who was Dean, and Gerard O'Brien, a partner in Craig Gardner, who lectured in Accountancy. They all decided that the BComm was not a top-class degree. They wanted to change it into a degree in Economics. They passed all sorts of regulations and disposed of the Commerce subject. They asked me if I would lecture in Economics and I said I was delighted to. I started lecturing on things I wasn't really interested in at all, such as the economics of the farm. They then added on a bit of accountancy, so I was lecturing in Economics and Accountancy. I had a great time lecturing in Elementary Accountancy to people like Laurence Crowley. Alex Spain was a student – all sorts of people whom I got to know very well.

Turning the BComm into a sort of Economics degree didn't quite work. They had me for one thing and I was not very keen on it being an Economics degree.

I made great friends with Paddy Lynch, who was 10 years older than me. Paddy had been Secretary to the Taoiseach. John O'Donovan came from the Department of Finance. I was able to convince Paddy that there was more to the BComm than economics and that there should be some elements of business studies in it. Paddy progressed that through the Commerce Faculty against great opposition. The President, Michael Tierney, always took the chair at a faculty meeting – a practice that continued up to recently.

I got to know him quite well even though I was only a kid really. Tierney took some interest in me because, I suppose, I fought quite a bit. I think he admired that and also the fact that there was somebody willing to step into the retiring professor's shoes, not that there were any shoes.

I also talked to Gerard O'Brien, who did not believe in business studies at all. I got on well with George O'Brien – Pat and I used go out with him at night. I did not get anywhere with John O'Donovan nor very far with Jim Meenan. Gradually, the atmosphere changed and, about 1954, they put a business subject in the BComm. I was given it and could do completely what I liked – nobody had the slightest interest in it. I was able to design two undergraduate courses in the first and second years of the degree. There were two lectures a week in second and third Commerce. I thought I would be able to develop things in a step in the right direction. I was working in a university that did not approve of business studies and I had to be very careful. I was a nobody – I had no statutory position.

In 1954, a request came from the Department of Industry & Commerce, where Norton was Minister, to George O'Brien, to tell him that there was a European Productivity Agency mission going to the States and could he recommend somebody to go on it. I was nominated to go on what was called EPA 229. There were about 15 Europeans, a couple of English and me. The idea was that we would spend some time in a university in the US and then go around business schools. We were to see what the business schools were doing and if that could be translated into our own countries. I was lucky because the Germans and the Scandinavians did not like the English participants. Somebody was needed to act as secretary to the mission. I became a sort of organiser and had to produce a report.

We were in the States for five months, which Pat didn't like – we got married in 1950. She stayed in Ireland and perfected her skills. I admired her grasp of reality and her agreement for me to go to the US. A problem was that Pat did not drive – I left the car in the driveway in our house in Ranelagh. When I came back, she could drive.

We spent one month out of the five in the University of Syracuse, doing an actual course. It was not very good but it broadened my mind to the range of subjects that could be done in a postgraduate degree. My companions on the mission were all pretty senior – 30 to 35 – and were very critical of the American professors. At the end of it, I wrote a long report. It went into the files in the EPA. I presented it to UCD, who had no interest in it. George O'Brien put it in a drawer and that was that. But writing the report gave me ideas that I could do something useful in UCD.

At this stage, the IMI was working away with its post-experience short courses. I was very interested in seeing the way thinking was developing there.

In the period following the EPA mission, funnily enough, I got very close to Michael Tierney. When I had difficulties, I'd ring him up and he'd say come and see me. He had an office in Earlsfort Terrace. I'd go in and sit at the fire and talk to him. I slowly introduced the topic of graduate business studies. In contrast to what I had been told, he was quite interested. He talked to George O'Brien, who was neutral. Paddy Lynch talked to him quite a bit. The first thing I proposed to him was that I would run an MBS (Master of Business Studies) to follow immediately on a primary degree. It would be for BComms who wanted to concentrate on one subject for one year, like Marketing or Industrial Relations.

At this stage, the College strengthened my position by making me a part-time lecturer, but I was still working in accountancy, which I didn't like at all.

I recruited Tony Cunningham who had just got his doctorate in Cornell. He got a job as lecturer in Marketing. This was an enormous step forward. He started to run the Master of Business Studies with me. A number of peculiar things started to happen. Des Hally became lecturer in Accountancy. You ask me if I was the boss. I was in a kind of way – a boss without authority. George was the boss but George didn't care. Pat was secretary to George O'Brien at this stage. She did his letters and looked after him. His method of dealing with Pat was that every morning she would have coffee with him in Bewley's. He brought his post with him. They'd sit in a corner, George would open the post, hand it to Pat and tell her what to do. That gave me another link to authority.

That MBS, incidentally, had to go through the whole hierarchy – the Commerce Faculty, the Academic Council, which consisted of all the professors in the College, then to the Governing Body, which was composed of County Councillors and God only knows who, and from the Governing Body, it went to the Senate of NUI.

I saw I couldn't get anywhere unless I engaged in the political process in UCD. That meant that I had to consider how you get power. The first thing was that I had to go full-time. The College agreed, with the title Lecturer in Economics (Business Administration). That made me a member of the Commerce Faculty, which was an enormous advantage. Towards the end of the 1950s, I began to talk about doing postgraduate work for people who might not have had a BComm or a BA. That was very difficult to get across. Everybody said "No".

I kept at it. I kept talking to Tierney. I was now also lecturing in the Engineering Faculty, giving final year engineers a flavour of business. I got to know the engineering professors very well – people like John O'Donnell, Michael Hogan, Pat Leahy. Michael Hogan was a great friend of Michael Tierney. He was a powerful guy in College on all the various bodies, including the Senate of the NUI. He, with Michael Tierney, and Joe McHale, the Bursar, would have been the people who put Belfield together with Pierce Purcell. Michael Hogan was quite interested in my doing something in the post-experience field.

In the early 60s, I wrote a proposition for a postgraduate course – the one thing I could not call it was an MBA. People in College knew enough about an MBA to think of it as the dreaded American business school thing, which they would not let near the College. I foosthered around with it and called it all sorts of things and got nowhere. Finally, I got to a stage with the Commerce Faculty that, if I wanted to do it, they would not stand in my way. Michael Hogan thought the whole thing was marvellous but asked what I was going to call it. I said I was a bit at sea. He said, "There's a great degree in the United States called an MBA. Would you think of calling it that?". I said I'd have to think about that very seriously. He said he would push it through the University. In 1964 we started it, at which stage the College gave me permission to get a few more people. I got Jim Doolan for Finance. (Jim Doolan subsequently was the first person to hold a Professorship of Business Administration in UCG.)

In the 1960s, I began to accumulate a few more people. Joe McHale told me I could not replace Jim Doolan – Joe wasn't too keen on business studies anyway. I proposed another few and got Brian Hillery for Industrial Relations. Brian worked with one of the American banks in Dublin. At that stage, I decided the only way of developing the school was to get some Chairs. I had been promised a Chair myself by Tierney. When the Statute came up, there were two Chairs, one in Social Science, which went to Jim Kavanagh, later Bishop Jim. They decided not to make the business administration appointment, so I was left as lecturer. When Gerard O'Brien, who lectured in Accountancy, retired, they decided that, to hold Des Hally, they would have to give him a Chair. I made a strong case that there would be holy murder if Des Hally got a Chair before me. Jerry Hogan was now President. He was Michael Hogan's brother and had been Registrar. He thought my case was fair enough and, in 1971, the Chair of Business Administration went through with the Chair of Accountancy.

During the 1960s, there were a few other factors that contributed to the success of the MBA. One was that there was enormous interest from the business community, particularly from people in their late 20s – people like Richard Hooper, Tom Toner and Enda Hession. They became a great source of strength to me. The course *had* to be good simply because it was for good people. They told everybody how good the degree was.

I was working closely with Tony Cunningham and both of us went to all the lectures. This was in sharp contrast to what happened in other faculties. The standard came up.

At the time I got a Chair, I decided there would need to be significant additional Chairs. I approached John Donovan, Managing Director of Esso in Ireland, a great IMI man. Esso sponsored a Chair in Industrial Relations, which went to Brian Hillery. I went to Don Carroll. He put up the Chair in Marketing, which went to Tony Cunningham. They were the first sponsored Chairs in UCD.

Some members of the Business academic staff applied for, and were appointed to, senior ranks in other Irish and foreign universities. In one instance, when I was a member of the assessment board, the candidate was asked why he wanted to leave UCD. He said that he wanted to get away from that man – me. He got the job.

Once I became a Professor, it was different – I had status and was a more powerful member of the Commerce Faculty and was elected to the various College bodies. At that stage, all the different bodies were filled by election. I was a member of the Academic Council and could talk there. From the Academic Council, because I talked so much, I was elected to the Governing Body. From the Governing Body, I became a member of the Senate of NUI. There was enormous opposition in the College to making any changes in the MBA, mainly from Arts professors, led by Maurice Kennedy, who was Registrar for a lot of this period, from Ruairí de Valera, who was Archaeology, from some of the Social Scientists. Cardinal (then UCD Professor) Desmond

Connell played a major role in questioning the place of graduate business studies. He had a powerful voice in the ear of Tom Murphy

I then began to run short courses with American professors. We brought over four Harvard professors for two-week courses. We put people up in the old Intercontinental Hotel, now Jury's. One course was led by Ed Bursk, editor of the *Harvard Business Review*. All sorts of people came on those courses – people like Tony O'Reilly.[24] We had great fun. We had no buildings for it – I worked out of the back of the Medical Faculty in Earlsfort Terrace. I told Tom Nevin, the Dean of the Science Faculty, and he gave me some rooms in the new Science Building in Belfield. Ed Bursk, who was a little Bostonian, was taking a session and Jerry Hogan, then President, told me he'd like to come to one of those things. He came at 2.30 and sat at the back. Bursk did not know who he was. The first thing Bursk did was to peel off his jacket and throw it in a corner. I asked Jerry Hogan what he thought of the session. He told me the case study was very interesting but he said, "It was the first time I ever saw a professor take off his jacket". Of course, at that stage, we all wore gowns. I held three or four of those courses in the College and they did a lot for business studies because of the prestigious professors.

I continued my connection with IMI during that period. I considered it very important with what I was doing in College.

I asked Michael Smurfit if he would put up a Chair in Corporate Strategy. He did, and Enda Hession was appointed. The College put up a Chair in Statistics and Quantitative Methods, which Harry Harrison got. Gradually, we built up a set of people who were very bright. It was great to have them to work with.

We moved to Belfield in 1968. We were first into the new Arts Block. Harry Harrison did a good job on the quantitative side and began to introduce computers. I did a lot of joint lecturing with Des Hally, who was truly brilliant – two of us in the classroom. We did case studies that way – he'd take one side and I'd take the other.

I did a lot of work abroad – I went with Tony Cunningham to places like Thailand, India and Kenya. I did some work in South Africa with Martin Rafferty.[25]

---

[24] **Chapter 12**.
[25] *Out On Their Own* (1991).

All this helped the vision of Business Studies in UCD. The College was well aware of everything I was doing.

The next important thing, from my point of view, was the appointment of Tom Murphy as President in 1972. He was a great supporter of Business Studies.

At the end of his period, I ran for the Presidency against Paddy Masterson, who beat me out of sight. That was fair enough because I was coming from an area which was not very popular in the College. Paddy beat me at the Academic Council level by something like 20 to 10. I decided then not to go the next step to the Senate of NUI. I left the race. I was told by everybody in the Senate that, had I stayed in the race, I would have got it. Colm Ó hEocha, President of UCG, thought I was an absolute idiot to quit the race.

In 1986, when I was 60, I decided I had done my job, I had created the Chairs, I had created the degree. We were at the stage of talking about a new building on the Belfield Campus. However, the Carysfort situation turned up and Paddy Masterson rightly grabbed it. It has turned out to be a wonderful campus.

I believe the Business Schools have been a great success and I'm happy with the part I played in helping form them. I get satisfaction that something I set out to achieve, was achieved. But there were times I felt it would not work.

When I left College, I held a number of directorships. I was, strangely enough, a director of Irish Shell and Bord na Móna. When I retired, I was approached to be Chairman of Green Property. I worked in Green with John Corcoran, who was managing director. We bought Blanchardstown. It was very rewarding for Green (and it was very rewarding for me). Blanchardstown is now worth many hundreds of millions, totally owned by Green. John was succeeded by Stephen Vernon, a London property man, a marvellous guy. He still runs Green. It's not a public company now. I was then asked to join the Board of First National Building Society. I was invited by Harry Robinson, the solicitor. Meetings were at 4.30 in the afternoon. I sat at the boardroom table and was handed a big file. I looked at the results. The detail was unbelievable. Gerry Creedon was chairman. They ploughed through everything, talking about each branch and the amount of money it had taken last month. Awful stuff! At the end of the meeting, I took up the file to put it in my briefcase. The Company

Secretary, said, "What are you doing with that?" I told him I was taking it home. He said, somewhat frantically, "You can't take it home! That's First National Property and remains here". He won the argument – naturally. Strangely enough, I was supported by Matt Macken, who was on the Board. Matt was the ex-Dublin City Manager. I did a deal of work with First National, with, I must say, a lot of co-operation, to adjust the Board meetings and to talk about real things. They had the ridiculous system that the chairmanship revolved around the directors once a year. It came to my turn. It was agreed that I would stay as chairman for a few years. They were two solid directorships, in First National and Green.

I was a director of Brown Thomas Group under the Maguires and, later on, the Westons. Galen was, and is, a great chairman and a very good person to work with and I think I made a contribution to the success of the Group.

I wrote a lot around that period about boards of directors. That's now been taken up in UCD and they have the Institute of Directors Centre run by Professor Niamh Brennan.

Right through my whole career, I was interested in racing. In fact, I wrote a book about it. Somewhat to my surprise, it turned out to be an important book. I was then asked to become a member of the Turf Club, where never an academic had set foot. From that, I was nominated to go on the Killanin Commission – I worked in it with Lord Killanin for four years. Killanin was an unusual chairman. He let everybody hold the floor for as long as they liked. The meetings went on for hours, very boring. In the middle of the work, Michael Killanin had a bypass and I became chairman. I got an awful lot done in three months. He came back and we wrote the report. It was an important report for the racing industry. It led to the creation of the Racing Board – I was put on it from the Turf Club. Denis Brosnan[26] was Chairman. Then, to my astonishment, I became Senior Steward of the Turf Club, the top job. You are the final arbiter – difficulties can come right to the top but, I am glad to say, not many in my day.

I very much enjoyed the whole racing scene. I went racing every Saturday and sometimes during the week and went to many meetings abroad. I learned a lot about people, let alone horses. I was never

---

[26] **Chapter 2.**

seriously interested in backing – I had the odd fiver. Now I look at racing on television.

I knew all the trainers and owners and I'd meet them before a race and they would all tell you they were going to win. You learn about human nature. If a good trainer tells you that he has a horse that will be in the first three, the chances are the horse will, at least, come fourth. But if they tell you they are going to win, they really are going for a win. However, they can't all win.

During the period we've covered, I was also a chairman of the National Institute for Higher Education, Dublin, which became DCU. I worked closely with Danny O'Hare, the first President. I was responsible for the move to Glasnevin. We started in a few rooms in Grand Canal Street. I hired Danny. I had done a lot of work in UCD with the Vets and the Ags and, when the Ags Building was built in Belfield, I knew that their building in Glasnevin, the old Albert College, would be free. I was friendly with John Wilson, the Minister for Education. He agreed with the move to Glasnevin and, as Chairman of the Dublin Board, I was also on the Board for Limerick NIHE,[27] while their Chairman was on the Dublin Board. I worked with the HEA during that period and chaired two Government Commissions – one on Dublin City traffic, which was responsible for bus lanes, then another commission on freight in the Irish ports. I must have got that because I taught economic geography.

Finally, a significant influence has been my wife, Pat. When I was struggling in College, she was a great backup. She worked closely with me. She had a few miscarriages and ultimately produced Lucy in 1967. Right through, she has been a model of consistency and support. Since she came from an academic background, she understood what I was about. It was possible to argue my cases with her as they came up. Many times she changed my view because, at times, I was a bit too difficult or pugnacious. She was prepared to tone it down – and I did what I was told.

---

[27] **Chapter 17.**

9

HUGH MACKEOWN

Musgrave Group

We are confident that, so long as we keep the kernel of the business going and successful, we can ride almost any storm.

HUGH MACKEOWN is non-executive Chairman of Musgrave Group plc.

He was born in 1941 in India to parents from Cork. His father worked in the Indian Civil Service.

He has four sons: Philip, Keith, Scott and David.

He was educated at Radley College, England and at Trinity College Dublin, where he graduated in History and Political Science and gained his colours in golf, rugby, tennis and squash.

He joined Musgrave Brothers Limited, his mother's family company, in 1965 and took charge of the company's new wholesale warehouse. In 1968 he was appointed to the Board, joint managing director in 1971, and managing director in 1972. He resigned as managing director at the end of 1996 and was appointed to the position he now holds of non-executive Chairman.

He was the founder chairman of the Wholesale Grocers' Trade Association, IADT, which later amalgamated with RGDATA, The Retail, Grocery, Dairy & Allied Trades' Association.

He was previously a non-executive director of Eagle Star Insurance Company and of the Ulster Investment Bank.

He played golf for Ireland in the European Championships and the Home Internationals in 1973 and at senior level in 2001 and 2005. He won the 1982 British Championship in 18-foot national sailing dinghies in Findhorn, Scotland.

*T*his is the only story in the book of an old – very old –
family business. The Musgrave Group, under the distinct
SuperValu and Centra banners, both throughout Ireland
and increasingly in the UK, is now so big and spread that we
would not think of it as a family business. While it has changed
unrecognisably over the years, what has not changed are the
enduring family values. Hugh Mackeown's unswerving
determination to maintain those values is the keynote of the
chapter. Over a 120-year span, there were four family chief
executives. Hugh Mackeown says unequivocally, "That gave us
continuity in the personality of the company. It gave the company
an individual style. It involves high levels of performance and
integrity". In the background was the non-conformist ethos.

Hugh Mackeown has the lean and aristocratic mien of someone
who, in Alan Clark's memorable definition, did not have to buy
his own furniture. His courtesy, his public school education –
Radley – are palpable.

They were a reminder to me of the telegram sent from Henley
Royal Regatta by the headmaster of Shrewsbury School: "Eton
beaten. Radley badly. Shrewsbury lose". The friends I made in the
London Rowing Club were from public schools. Contrary to (at
least Irish) popular belief, they had a sense of fairness, of
directness, of duty, and a self-confidence that was never
overbearing. You can see that in Hugh Mackeown.

A distinguished golfer and sailor, there is no sign of his 64
years.

The conversation was recorded in Hugh Mackeown's office
in the Musgrave Group, Ballycurreen Industrial Estate,
Airport Road, Cork, on March 21, 2005.

HUGH MACKEOWN

The origins of the company were from 1876. Two brothers came to Cork – we think from Leitrim – to set up a grocery shop. They did very well considering that, within 20 years, they were investing in a hotel and various other businesses, all in Cork – I think the geographic strand is an important one. Having opened retail shops in North Main Street, they expanded out to McCurtain Street. They opened a shop in Tralee, which did not do particularly well. They also went into the wholesale end of the business, which presumably had more potential. Things progressed pretty well up to the First World War, a prosperous time for Ireland.

My grandfather, John L. Musgrave, took over the running of the company some time in the early 1900s. He had a fantastic record. He lasted into the 1950s. During that period, he had two world wars, the War of Independence, a civil war, the Emergency and a great depression. From, say, 1916 to the 1950s, Ireland had a depressed history. He brought the business through all that. He is the hero of the story, in that he helped the company to survive through those difficult years, while many family companies, after 30 to 50 years, with new generations coming in, tend to fade away.

A problem he did have was that he had a lot of brothers in the company. They diversified in Cork into different businesses: hotels, laundries, coal distribution and things I can't even think of. Different family members developed different businesses until the lack of central control and the poor performance of many activities, allied to the depressed Irish economy of the '20s and '30s, led to the company nearly going to the wall.

As a result, John L. cleared out the rest of the family, but obviously not his first cousin Stuart, who, like him, was the son of one of the original brothers. In effect, he eliminated his own brothers and their shares. How he did that I don't know. I imagine there was a sufficiently serious situation to enable him to swing it. From then on, there was a strict rule that only one member from each of the two branches of the family could come into the company. That worked OK in my grandfather's case because he had only one son, plus two daughters, one of them my mother. His first cousin, Stuart, had three sons and one of them came into the company. The other two became doctors and went to practise in England. Their families are still shareholders.

It was a fairly Draconian rule, but I have no doubt that it played a big part in the company surviving as well as it did – first of all, through the difficult times and, when things began to pick up, as well as the two family members, there was a need for professional managers. In the early 50s, my Uncle Jack took over. They were still very tough times. Bringing in professional management was important for the future development of the company.

Jack concentrated initially on tea – Musgrave Tea was well known. In the early '50s, it would have been vying with Lyons.

The wholesale business began to get into serious trouble. Competition had changed practices. You had the beginning of self-service and some retail co-ops were being formed. Jack went and looked at what was happening in England and Holland. There was a voluntary group trading in one stream with cash-and-carry as a parallel development. He was the first in Ireland to move into those two, about 1960. That was really the start of where we are today.

Because we were based in Cork and Munster, there was a tendency to take on diversification. My grandfather, because of events, had narrowed everything down, but Jack was looking to expand. We diversified into a lot of new, but related, businesses –shop-fitting, building, and on the restaurant side, which eventually proved not to be successful.

We also had the tea, left over from successful days, a sweet factory, and the Metropole Hotel in Cork. The hotel had been developed in about 1905. It was part of the buoyancy of the company in those days, a buoyancy that did not last beyond 1920.

By international standards – and I hesitate to say it – Cork is a small environment. If you want to expand, you have to go into new businesses rather than repeat the businesses you have – that was our policy then. Things were only beginning to pick up in the '60s.

In order to cover the whole of Ireland with our voluntary group, which was called VG, we got a wholesaler in the Dublin area, Garvey's of Drogheda, and one in the Galway, Nilands. Our first instinct was not to go out into these areas and do them ourselves but to get established wholesalers there.

Jack Musgrave was a major influence. I first came into the company for six months before I went to Trinity. I was working in the warehouse but had coffee with him every morning – at his request. It gave him a chance to indoctrinate me. I think he had me marked out for succession.

If you look at where we are today, it is actually a fulfilment of his principles. The fundamental principle was that you were trying to bring independent retail grocers to where they could compete head-to-head with multiple retailers. At that stage, multiple retailers were only starting. Dunnes were starting, Roches were quite strong in Cork in the middle of town, Feargal Quinn was getting off the ground.[28] You had, of course, H. Williams, Liptons, people of a slightly different category. Powers were just starting with Galen Weston.

It was a good indoctrination and that was the vision which we concentrated on to different degrees as time went by and circumstances changed.

The multiples were now steaming ahead. At times, you would ask yourself if we could do it, was it ever going to work. Progress was slow and the multiples were mopping up. The scale of our operation could not match theirs. But underneath it all, Jack's vision inspired what we were doing most consistently.

In the early '70s, he was anxious to do less and, in 1971, I was appointed joint managing director. I was in the company then only six years or so, having cut my teeth in the warehouse end of it, the logistic end. (I took History and Political Science in Trinity – absolutely relevant!)

That was me moving into the hot seat – it was a difficult transition. I was just 30. The company was much smaller than it is now. It was possible to integrate a family member into the company whereas, in the last 20 years, we have not succeeded in doing so. There is now no full-time family member working in the company since I became non-executive Chairman at the end of 1996.

In 1972/73, I became full MD. I went to some IMI courses and obviously there was a need for a long-term plan. It had never been

---

[28] *Out On Their Own* (1991).

done. It was all in the mind of the chief executive. I produced a plan, which indicated a concentration on the grocery business, geographic expansion and the elimination of some of our other businesses, of which the main ones would be the tea business and the hotel. There were others: shop-fitting, building, a sweet factory. We sold 40% of the tea to Brooke Bond and then, after a few years, we sold it all to them. Barry's Tea has done very well out of Cork. For us, the problem was that we were competing with our customers. The bigger we got, the more of a problem that became. We were also big sugar distributors along with Punch's and with Garavan's of Galway. There were some other arms to the business that were likely to cause trouble in the future. The Metropole Hotel had a good run in the '50s, and particularly during the War period. It was one of the leading hotels in the country, managed by Douglas Vance, a famous Irish hotelier. But being off the centre of the city with no parking, the future was not bright. I managed to persuade the other family members on the Board that we should sell it.

We exited from a lot of businesses. They did not give us much cash but we were fortunate in that my grandfather, who was a bit of a whiz on the stock-market, had built up a reserve of investments. That money enabled us to expand into Dublin in 1972 with the cash-and-carry. We built from scratch a warehouse of over 100,000 square feet. It had quite an impact. It was our first move out of the Munster region. It was the project on which I cut my teeth. I either fell or thrived with it. One of our directors, Pat Hickey, wanted to move to Dublin to manage it. Our two heads were on the block.

Jack was so concerned about it that he talked with Martin Rafferty[29] and his friends about it. They were BWG – Brooks Watson Group – a shell company they had then, but at that time, Spar were in the throes of combining all their Irish operations in BWG. The talks did not go very far. It would have been a shame if it had happened because we would have lost our identity. Spar, as you know, or rather BWG, ran into tough times. They were strapped for cash. They were also builders' providers and they appeared to run the Spar operation as a cash cow. That meant they could not invest and do things we were able to do.

---

[29] *Out On Their Own* (1991).

Our Dublin cash-and-carry was an outstanding success. Cash-and-carry was the story of the company in the 1970s. We built another one in Dublin. We built two big cash-and-carries in Munster, one in Cork and the other in Limerick.

The '70s were tough for us but we kept things going. We realised that what we had to do was to separate out the bigger VG retailers from the smaller ones. They were all getting tarred with the same brush. Even the big retailers were considered by the public to be in no way the same category as the major multiples like Dunnes, Quinnsworth and Superquinn in Dublin. The '70s nearly went by, before we took the steps that had to be taken. The '70s belonged to the cash-and-carry but, in the mid-'70s, we took over a food-service company, Smiths Stores. With it, we got a bright young man, John Smith. He provided a lot of impetus to the replacement of VG.

Towards the end of the '70s, we decided to split VG into two groups. The bigger stores would become SuperValu Supermarkets and the smaller stores, Centra Convenience Stores. It was a difficult enough job. John Smith had with him Seamus Scally, for whom we're having a party this very evening as he retires from the position of Group Chief Executive. Seamus was originally Sales & Marketing Director. We pushed through the change, which, naturally, some retailers resisted. They were nervous about it. Our colleagues in Drogheda and Galway were reluctant, slow to move.

The early '80s were very tough – the best thing that ever happened, because people are readier to accept change when things are not going so well. By the mid-'80s, when H. Williams got into trouble, we were in a position to take advantage of the changed situation, having already acquired the franchise for the Dublin market. In the end, we bought 15 of the H. Williams stores in the Dublin region. This gave us a lot of credibility, both with retailers and our suppliers. That was the basis for everything that came after.

In the late '80s, we purchased Nilands in Galway. We had decided at that stage that the only way we were going to develop SuperValu satisfactorily was as a national group, which we needed to control ourselves. Nilands did not want to sell. Eventually, we were able to do a deal with them. It was pretty expensive but they had worked hard at their business. We now had access to the whole 26 counties for our own SuperValu and Centra franchises. We should not really talk about *our* retailers. They are fiercely independent people, and rightly proud of what they have achieved. What we often do is buy stores from somebody else and then invariably sell them on to independent retailers. We act as a conduit.

Now we regard Ireland as one market.

In the early '90s, interest rates went up to ridiculous levels for a short period. Some of our retailers got into trouble. A SuperValu store in those days would have been worth £2m or £3m but all the franchisee would have in it would be £200,000 or £300,000. He was very highly geared and vulnerable to interest rate hikes. It's hard to look back on that now when we're stuck with interest rates that may be too low but very nice for anyone who wants to invest.

Once that period in the early '90s went by, we were on a roll. We developed SuperValus in every county of the Republic, and in the North of Ireland. They got bigger. The business mushroomed right through to the present time.

We had done the ground work in the late '70s and early '80s. When things looked up, we were in a position to take advantage. They were the golden years. Life is inevitably going to be more difficult now with the bigger chains coming in from abroad but, at this point, we have helped to bring first-class food retailing to practically every town and village in Ireland, in many of which the multiples had no interest.

The things that helped us in those days – and I think, rightly – would have been the Groceries Order and the cap on superstores. The Groceries Order would mainly have been the ban on below-cost selling. Tesco came in and purchased Three Guys, which was Gubay. They bought a few more stores and then decided that they did not like what they were doing and sold to H. Williams, who became a conglomerate. They began to expand and look a little bit aggressive, and Dunnes are reputed to have gone after them with very low prices and put them to the wall. As a result of that and of other arguments, the ban on below-cost selling was brought in. It's an absolutely right thing to have. Received wisdom is very slow to recognise predatory pricing. The reality is that a multiple chain with, say, 100 stores can pick a town where there is a successful independent retailer with one store. They can open a supermarket in that town and sell at very low prices just in that supermarket in that town. They have another 99 stores to give them the funds to do that. And they can put that retailer out of business. A *Panorama* programme in Britain verified that several years ago. I am told that recently in England, Tesco tried to put one independent store out of business but he made such a fuss that Tesco backtracked. I believe the Competition Authority had their heads somewhere out of where they should be. They just did not understand. Politically, perhaps, they don't want to know. The truth of the matter is that, when the day comes that all those people have been put out of business and there are two or three dominant supermarket chains, where's your choice? Where's your true competition? It's not going to be there. The dominant chains will cosy up – informally – they won't even have to talk to one another. It will just happen. Prices will go up. There will be nobody there to rock the boat. That is going to happen – I don't have a shadow of a doubt about it.

Then there's the question of vast hypermarkets. If you have four or five towns with populations of 5,000 within 20 miles of one another, do you want this vast hypermarket in the middle of them, perhaps in the countryside, with everybody driving to it on a predatory pricing basis? They have 100, maybe 1,000 stores across the world and they can sell at any price they like, assuming below-cost selling is not there. They can mop up the business from all that area. People will drive 10, 15, 20 miles if the offer is right and suddenly you have no grocery supermarket shopping in four or five towns in the region. Is that what people want? Our experience is that the politicians are very conscious of this issue. When we have gone and made our case to TDs, we have had huge acceptance. There is a statistic trotted out that 40% of small towns and villages in Britain have no grocery shop. That's the alternative we're facing.

Dublin is a different case. The hypermarket idea is still prevented, except for the IKEA development. It will be part of the regeneration of Ballymun. Even though it doesn't apply to groceries, it is a potential thin end of the wedge. IKEA bluffed its way in. They said if we can't have a 200,000 square foot store, then we won't come in, while, at the same time, they had decided in Britain and other places that they would develop smaller stores because they were not able to get permission for the big ones.

I can understand that there is consumer pressure for an IKEA store, and there's the danger of one opening in Newry instead of in Dublin, but it is a dangerous precedent.

Those two areas are of concern to us. The independent retailer, no matter how good and efficient he is, is at a potential disadvantage when faced with the multiple competitors, because of unfair trading practices. The large independent retailer is the backbone of our business.

However, it's a struggle that's been going on for 45 years, since 1960. We expect to win that battle for the next 10 to 20 years. I don't want to be immodest but I think we've done a very good job in developing our services, both logistic and advisory. When the retailers saw the potential, it brought out their skills and they really applied themselves.

As prosperity spread through Ireland, there was scope for a much higher quality operation in medium-sized towns, which the multiples turned their backs on. There was good potential there, a gap that we exploited. For 10 years, we were the only people in that gap. That has changed. You now have Dunnes opening convenience supermarkets and stores. You have Tesco prepared to go in at almost any size, as they have done in Britain. You have Spar moving up into Eurospar. Spar, incidentally, are now independent. They bought themselves out from Irish Distillers after Richard Burrows[30] had bought BWG. That niche of the market is now more congested. For the size of store in which we are interested, the franchise option is *the* option where, preferably, you have the owner-manager on the spot. The large chains, Tesco and Dunnes, are not going to put their best managers into a store of 5,000 square feet. If you can get a good, highly-motivated franchisee who is interested in good quality and service, I'm sure it's the right option – so long as you do not have predatory pricing.

The successful selection of franchisees is a matter of contact and experience. Very often, they are multiple managers who want to get into business on their own. Sometimes, they are existing retailers in the village or town who maybe have a son or daughter who is showing enthusiasm. Sometimes, they are former Musgrave employees.

It's not simple or straightforward and it does not always work.

If the franchisee is not living up to our quality standards, we talk, persuade and cajole and if, at the end of the day, that doesn't work, then the sign comes down. That does happen. It's a human

---

[30] *Leaders* (2001).

relationship issue and you have to keep working at it. It's an intense partnership.

I believe that, when some people talk about partnership, they don't know what they're talking about. It was a buzz word five years ago. For us, it is partnership in every sense of the word – it's like marriage, you are totally dependent on one another. If they fall down, we fall down, it's, if that's the word, a symbiotic relationship. There are some things you say to independent retailers and there are some things you don't say. They are naturally proud so it's all got to be handled carefully – but firmly.

One of the things we have not done is to duck out of difficult confrontations with retailers when necessary to maintain standards.

We have two kinds of stores. We have trolley-shop stores where somebody comes in and fills up the trolley with groceries for a week. We have 175 SuperValus in the Republic. 90% of them would be trolley-shop stores. Centra, the convenience stores, are basket stores, where somebody comes in and picks up a small number of items. There is a clear differentiation between the two. That distinction was where we took a jump ahead of our wholesale opposition. We made the distinction and stuck to it firmly in our advertising and marketing. We have a SuperValu sales director and a Centra sales director, and a marketing director for each. They operate each brand with a distinct mindset.

SuperValu is competing directly with the multiple. That's its target. It's got to price itself to do that. It has to have the range and the quality and it's got to have good parking, and so on. On the Centra side, it's convenience. How can we make things easier, simpler, quicker?

Price-sensitivity is always an issue. One of our supermarket franchisees was telling me yesterday that the customers can never accept that our prices are competitive, simply because of the background. They tell him that, because he's buying from Musgraves, he can't be cheaper. His latest one was someone said that, because he was not buying from Musgraves, he couldn't be cheaper! Now he has a Dunnes and a Tesco four or five miles up the road, big ones. He's always concerned about price. I said to him, "Just look at the way your business has grown". He is the biggest individual store that we have: Barry Collins in Carrigaline – an old friend of mine. I said to him, "Are you a little more worried about price than you have to be? It's always a factor, but there are other factors and your business has grown phenomenally". What I said is borne out by surveys, which emphasise other things like hygiene and convenience, friendly service, perhaps a little less as the independent stores get bigger and the personal contact tends to fade.

Price is only make-or-break if it reaches ridiculous proportions. If a store sells for 50 cent something that usually costs 80 cent, then people get excited. If it's normally 80 cent and somebody sells it for 77, people don't get all that excited.

In these big display ads, particularly on Sunday, there is a huge emphasis on price. That is not so much about actual price as about image, so you won't get people saying, "I won't go near them – they're robbers". You've got to establish a price image so that people recognise that you're in the ballpark. If you are 3% more or less, a lot of people don't notice that. Studies have shown that 20% of shoppers are absolutely focused on price. The other 80% are more wishy-washy about it. It's not a matter either of how much money people have – it's a matter of their temperament. In Germany, what are known as the hard discounters, very cheap, very restricted range, unfamiliar brands – Aldi and Lidl are of that ilk – they have found they are very successful in middle- to upper-middle-class areas. They do every bit as much business there, maybe even better, than they do in lower-class areas. Lidl advertisements are nearly all non-foods – there was one in yesterday's *Sunday Indo* which was all about gardening. When they open in a town in which one of our independent retailers operates, if the retailer is good, they don't hit him seriously. They might just stop his growth for a year, but not permanently. Each Aldi or Lidl store is quite small and when they came in, we or RGDATA did not object. The media got a hold of that and said oh, they were asleep, why did they let that happen? It wasn't right for us to object to them. First of all, they were not selling below cost and, secondly, they weren't too big. What we say to the politicians is that two of the cheapest operators in the world have come into this market. We asked the politicians if that is not a competitive, open market? While the housewife goes to a Lidl or an Aldi, she has to go to the other store. Price is a complex thing but, don't misunderstand me, you can't disregard it.

We bought a chain in the south-east of England called Budgens. We planned to sell the stores to franchisees – 150 stores in mainly small towns, basket stores if you like. We then got an offer from Londis to purchase them. They are the only retail franchise co-op in Britain. They are totally separate from Londis in Ireland. They have something like 2,200 stores, from Land's End to John O'Groat's. Budgens cost us quite a lot of money. We were not looking for another purchase quite so quickly, but it was too good an opportunity to miss. We put Budgens and Londis under one management. Budgens will be the SuperValu – the bigger trolley-shop stores – and Londis will be the smaller, convenience basket-stores. We have four distribution depots in Britain now.

Our future is to keep our operations in this country going – obviously very successfully, and to try and replicate throughout Britain – 55 million people – what we've done here. We're coming into a very mature market in Britain in the heel of the hunt. It is probably the right place to go and start in against the Tescos and the Asdas to try and return independent retailing to a decent level.

Many years ago, we developed into Spain. Our theory then was that, being a less mature market, the opportunities would be greater for us. Spain had become quite backward under Franco – things were only really coming through in the late '70s or early '80s. We bought in 1994 – it was still relatively backward then. There were a lot of hypermarkets and old traditional shops but nothing in between. In practice, it has proved very difficult because the Spaniards did not take to the franchise concept. We can't get good franchisees, so we're now developing a few of our own stores. This may change in time – maybe franchisees will come through. It was hard to get people who had the integrity and the willingness to put in the time and the work.

However, we did learn a valuable lesson. After that, we went to Russia – another immature market. We did not like what we saw there. We looked at Poland, nothing like as bad as Russia, but we were beginning to realise that immature markets just did not work. This is why we got to England *via* Spain, Russia and Poland, rather than direct. We came to the conclusion that a mature market suited us better. You need a prosperous community that will be happy to pay for that little bit extra in the way of service and convenience.

The influence of the Musgrave family on the business has been critical – what you are talking about here is ownership. People tend to underestimate the importance of ownership in the style of a company, the things it does and why it does them. We had family chief executives for 120 years, four of them. That gave us continuity in terms of the personality of the company. It gave the company an individual style. The reason we are in the business is because of the style. You supply the same customers day after day, year after year. There is a huge difference in that kind of business by comparison, say, with construction or property development. There you go in, you do your job, and you clear out. You may never deal with the same client again. That gives you a different, sometimes offhand, attitude. We *know* we're going to see the customer again. It involves high levels of performance and integrity.

With the Methodist background and the non-conformist style – a lot of shopkeepers were Methodists in years gone by – there was the basis for the Musgrave style.

The family business encourages long-term thinking – it's absolutely central. For example, if we were a public company, we would have had to look three or four times before we did Budgens and Londis and we might well have said "No". For us, it was just a question of can we, in five or 10 years, make a success of this business? Because we do not have the stock-markets breathing down our necks, we can take that sort of risk, and even, ultimately cope with failure, if that is the way things turn out. But I don't for a minute believe that is likely to happen.

We can be confident that, so long as we keep the kernel of the business going and successful, we can ride almost any storm.

If we anticipate difficulty, our shareholders will understand that we will work our way through and out of it and you'll get a continuity of the same style as long as the family maintain their input. It's not just financial. It's also psychological and style. What we are working hard at at the moment is our family relationships. We have family assemblies and councils. We're developing a family constitution. If we cannot keep the commitment of our 50 family shareholders, their interest and their input, their willingness to see the thing continue, their pride, then we're not going to be able to maintain ourselves as a private company.

One of our principal objectives, which people never believe, is that we are going to remain private. That's written down in black and white. It's up to those 50 shareholders to establish a constitution to keep the relationships which will enable that to continue and empower the full-time executive management. The management will know that there are shareholders there who have the same commitment, outlook and style as the family traditionally had.

In seven years, I expect to hang up my boots finally. I will be giving much of my time to ensuring that, out of the next generation, we can get people who can take my and Peter's and Stuart's places, the two other family directors, ensuring that the executive are properly motivated and encouraged. It will be a difficult transition. We recognise that and are working hard at it.

PÁDRAIG Ó CÉIDIGH

AER ARANN

*Our original vision was a safe, reliable, profitable
service to the Aran Islands. Then the vision became
Ireland's internal airline. Now the vision is to be the
best regional airline in the world.*

PÁDRAIG Ó CÉIDIGH was born in Spiddal, Co. Galway on May 23, 1957.

He is married to Caitlín Costello and they have four children: Emer, Cathal, Triona and Fainse.

He was educated at the Jesuit College in Galway, Coláiste Iognáid, and took a bachelors degree in Commerce at UCG. He studied accountancy with KPMG in Limerick and is a qualified solicitor.

He owns Foinse, the national newspaper in Irish. He took over Clódóirí Lurgan in 1996, a printing company based in the Connemara Gaeltacht.

He bought Aer Arann in 1994. It was then a small airline serving the Aran Islands. It had an annual turnover of £250,000 and had never made a profit. It employed eight people.

The airline is now one of the fastest growing regional airlines in Europe, with a turnover in excess of €94m and passenger numbers of just under one million for 2004. This was an increase of 59% on the previous year. The airline now operates over 500 flights a week, with a fleet of 10 ATR aircraft across 17 UK, six domestic and two French routes.

He was named Ernst & Young Irish Entrepreneur of the Year 2002 and represented Ireland in the Entrepreneur of the Year Awards in Monte Carlo in 2003, where he came second overall.

Aer Arann was awarded the European Bronze Airline of the Year Award for 2004 by the European Regions Airline Association.

Through Aer Arann, he supports national and local charities.

*T*he conversation with Pádraig Ó Céidigh brought me back.
*I got my secondary education in Coláiste Iognáid, where
Pádraig went to school and subsequently taught. In my
day, it was all-Irish and a bit prurient – black priests with black
hats on black bicycles patrolling the streets of Galway to catch you
out after 7.00 pm. Presumably at 7.15, you could be up to no
good. I was chastised for reading* The Three Musketeers, *for
chortling over a phrase "as confused as a Jesuit in Holy Week".
However, I had superb French and English teachers. Like Pádraig,
I went back to teach there for a while after my MA, until I came to
Dublin and lived happily ever after.*

*The "Jes" Pádraig taught in is a different place now, bi-lingual
and co-educational. In my day, girls would have been regarded
(hopefully) as occasions of sin.*

*Pádraig enjoyed teaching but I can well understand his need to
move on. Unless you have a true vocation, the discipline of the bell
and the repetitiveness of the prescribed courses can be
constricting. "Looking back on it now", he says, "it was inevitable
I was to leave teaching and develop skills in another avenue – in
the world of business and risk".*

*Pádraig Ó Céidigh did not arrive with a leap and a bound from
teaching school to running and owning a regional airline and
being Entrepreneur of the Year in Ireland and Europe. His dream
literally came to him on Christmas Day 1993, when, after dinner,
he went for a walk by a half-finished airstrip in Connemara. He
said, "I stepped into a dream", a dream he achieved resoundingly.*

The conversation was recorded in the author's office in
UCD, on November 30, 2004.

Pádraig Ó Céidigh

On a fine June evening in 1969, Colie Hernon composed a letter to the editor of *The Irish Times* from his home on Inis Mór. He spoke from the heart for his island friends to get help to set up an air service between the Islands and the mainland. He did not realise that his letter would lead to Aer Arann.

A number of Galway businessmen read the letter, were intrigued by the possibility and decided to invest. The first commercial service operated by Aer Arann, with a nine-seater BN2 Islander aircraft, took place on Saturday, August 15, 1970. This was a great event in the lives of the islanders. In true Aran tradition, one of the best parties ever held on the island took place on the night of the inaugural flight. The Chief Pilot, Bill Wallace, said the weather was too bad to make the return flight that evening. There is no account of when the weather improved sufficiently – it did not appear to cause any customer complaints.

This airline would become the lifeline of over 1,000 islanders. Thirty years later, it would expand to become one of the best and fastest-growing regional airlines.

In the early days, the airline operated from a number of different mainland locations. The local Inis Mór beach became the landing strip. Later, a proper airstrip was developed on each of the three Islands.

The airline always struggled to make a profit. It was set up originally as a community facility. There were some attempts to create an internal air service around Ireland which, for various reasons, did not work. In 1982, the airline was sold to Tim Kilroe. Tim was Irish, from the Mayo/Roscommon border, went to England at 17, made his way up through the construction industry and became a successful businessman. He owned hotels such as the Four Seasons near Manchester Airport, a lot of property and had a keen interest in race horses. One of those horses. *Forgive & Forget*, won a Cheltenham Gold Cup, but later had to be put down.

Tim set out to manage Aer Arann from his head office in Manchester. The airline got a licence to fly a scheduled passenger service cross-channel. This was revolutionary, because, at that time, nobody had challenged Aer Lingus on their UK services. Aer Arann never took up the opportunity given to it by the licence. I believe that paved the way for Ryanair's strategy two to three years afterwards.

Aer Arann was still not making money. In the summer months, it started flying passengers between Shannon, Derry and Galway into Dublin.

In 1992, Tim Kilroe decided to move from Galway airport and develop his own airstrip and passenger facilities in Connemara. On May 1, 1994, he sold me Aer Arann as a going concern.

I was born in Spiddal in 1957, a small, closely-knit village in the heart of the Connemara Gaeltacht. My parents moved back to Spiddal to raise a family after a number of years working in London. There were five of us – I was the eldest.

After the local Spiddal primary school, I followed some of my friends to the Jesuits' Secondary School in Galway city. This was a new and very different experience for me, probably the most important learning experience of my life.

That was followed by a Commerce degree in University College Galway.

I went to work in Limerick as a trainee accountant with KPMG, then Stokes Kennedy Crowley. I was not comfortable there for a whole lot of reasons. They were a great company to work for, but, I could not settle in Limerick. I was deeply involved with the community in Spiddal and, more importantly, my girlfiend was in Connemara. I moved to a firm of accountants in Galway, Thomas P. Burke & Company.

One day I bumped into my former headmaster, Father Paddy Tyrrell. Over a coffee, he suggested that I should consider teaching as a career. Thus began my next experience, teaching in the Jes. I found it difficult at first, not because of the work, more due to the fact that most of the teachers had taught me a few years earlier. However, I settled fast. Every day was a new experience, and every student a new challenge. I got great satisfaction from teaching young people – I have never met a young person without potential. Teaching is the art of enabling people to tap into their potential.

I began to read and learn more and more about how to become an effective teacher and how to help people develop learning skills. During the holidays, I would go to the UK and elsewhere to do courses at my own expense. I learned to teach more effectively, but then I discovered that my role was not to teach, but, instead, to facilitate learning – a different focus. I would help students to have the confidence to go and learn to create things for themselves instead of stuff being imposed on them. In other words, we developed self-directed learning for the individual student and not a shrink-wrapped teaching structure.

I had no problems in the classroom but the staff-room gave me headaches and, as the years went by, this frustration increased. I felt restricted there. Some teachers were committed and professional but there were some who were less than that.

Looking back on it now, it was inevitable that I was to leave teaching and develop skills in another arena – in the world of business and risk. We had just got our Easter holidays and Caitlín and I went for a walk by the sea beside our home. She turned to me and said, "Pádraig, take a career break. You're getting more and more depressed, fed up at the constraints of the educational system. You're not comfortable in that space. You used to be, but you're not now. You're not yourself, and you can't do a good job if you're not yourself". She was on the button. We mapped out my options. They were limited. I had worked as an accountant and was a qualified solicitor. With four young children, a wife and a mortgage, I set up a law practice, no clients but plenty of ambition. I felt that there could be a good market for a local Gaeltacht law practice. At first, I used a converted garage at home, then I rented office space in Galway city.

I had also been running a Summer Irish college. I was Chairman of the Community Development Council. The local Irish College had gone bust. Nobody was willing to invest their time and money to revitalise it. A friend and I took it over. In the first year, we had an enrolment of 200 students. During the next five years, we had 1,200. It was important for the local economy. Its future was secured.

Let me go back a bit, to Christmas Day, 1993. We would always go to midnight Mass. Then we would go down to my parents' house for Christmas dinner and at 3.00 or 4.00 o'clock over to Caitlín's parents' house. I would go for a long quiet walk. The walk brought me to a half-finished airstrip in Connemara down by the sea shore. It was about 18 miles west of Galway, built on a bog, the last place on earth you would imagine an airstrip. There were JCBs and rock-breakers and big holes in the ground. I must have been walking up and down that half-finished runway for two hours. I lost touch with time. I was away in dreamland. I was just thinking how amazing this thing was – imagine an airplane taking off from this place. It was crazy but brilliant at the same time. I could have been in the same mind-space Colie Hernon was in 24 years earlier when he searched for words to express his plea for help for an air service to the islands.

That went into my sub-conscious. In 1993, Aer Arann moved their operation from Galway to this new airport. Tim Kilroe had had a row with the board of Galway Airport. It was settled to Kilroe's satisfaction on the steps of the High Court. He maintained that the board of Galway Airport did their best to get rid of Aer Arann. It was a power struggle and the airport was always looking for more money. They eventually squeezed Aer Arann out of Galway. Kilroe had enough of it, so he built his own airport. That was when I stepped into the dream.

In 1993, I flew out to the Arann Islands twice. I was struck by the friendliness and professionalism of the staff. One night, I saw Máire Geoghegan-Quinn on television. She was Minister for the Gaeltacht, talking about the consequences of Tim Kilroe's decision to sell the airline. This caused major concern to the islanders as they were happy with Kilroe's operation.

In April of that year, I contacted Tim and asked him if he would sell the airline to me. I had no money. I was married. I had four kids, the youngest was only three months. I knew nothing about airlines. But that never seemed to be a major issue.

I phoned Tim twice or three times and then everything went quiet. He continued running the airline. In September, I phoned him again. He said he had moved on and was not now interested in selling. So I said, "Could I go over and talk to you anyway?". He told me his financial controller, Roger Haydock, would be in Ireland the following two weeks. Kilroe would arrange for me to meet him in the Connemara Coast Hotel in Furbo.

I met Haydock, a man with glasses, in his late 40s, a big long black coat, very swanky looking. I felt overwhelmed by his presence. But, after a few minutes, I settled and found the guy to be pleasant and interesting. I spoke to Kilroe a few more times on the phone. My brother, Seamus got married on December 23, 1993 – I was best man – and throughout that day Tim Kilroe and Roger Haydock were trying to phone me. They wanted to sell the company to me. On Christmas Eve, I phoned Kilroe and went to Manchester on December 28 to meet him. We shook hands and did the deal. Tim was like me, a handshake and word of mouth commitment was all that was required to create the contract and the commitment. We agreed that the whole purchase would go through on May 1. I was really nervous. For the first time, what I had got into really scared the daylights out of me. I knew nothing about the aviation business.

I did not have the money to do a go-it-alone. The banks wouldn't give me the financial support I needed. I re-mortgaged my house, everything I had. I took in a partner, Eugene O'Kelly, an anaesthetist in Galway, who became a friend. He came up with some of the money and then we got a couple of hundred grand of a loan from AIB in Galway against the property of the airstrip. I figured out that we could pay it back over a seven-year period, all going well.

Later on that summer, there was a problem with an engine on one of the Islander aircraft. We had to replace it. It cost about £15,000, which we did not have. Two members of the staff approached me, separately and independently, both of them not long married. They had some money not yet drawn down on their mortgages that they were willing to give me to buy the engine. Marie Mulrooney had spoken to her husband, Gearóid, to draw down more money from their mortgage to get the engine. Separately, Peter McKenna, an engineer in Aer Arann at the time, had built a house and had not drawn down his full mortgage. He and his wife, Keelin, were also willing to provide. I thought to myself, with staff like that, it's hard to go wrong. Both Marie and Peter have been instrumental in the growth of Aer Arann. They are great people and great friends.

We turned around the company quickly and made it profitable - well, marginal profits, £15,000 or £20,000. There had been Government subvention of about £150,000 from Údarás na Gaeltachta. To be honest with you, this was completely inadequate to provide anything like a decent service – everything was done on a shoestring. The staff were not being paid the salaries they were entitled to. All along, it had been Kilroe putting in more and more money. It was a personal subvention from Kilroe, as well as a State subvention that kept it going.

I tried to commercialise Aer Arann. This was not easy, as fixed costs were very high, so I did two things. First, I had to let go some of the senior management. I took on the role of Managing Director, doing the work that three of them had been doing beforehand. I saved considerable salary costs at the top end, plus the law practice was beginning to do reasonably OK. Second, our aircraft were maintained in England. I thought this was crazy, because we had mechanics and engineers in Connemara. Peter McKenna, a young and ambitious Athboy man, became Chief Engineer. Instead of maintaining the aircraft in England, which was costing us a fortune, we now maintained them ourselves in Connemara. Then we started maintaining other privately owned single-engine aircraft around Ireland.

We reduced cost significantly and started increasing income. I thought the third party maintenance work would pay but it didn't – we were busy fools. After two years of hard work, we were not making a profit on it, so I decided to stop. The best thing to do when you are on a dead horse is get off.

Revenue and increased passenger numbers were the second part of the strategy.

Before I got involved, Aer Arann would advertise its services in magazines in Europe, for which we were spending £8,000 to £10,000 a year. We were advertising to the wrong people in the wrong place. I knew that 1.5 million tourists came to Galway every year and about 250,000 people went to the Aran Islands, the vast majority by boat. There were only 5,000 people flying to the Islands. We started putting ads around Galway city and signs up on billboards. The idea was to get the tourists who were in Galway to fly to the Aran Islands for a day. Passenger numbers started to grow.

Our revenue was increasing. We had reduced our costs. However, there was still a gap between revenue and costs.

One Sunday morning, I was at home. Mary Gilmore, who works with me, phoned to say, "There's a man here, a Mr. Larry Stanley with his wife. He's from Aer Lingus. I think you should meet him". He had flown for a day to the Aran Islands and spoke highly of the service. Larry got me thinking in a greater regional context: I was going to create an Irish Regional Airline.

My original vision was *to provide a safe, reliable and profitable service to the Aran Islands*. Number one was safety. If we were going to fly at 10 o'clock in the morning, we flew at 10 o'clock, but if it was not safe, we ain't flying. I quickly realised that we could achieve those objectives, particularly with the really good people we had in the company. All they needed was direction, support and, most of all, leadership.

To run an airline, you don't have to know how to fix an aircraft, or how to fly one, or how to do a booking. What you need to know is how to create an environment in which people can do the best themselves, exactly the same formula I developed in my teaching days in the Jes. My role in Aer Arann is not to lead, but to facilitate leadership. Same thing – different environment. The people in Aer Arann motivate themselves and each other. They have a significant say in how the company should develop.

From the original vision of flying safely and profitably to the Aran Islands, I began to realise that we could do a lot more, building on the fact that we had turned around an airline that was forever losing money. In three months, we had started to move the tide in the opposite direction, with people who had a lot more talent and ability and skill than they realised. All I was doing was creating the opportunity for them to realise that potential, which, in the past, had been capped, not tapped.

I figured out that Aer Lingus could not be all things to all people. For the first time, I started to think about a business model. I could not afford to get advice from aviation consultants. Number one, I didn't know where to go, and number two, I had no money anyway. It was just like getting a blank canvas – you get paint and a brush and start painting. When you are painting, maybe a blob of paint goes somewhere you don't want it to. You rub it out and start reshaping it. At the end, you've created a painting that has structure and form. By trial and error and moving on, I had to create the business model myself.

We could not afford big mistakes. Even minor ones were expensive setbacks. I suppose I never considered that it was risky. It was just what I wanted to do – and that was that. It was not relevant whether people believed in me or not. That would not stop me, as the people most important to me did believe in me. That was all that mattered.

I figured that Aer Lingus would make a lot more money if they did not fly internally at all, if another airline flew internally and dropped the passengers at the Aer Lingus aircraft. I could see Ireland as a green field. Aer Lingus wanted to take people from all parts of that green field and bring them to other parts of the world, but a business model that was all things to all people could not be financially viable. They had to refocus and I decided to try to help them to see this new, different model.

If a senior person from Aer Lingus, like Larry Stanley, comes down to me and talks in a complimentary fashion about our service, that means we're on somebody's Richter Scale. Larry is now a non-executive director on my board. I started knocking on the doors of Aer Lingus but, with whatever little attention they paid to me, they thought I was crazy. I am sure that they had seen many budding entrepreneurs with great ideas – few, if any, of those ideas worked. I was just another of those people.

A PSO is a public service obligation to fly passengers around the country to peripheral areas, to areas which, but for the Government subvention and support, would not have an air service. The PSO model is in every country in Europe – there are six such contracts in Ireland. I decided to bid for them around 1997. All we had was two nine-seater aircraft. We didn't get the contracts – thankfully. Aer Lingus got them. But there was serious interest in our submission in the Department of Transport. I figured out that there was potentially an opening for us as a dedicated regional airline.

Ireland Airways, an airline based in Dublin went out of business. They had been operating the Dublin-Donegal PSO contract. The Department contacted us and other airlines that had previously put in submissions to consider bidding for this defunct route. More or less on the back of an envelope, we prepared our figures as best we could.

I was in the Great Southern Hotel in Galway on a Friday morning in March 1999. By this stage in my career, I had a mobile phone. I got a call from the Department of Transport: "Pádraig, we have good news and bad news. Which do you want first?". I said, "The good news". "You've been awarded the contract from Dublin to Donegal. And it runs up to December 31 next." I asked what the bad news was. They told me the Minister was under pressure to get the service up running fast. They wanted it to start Monday morning. I had no pilot, no airplane, no cabin crew. The contract required 19-seater aircraft. My nine-seater Brittan Norman Islander aircraft were no good to me.

I had anticipated something like this, but I had hoped for two months notice in order to get up and running. I contacted Tim Kilroe in Manchester, who still had an airline called Air Kilroe. He was flying 19-seater aircraft around the UK. I asked him if he would lease me an aircraft, pilot and all that went with it, to fly to Donegal on Monday morning. He said, "Fine", and he did. The aircraft would leave Manchester in the morning, empty, fly to Dublin, fly passengers from Dublin to Donegal at 12 noon, back at 3.00 pm and fly to Manchester that evening.

I was losing a lot of money, but, at least, we had started service. There was a cap on what you could charge – it's a very competitive contract. The airline that requests the smallest possible subvention gets the gig, so you cut your costs as tight to the bone as possible. That's why a number of airlines have gone bust flying these services. That was the first time we flew out of Dublin Airport. We did not have a desk. We had a fellow at Arrivals, standing on an orange box with a sign and saying, "Anyone for Donegal?" The same thing at Departures, "Donegal? Over this way, lads." We had no advertising or marketing and there were six or seven passengers on the 19-seater aircraft.

I noticed that there was a 36-seater aircraft – a Shorts 360 – at Dublin Airport, which flew to the Isle of Man once a day and back in the evening. It was there all day, sitting on the tarmac. It could not have been making money. It was owned by BAC Express in Gatwick. BAC operated aircraft and also leased them. They wanted to lease me an airplane that was on the ground over in England. I told them that I would lease the aircraft that was parked at Dublin airport for most of the day, not the one in the UK, provided they would subcontract their Isle of Man rotations to me. They agreed with me that they were losing money on it but that it was part of an overall contract. I said, "Sub-contract that to me and give me the airplane". They did. At 7.30 in the morning, we would fly business people (who became well-known since) out to the Isle of Man, back at 9.00 a.m. At 12 o'clock, we'd fly people up to Donegal, back at 3.00 p.m. and at 5.00 o'clock we'd go out to the Isle of Man. Between the two contracts – to the Isle of Man and to Donegal – I was breaking even.

Then one day, not long after I started operating the Shorts 360, I met Seamus McBrien of Target, at a football match in Croke Park. A mutual friend introduced us. Target are a courier company. Seamus was flying freight to Coventry at night. We struck a deal. I bought a white (well, off-white) Hiace van for a hundred quid. We had to take the van out to the airplane, unscrew the seats and put them in the Hiace, then fill the aircraft with freight and take it to Coventry. The airplane would come back from Coventry between midnight and two o'clock in the morning with more freight. The seats had to be reinstalled to be ready for passengers to the Isle of Man the following morning. That was it, four years ago.

Then, in 2000, we tendered for the PSO contracts for all of Ireland – for Galway, Kerry, Sligo, Donegal and Derry.

We had a number of commercial agreements with Aer Lingus, the most important of which was the use of their reservation system called Astral. Under this agreement, passengers could book Aer Arann flights by using the Aer Lingus reservation system. This meant that Aer Lingus received the income from passengers and then passed this on to Aer Arann after taking their commission. This caused significant cash flow problems for us in the early days. But there were further unforeseen implications, which brought us to our knees. When we built our business model for the PSO application, we assumed that people would have paid €1.2m in advance for tickets with Aer Lingus on the Astral reservation system. This would give us good cash flow/forward sales revenue on commencement of services in January.

We had seriously miscalculated. Aer Lingus had put a block in their booking system, which meant that passengers could not book flights in advance. We were not made aware of this change until it was too late for us to do anything about it.

We tendered for and won the tender, still unaware of the change with the Astral system. We were to fly between Kerry and Dublin three times a day, Galway and Dublin four times a day, Sligo twice a day and Knock to Dublin once a day. We were still flying to the Aran Islands using the Brittan Norman Islander aircraft.

I remember Jackie Healy-Rae, a local TD, saying, "That Pádraig Ó Céidigh is a nice Connemara lad but we don't want him flying those bloody aircraft up to Dublin. We want Aer Lingus. Aer Arann is degrading the service to Dublin". There was a serious amount of that stuff coming out from the local Kerry media. Anyway, we started the Kerry flights. They didn't want me in there. I could understand it – there was a lot of comfort in having the flag-carrier.

I decided to use ATR aircraft – 50-seater and 70-seater turbo-props made by Airbus Industrie in Toulouse. They are good and popular airplanes. I went to Toulouse to try and strike a deal with the President of ATR.

After a long wait, I was brought up to the fifth floor of one of the most famous aircraft manufacturers in the world. The boss was a man in his early 40s. His office was huge, graced with hand-carved furniture. The far end of the room was dominated by a big mahogany desk, with a map of Europe hanging on the wall behind it. He said, "I do not usually meet people like you but I've heard about you. You are amusing, a crazy Irishman". I said, "How do you mean crazy?". He said, "You come over here to France, to meet me, looking for airplanes, and you've got no money?". I said, "You're right". He said, "You're crazy. We don't do that. Who do you think you are? We don't do business like that".

I walked behind his desk to the large map on the wall, took one of his red pins, and stuck it in the map on Dublin. I said, "If you want your aircraft there, I'm your man. If you want something, and I want something, I ain't got everything you want and you ain't got everything I want – let's see can we work on something together". You know something? That helped turn his mind. Now we are one of the largest ATR operators in Europe. They have a promotional brochure saying "You too can build an airline like Aer Arann if you use our aircraft". That French flag I put on the map helped them to develop activity for ATR aircraft – around Europe, in particular. Now other airlines are copying our model – well, trying to.

The contract had a start date of January 17, 2001. I leased two ATR42 aircraft, which were scheduled to arrive in Ireland the previous week. On January 14, no sign of an aircraft. The following day, one aircraft arrived. The second arrived the day before the contract commenced. I had a plan B in case the aircraft were delayed, where we could call on another airline to provide the service until our aircraft arrived. I was praying that they'd come in on time. All the media attention was on us – you could feel the heat. Peter McKenna was in France organising the delivery. I will never forget his phone call the day before the aircraft arrived. "Pádraig, it's going to happen, it's going to happen". The Irish Aviation Authority was fully behind us. They pulled out all the stops to help us make it happen.

I had contracted crew in because there wasn't sufficient time to train people up: they were French, Polish, Romanian, some English and some Irish. It was the fastest way of getting up and running.

The service started well but, in late January 2001, we realised that significant revenue was not coming in. We started with empty planes, simply because people could not book in advance. Losing €1.2m revenue was a huge hit for us. Do you know what happened then? When one thing goes wrong in aviation, brace yourself for a number of problems. Foot-and-mouth changed the aviation landscape for us. It meant there were less passengers flying in and out of the country. The third problem was of our own making, we miscalculated the "out of hours" charges the regional airlines were to charge us. It was much higher than anticipated.

In June, I contacted the Department of Transport and told them I would probably have to surrender the PSO contract by invoking the break clause. The more we flew, the more money we lost. I suggested they get independent auditors to satisfy themselves about our position.

I reduced my costs and got out of some of the routes. We re-tendered for the contracts. Next thing, September 11 happens. My brother and father re-mortgaged some property. They left a bank draft on the kitchen table and said, "Now turn this company around". This was the last thing I wanted to happen. It gave me cash-flow for a few months but the pressure was something else.

I was struggling from day-to-day. Aer Lingus were in serious financial difficulty and they were our biggest debtor (we were still using their Astral booking system). Plus, after 9/11, insurance went up by 450%, less people were flying, and all the creditors wanted money on the nail. The Department of Transport decided to run a short-term contract until the following July, about eight months.

Six or so airlines tendered for this new short-term PSO contract. The tendering has to be done through the EU and stamped with the approval of Brussels. It's a formal, structured process. We were successful in our tender – at least, for the short term. We tendered again in July 2002 for a three-year contract. We were successful on Galway, Kerry and Knock. An airline called Euroceltic was awarded Sligo and Donegal, and British Airways – Logan Air – got the Derry to Dublin contract. We had got half the contracts.

I changed the Board members. Paul D'Alton became Chairman – he was financial director of Bank of Ireland Group and Larry Stanley came on as a non-executive director. I appointed Peter McKenna my chief operating officer. I had a new financial controller, Fergal Barry, a 26-year-old lad from Cork. I changed my management team quite a bit. We managed to turn the company around. After a few months, Euroceltic went into liquidation. We and five other airlines tendered for those contracts and we were the lowest, so we were back in Sligo and Donegal. This meant a lot to me.

My strategy then was not to have the airline PSO-dependent. I wanted to roll out more commercial stand-alone non-PSO routes. A year-and-a-half ago, the PSO routes would have been about 85% of our business. Now it's less than 30%. The PSO routes are important to the company but the other routes are profitable and successful in their own right. We chose them more by gut feeling than by any scientific analysis. Many of the routes were totally new, without any prior history.

I now own 100% of the company. When I bought it, the turnover was about €250,000 a year. We increased turnover tenfold from €250,000 to €2.5m. In the past four years, we went from €2.5m to €90m this year. It's huge growth. Last year, we carried 620,000 passengers – this year, it will be about a million.

The population of Ireland is over four million. The population of America is 265 million. If we were in America, based on passenger numbers alone, we would be one of the top 20 regional airlines in America. We work really hard and are committed and proud of our airline. We are very ordinary people doing extraordinary things, based on the classroom strategy of people growth.

Remember our original vision – *a safe, reliable, profitable service to the Aran Islands*. Then the vision became *Ireland's internal airline*. Now the vision is to be *the best regional airline in the world*.

At a recent meeting of judges in Vienna, we got the bronze award for being the third-best regional airline in Europe. That means we're one of the top five or six in the world for punctuality, value for money, contribution to the community – all those things. That's huge for us – but the aim is to be Number One.

We got there in very difficult times. The aviation industry has never been as bad. In 2002, two out of every five airlines in the world went bust. We were close to it. I was hanging on by my finger nails with the help of some people who are very close to me – some great friends and great people in Aer Arann. It's not my vision any more, it's our vision. We have over 500 flights a week now. I don't have an office – anyway, there's no room for me. I'm on the go all the time. There are people who need an office more than I do. If I need to meet somebody, I'll find a free room and go in and have a chat there. That's why I preferred to come and meet you here in UCD!

In the foyer of our offices, we have a flipchart and every day we change the numbers on it: our on-time performance yesterday, which is critical, the number of passengers we carried yesterday, and our load factor – what percentage of our airplanes were full. Everybody in the company sees that. We want to get those figures as perfect as we possibly can. If we get them right, the money and profits will look after themselves. When I was awarded Ireland's Entrepreneur of the Year, I said that my passion comes from Aer Arann and Connemara. At the Christmas party, they gave me a present of a chess set. Written on it was: "Finite resources, infinite possibilities".

We started with a very simple vision. It was not that there was a huge long-term vision. It was developed by taking one small step at a time, as we started to paint the picture on that blank canvas. I am so fortunate to work with great people. As a result, Aer Arann was awarded the Bronze Award for European Regional Airline of the Year 2004.

Do you remember this?

> *The greater danger for most of us is not that our aim is too high and we miss it, but that it is too low and we reach it.*

11

JOYCE O'CONNOR

NATIONAL COLLEGE OF IRELAND

*If there is a lesson to be learned from the growth and
development of the National College of Ireland, it is that a
vision needs to be shared if it is to be realised.*

PROFESSOR JOYCE O'CONNOR is President of the National College of Ireland since 1990. She is the first, and only, woman President of a third-level institution in Ireland.

She was born in Bray, Co. Wicklow, on February 9, 1947. Her father was Michael Fitzpatrick, a dairy farmer. Her mother was Johanna Maher, a civil servant. She was first in a family of two. Her brother is Sean Fitzpatrick.[31] She is married to Pat O'Connor. They have two children: Aoife and Rory.

She was educated at Loreto, Bray and at UCD, where she took an MSocSc and a PhD. She participated in the Programme for University Presidents at the Harvard University Institute for Educational Management in 1995 and 2001.

Among her previous appointments she was:

- Head of the Department of Languages & Applied Social Studies at the University of Limerick (1987-1990);
- Adjunct Associate Professor (Research) at Worchester Polytechnic Institute, USA (1986);
- Senior Research Fellow, UCD (1971-1976);
- Lecturer, St. Patrick's College, Maynooth (1970-1971);
- Lecturer, Milltown Park Institute of Theology & Philosophy (1968-1970);
- Research Fellow Department of Psychiatry, UCD (1968-1970).

She is:

- Chair of the Further Education & Training Awards Council (FETAC).
- Chair of the Dublin Inner City Partnership.
- Chair of the Expert Group on Mental Health Policy.
- Chair of the National Guidance Forum.
- Member of the National Qualifications Authority of Ireland.
- Council member of the Dublin Chamber of Commerce.
- Non-Executive Director of Cement Roadstone Holdings (CRH) Plc.

---

[31]   **Chapter 5.**

She has served as the Irish representative to the World Health Organisation and chaired the WHO expert committee on Alcohol & the Workplace. She was an Eisenhower Fellow, in recognition of leadership potential. She has received a number of awards, including recognition by the International Institute for Alcohol & Addiction for her research on drinking behaviour and a recent award from the International Centre for Alcohol Policies. She was awarded an honorary doctorate from the Dublin Institute of Technology.

She has published on the care of older people, age discrimination at work, carers, innovation and enterprise, and drinking and smoking behaviours.

I n 1982, that old rabbi, Kenneth Galbraith, wrote: "Nothing or not much happens in response to a report. Something happens only when someone obsessed by belief fights the proposal through". I put this on the first page of Lifelong Learning, the report of the Government Commission on Adult Education, in the sure and certain knowledge that no one was going to fight the proposal through. A few years later, I was called by Paddy Galvin[32]to talk as an "expert" or some such to a Government-sponsored committee on management development. At the end of the meeting with them, which I enjoyed, I said they too would enjoy the work, learn a lot from one another, and nothing would happen.

Joyce O'Connor was obsessed by a belief in the potential of the individual. She took the National College of Industrial Relations, which nearly went under, and made from it the National College of Ireland, with its splendid campus in the Financial Services Centre in Dublin. Here again is an illustration that it takes an individual, not a committee, to remove mountains.

The difference between the job of chief executive and one anywhere down the line is that the top job is both vulnerable and highly political.

There are echoes here of the way our other two academics, Michael MacCormac and Ed Walsh, operated in the Byzantine world of universities, where the more straightforward rules of profit and loss cut little ice. Joyce O'Connor knew that she could not get anywhere without building alliances with powerful constituencies. The chapter is a magnificat in praise of the people who helped her.

Her motto might well be taken from the final words of Robert Burton's Anatomy of Melancholy: "Be not solitary, be not idle".

---

[32] *Management Journal* (1991)

The conversation was recorded in Joyce O'Connor's office in the National College of Ireland, Mayor Street, IFSC, Dublin 1, on December 17, 2004.

Joyce O'Connor

I have always viewed education as a means of giving people life choices. Ever since my time as auditor of the UCD Sociology Society, I have had a strong belief that access to education is vitally important in developing an individual's potential and that academic aptitude is related to the person and not to their address. My interest in social issues in general and educational access in particular was nurtured by my parents who gave both my brother, Sean Fitzpatrick,[33] and me tremendous support in everything we undertook. They encouraged us to fulfil our potential. They instilled in me the belief that everyone can realise their full potential if they are given support and encouragement.

That's the basis of the vision we have implemented at the National College of Ireland. Today, our state-of-the-art campus in Dublin's International Financial Services Centre provides the hub for an innovative and unique programme of work in academic development, teaching and research. Through our campus, our network of 40 off-campus centres, on-site educational hubs within industry and in the community, and our online programmes, we are committed to enabling learners, in a flexible and accessible manner, to avail of leading edge programmes in business, management, human resource management, financial services, information technology, maritime management, humanities and related fields.

Looking back to 1990, when I first joined the National College of Ireland, it would have been impossible to predict such a future. At that stage, the College was at a crossroads. Its continued existence was in the balance.

It had been established 40 years earlier, in 1951. It was founded by the Jesuits as a workers college, along the lines of Ruskin College in England and many others worldwide. It was very much part of the Cold War. Communism was seen as a major threat. The establishment of educational institutions in competition with those backed by

---

[33] **Chapter 5.**

communist or socialist organisations was seen as part of the war against Communism.

It wasn't as simple as that in Ireland. There was a genuine need for the education and training of workers in industrial relations practices. The Labour Court had been established a few years earlier and industrial relations were becoming a far more complex area. Over subsequent years, the College played a major role in professionalising industrial relations practice, with thousands of trade union and employer representatives gaining qualifications there.

Originally called the Catholic Workers College, it had changed its name to the National College of Industrial Relations during the 1970s. What attracted me in 1990 to leading the College was the potential to make a real contribution to Irish education, in particular to offer access to education to a diverse group of people.

At that time, there was a shortage of third level places. Large numbers of both young and older people were unable to have access. I saw the opportunity for the College to make a difference. I went to the interview for the job with a vision of the College offering access and opportunity to learners of all ages and backgrounds by delivering full and part-time courses in a range of subjects wider than industrial relations.

The College was already offering degree and diploma level courses. It was just a case of expanding the range, reaching out and encouraging people to return to education, either on a full- or part-time basis, as well as taking in school leavers.

I was lucky, and have continued to be lucky, to have had support from inspirational people. Members of the Governing Body have included Paddy Moriarty, Paddy Galvin, Ita Meehan, Brendan McGinty, Peter McCloone, Eoin O'Driscoll and Denis O'Brien[34], amongst others who have throughout the years shown commitment to the mission of the College, its belief system and the strategic part it could play in Irish education.

I was lucky in the timing. By appointing the first non-religious head of the College, the Jesuits had already made a decision about its future – either it was going to grow and develop beyond its existing remit or it was going to close.

---

[34]   *Leaders* (2001).

As I said, the continued existence of the College was in doubt. Courses were subsidised by the Jesuits. Fees were set uneconomically low. The staff complement was 12. We had 500 students and five courses in industrial relations and human resources.

We set about developing a clear vision and mission for the College. We expanded the range of courses and developed off-campus centres around the country. We built relationships with communities whose members usually didn't go on to third level education. We developed alliances with the business world and the social partners. We built bridges between communities, the College, and business.

We also had a vision of the future of education. Lifelong learning is a term which is almost over-used today, but that was our vision 15 years ago. We saw the future as one where people continued to learn and develop throughout their lives and where education was firmly centred on the needs of the learner rather than on the institution.

All the other institutions were focused on full-time students. We had a completely different focus. Educational opportunity begins at primary level and in the home. We built links with communities and helped parents with children in primary and second level schools to keep them in school so that they could go on to third level. We also looked beyond school-leavers, to others who didn't have the opportunity to go to College, and reached out to them through the off-campus centres and the part-time programmes.

This vision was facilitated by the deal we negotiated with the Jesuits. They agreed to pay off the past debts of the College, the pension underfunding, and transfer the land and buildings to NCI on the condition that we got Government backing and set up a true social partnership. We had already got funding from the Department of Labour. Atlantic Philanthropies enabled us to develop programmes that were specifically designed to offer individuals access routes back into education. Our "Parents in Education" and Foundation programmes are examples of these initiatives.

Mary O'Rourke, Minister for Education in 1991, played a significant role when she made fees free to full-time students of the College. But the major role was played by the social partners who came together, worked on the vision and backed it all the way. Ultimately this resulted in our receiving funding of £600,000 from the Department of Finance in 1993. The previous Minister for Labour, Bertie Ahern, who was Minister for Finance at the time, was very important in obtaining that funding, as was the support of Sean Cromien, Don Thornhill and Niamh Breathnach. IBEC and ICTU, and people like Billy Attley, Christy Kiernan, Phil Flynn, Peter Cassells, John Dunne, Tony O'Brien, Declan Madden, Brian Patterson and Ita Meehan gave powerful support.

It was not a lot of money, but it kept us going and it put us on a sounder footing. That really was the beginning of the development of the College. Growth since then has been substantial. Our turnover increased from £680,000 in 1990 to €14 million today.

We couldn't realise our ambitions in the accommodation in Ranelagh. We had to expand. We applied for planning permission but the local residents had strong objections. We eventually got permission from An Bord Pleanála but with strict conditions attached – for example, we couldn't operate after 9:30pm and we had to limit student numbers to 400. We could not fulfil our mission with that, so we had to rethink our options.

The first option we looked at was to become the new Institute of Technology planned for Blanchardstown. This was 1998, following the Government decision to develop an IT there. Despite our best efforts, we were unable to meet the Government's requirements while preserving our own mission and vision. While we were not chosen, the process that we went through was invaluable in preparing us for what was to be the next phase of our development. We knew we had only one option, to move.

We had several offers from established universities. They wanted us to focus exclusively on our community-based or adult education programmes. That would mean giving up on our vision. We had to look for a new site.

That was when the opportunity to move to the Docklands came up. The Dublin Docklands Development Authority asked all the universities and colleges to tender for the establishment of an educational centre on the north docks. Our proposal was accepted. We then had to set about raising the funding required.

We sold our site in Ranelagh and we fundraised from the business community. The support of the business community was fantastic and critical. Our Governing Body had been clear that we couldn't go out and borrow the money. The task was to get the resources with no borrowing and no risk!

We had to be imaginative. We worked with developers such as Paddy Kelly and Ged Pierse and they not only backed us but bought into our vision and mission. So did Anglo-Irish Bank, which financed the deal – Kieran Duggan of Anglo was the mastermind. Today, we own all of our €100 million College campus. The support and belief in our mission from key business figures such as Michael Smurfit, Donal O'Connor, Gary McGann, Pat Molloy, Niall Crowley, Sean Fitzpatrick (the brother!) and Denis O'Brien were really important.

We now have a state-of-the-art, purpose-built college, which has become part of the community here in the north inner-city. We are working closely with local community organisations. The facilities in the College are at their disposal. We have set up an early learning centre to bring access and opportunity to the children of those local communities. We have set up the Learn 3K research centre, which is rapidly developing into a centre of excellence for educational research. The centre is looking at the key issue of our ability to learn how to learn. We are also developing our arts and culture strategy, which has been inspired and influenced by supporters of the College like Norma Smurfit, Paddy McKillen and Paddy and Veronica Campbell.

It has been an exciting 15 years – the journey continues. But the journey so far has only been made possible by the support we got.

People like Phil Flynn, Christy Kiernan, Peter McCloone and Billy Attley played a very important role in delivering the support of the trade union movement; ministers including Bertie Ahern, Micheál Martin, Mary O'Rourke, Niamh Breathnach and present ministers. Many others have shared our vision, as have numerous public servants and, of course, the staff of the College.

When we first set our mission and vision 15 years ago, it was ahead of its time. The concept of education as a cradle-to-grave process may be widely accepted now but it was new then.

It took hard work and perseverance to make that vision a reality. The local community were terrific and I got great support from people like Gerry Faye, Seanie Lambe and Fr. Wall.

Another group which was influential in our development was our International Committee, which includes some of the finest international educators. Throughout my career, I maintained contact with Ivy League universities, but particularly with Cornell, and developed a relationship with Prof. John Hopcroft. He was enthused by what we were doing. John offered to chair our International Committee and introduced me to a group of eminent US academics who also came on board, such as John Guttag. who held the Chair of Computing Sciences at MIT,[35] John Hennessy, President of Stanford, Steve Director from Michigan State and Ed Lazowska from Washington State University

My belief that all people can develop has also been sustained by my husband Pat, who, as headmaster of St. Enda's in Limerick, set up a community-based initiative to raise funds for a support infrastructure for young people in the area who would not have had previously a chance to go on to third level education. Pat and I share the same beliefs.

The National College of Ireland has not just been some grand experiment in social engineering. When we look at the competitive challenge facing Ireland today, continuously moving up the value chain is where the future lies. This can be achieved only through lifelong learning.

The College has created a model for the provision of this continuous training and education. Through the Learn 3K Research centre and our International Centre for Education & Learning Technologies (ICELT), which provide a unique rarefied environment for companies identified in the field of innovation in Education and Learning space, we are constantly developing new methods of learning which will blend in innovative ways the traditional classroom model with new technologies.

The true meaning and value of our mission and vision are that it is never fully realised. There are always new horizons. Access to education is still a major issue and we will continue to work to play our part in resolving it.

If there is a lesson to be learned from the growth and development of the National College of Ireland, it is that a vision needs to be shared if it is to be realised – it cannot be the property of an individual. One individual can provide leadership but that person will need support and encouragement if they are to lead over a sustained period. This

---

[35] Massachusetts Institute of Technology.

shared vision in partnership with business, trade unions and community is the cornerstone of the success that NCI has achieved. I have been fortunate that my vision has been shared by many others and that they have been there to offer their support over the years and into the future.

12

SIR ANTHONY O'REILLY

Independent News & Media

You try very hard. You win some but you don't win them all – but you must try to the very end.

SIR ANTHONY O'REILLY was born in Dublin in 1936 and educated at Belvedere College, at University College Dublin and at the Incorporated Law Society of Ireland. He earned a PhD in agricultural marketing from the University of Bradford.

He is married to Chryss Goulandris. He has six children: Susan, Cameron, Justine, Gavin, Tony and Caroline. His two homes in Ireland are in Kildare and in West Cork.

He has major business interests in Ireland, the UK, Europe, Africa and Australasia. He is Chief Executive and the largest shareholder of Independent News & Media plc. INM has market-leading newspaper positions in Australia, Ireland, New Zealand and South Africa. The Company publishes over 165 newspaper and magazine titles and is involved also in radio, outdoor advertising, internet, e-commerce and mobile information.

INM manages turnover of over €1.6 billion and gross assets of €3.4 billion. The annual compound return to shareholders with dividends re-invested has been 19% p.a. since Sir Anthony became the majority shareholder in 1973.

He is Chairman of Waterford Wedgwood plc and, with his brother-in-law Peter Goulandris, they are major shareholders.

He is Chairman of eircom plc.

He retired as Chairman of the HJ Heinz Company on September 12, 2000. He was the first non-family member to serve as Chairman. When he became Chief Executive Officer in 1979, the market capitalisation of Heinz was $900 million, compared to $15 billion when he resigned as CEO in 1998. The total shareholder return was 22% annually from 1978-1998.

He was Managing Director of the Irish Sugar Company from 1966 to 1969. Before that, he served for four years as Chief Executive Officer of the Irish Dairy Board. He launched the international food brand, "Kerrygold".

In 1988, he was conferred with the Order of Australia for services to Irish/Australian relationships.

He is Chairman and co-founder of The Ireland Funds.

He was knighted by Queen Elizabeth in 2001 for his consistent work over 25 years for peace in Northern Ireland.

He played rugby for Ireland 29 times and for the British and Irish Lions team 10 times. He was a member of the winning Lions Tour of

South Africa in 1955 and of the Tour of New Zealand and Australia in 1959. He established unbroken scoring records on both tours.

I *first met Tony O'Reilly in 1962 in the burgeoning IMI in Leeson Park. He had driven from Cork at a speed then permissible to lecture on, of all things, time and motion study. I'm sure the participants learned something about time and motion. My memory is of two things – the peals of laughter from the conference room and the fact that his handouts, which were duplicated on the IMI's old Gestetner wax paper machine, had the centre of all the Os missing.*

By 1987, I had joined the Board of the then Independent Newspapers plc. I was talking to Tony for the first book in the series. I told him I could not think of a title, but that I was enjoying myself. He said, "That's because you've been in good company". That was the title.

Eighteen years ago, Tony, who was domiciled in Pittsburgh, said, "I sense that Ireland is a fully-integrated paid-up member of a rather vulgar, interesting, fast-moving and exceedingly bracing Western society which, I suggest, now stretches in a band from Tokyo through San Francisco, Los Angeles and New York, and Galway and Dublin to London and Frankfurt, and is inching its way day-by-day towards Moscow".

This chapter is essentially about Independent News & Media plc, with an hilarious reference to his time, nearly 30 years, in Heinz.

Independent News & Media celebrated its centenary this year (2005). When Tony O'Reilly took over in 1973, there were seven titles, all in Ireland. Today, it publishes 175 titles in five countries and has added radio, TV, outdoor advertising, distribution, contract printing and the Internet. It employs 11,000 people and will now (2005) be associated with 3,500 more from India.

Tony O'Reilly nailed his visionary colours to the mast 32 years ago. His original letter to Independent shareholders set out with remarkable clarity and foresight the vision he has now achieved. There is an extract from the letter at the end of this chapter.

He hugely enjoys the business. He once said to me: "You couldn't have a more satisfying way of making money – meeting people, talking to people, enjoying their company". He makes enduring friendships. He is an international business statesman but, to paraphrase Yeats: "Think where man's glory most begins and ends and say his glory was he had such friends."

The conversation was recorded in Sir Anthony's office at Independent News & Media plc, Independent House, 2023 Bianconi Avenue, Citywest Business Campus, Naas Road, Dublin 24, on February 9, 2005.

His biography is in *In Good Company* (1987), and comprehensively in *The Player* by Ivan Fallon.[36]

---

[36] (1994) London: Hodder & Stoughton.

Sir Anthony O'Reilly

I joined Independent Newspapers in March of 1973. It had a turnover that year of €12 million. The budgeted figure for our current year is €1.65 billion. The profits in 1973 were €1 million. Today, they are €183 million. That extraordinary history is really the story of clear, long-term objectives and the skills of three men: Bartle Pitcher, John Meagher and Liam Healy.[37] They were the essential and dynamic CEOs of the company over a 27-year period.

Investing in news media, and in particular, newspapers, is a very judgmental thing. My initial ambition was to attempt to create in Ireland a group that would consider media in the broadest possible sense – radio, television, print etc. – as a means for the profitable expansion of the company throughout the world. Shareholders agreed with this vision at an extraordinary general meeting on September 12, 1973, which merged the "A" and "B" shareholding of the company (see **Appendix** at the end of this chapter), and Independent was on its exciting, but uncertain, way.

The most important thing of all is, from a marketing point of view – and this is what my experience at Bord Bainne and with Kerrygold taught me – that newspapers in general are a series of discrete circles of influence. You can't give the *Cape Times* away in New Zealand. You can't give the *New Zealand Herald* away in Sydney. You can't give the *Sydney Morning Herald* away in Melbourne, you can't give the *Johannesburg Star* away in London or the *London Independent* in Dublin, or the *Irish Independent* in Belfast or the *Belfast Telegraph* in Dublin. So you have a discrete series of bulwarks around the world acting potentially as clear, regional brand leaders. The noble side of you says you can change nations, you can influence opinion, you can comment on a great range of things, but, if you want to make money for your shareholders, then well-run, low-cost, brand-leading newspapers will remain, at least in my lifetime, one of the most discrete, powerful, brand-certain, saleable products for the advertiser and the consumer.

---

[37] *Management Journal* (1993).

In 1972 when we joined the Common Market, commentators, notably Garrett FitzGerald, opined that a considerable number of industries in this country would simply die. We were going to have no more motor cars assembled here, no more shirts made, no more shoes, no more local brushes, suits, clothes and so on. It was going to be wall-to-wall Marks & Spencer or British Home Stores or Tesco. A group of us asked ourselves what product or service is reasonably invulnerable to imports in this dramatic new era. One of the answers was newspapers, both local and national.

The vision was an exciting one – geography, people, opinions.

The editorial tone of the Independent Group throughout the world is best described by Dr. Vinnie Doyle,[38] the editor of the *Irish Independent*. He described it thus: "We define the position of our papers as liberal, centrist and supportive of a mixed economy. We are against violence. We are for peace. It's what we stood for 100 years ago, and it's what we stand for today".

I believe the general conduct of our papers, provided they don't support violence, can be left to the editorial direction and the sense of history that each paper has. For example, if you felt that the *Belfast Telegraph* should not be as it is, you would be running counter to history. History has made that paper what it is today, a bridge between the two communities. We do, of course, have conferences and meetings with various people from all walks of life and political persuasion. The editors are often there and hear what our guests have to say. They may or may not decide to take any line advocated. I believe it's a healthy thing for the editors to know what a proprietor and Board think but not to feel that their views on any given topic should be the direction of the paper.

A classic example was a lunch in England with Alasdair Campbell, Tony Blair's closest advisor. Blair was detained in Belfast and had to forego the lunch. It was just before the Iraq War. At the lunch were Chryss and myself, Ivan Fallon, the CEO of our British papers, and seven writers, including Simon Kelner, the editor of the *Independent*, with Tristram Davies, the editor of the *Independent on Sunday*. I said, "Gentlemen, can we take a vote on the war in Iraq which now seems to be inevitable? I would just like to cast my vote – I'm in favour of war".

---

[38] *Talking to Ourselves* (1994).

Chryss said that she was in favour of war and so did Ivan Fallon. The seven writers voted against the war. Alasdair Campbell was going up to town later from Canary Wharf with Simon Kelner. He said, "That was an extraordinary lunch wasn't it?". Kelner asked, "What do think was so extraordinary about it?". Campbell said, "Your proprietor seems to have bugger all to do with the editorial direction of the paper". I took that as a compliment.

Each day is a new day in the life of a newspaper.

I remember Nelson Mandela ringing me up one day and saying in his huge voice: "Tony! I have a problem. Your papers have libelled me. They said I have feet of clay. I do not have feet of clay". I said, "What papers said that you have feet of clay?". "*The Sowetan* says I have feet of clay". I said, "It might be interesting for you to know that we don't own *The Sowetan*. *The Sowetan* is actually owned by your personal doctor, Nthato Motlana. He's the only one who would know if you had feet of clay! Motlana owns it lock, stock and barrel. We used to own it but we sold it to him". End of story.

We publish about 150 newspapers around the world each week. It is widely assumed that one knows what's going on in every one of them. The truth is more mundane. The Advisory Board, and the multiple company boards that operate around the world, are good assessors of what's going to happen in a given country. They assist our papers in their general sense of direction on many issues. They will know in general – but not in particular – what is going on in each of our publications.

When you think of the variety and distinction of the members of the Advisory Board and the people who come to address it, such as Nelson Mandela, Thabo Mbeki, Archbishop Tutu, Helen Clark – Prime Minister of New Zealand, John Howard – Prime Minister of Australia, and a host of others, you have a sense of its relevance and reach. At the very top, newspapers give you extraordinary access. You are involved to an extent – perhaps not as great an extent as you might think yourself – in nation-shaping. You are both a participant and an observer.

Before I joined the Heinz company, I was managing director of the Irish Sugar Company, and we had just formed Heinz-Erin. We lived down in Delgany in a house called Columbia, a wonderful house for parties. One particular party was given for an extraordinary woman, the 85-year-old Vira Heinz, wife of the son of the founder of HJ Heinz. Dr. Tom Walsh ran An Foras Talúntais, the Agricultural Research Institute, at that time and was a tremendously bright fellow. He made approximately eight speeches that night. He kept talking about the Heinz "outfit" like it was the Bar-B-Ranch. He said, "The Kellogg Foundation has been very good to us. I'd like to see the Heinz outfit doing the same". When Vira was leaving, we all line up in this wide hallway down to the steps of the house opening to the terraces cascading down to the sea. At the bottom of the terraces the limos are purring in wait. Vira was a wonderful, angelic, fragrant woman. She waves goodbye to all us "lovely people, so wonderful to have been here". With that, a great hairy hand comes out of the crowd and grasps her around her waist. It was Tom. He bends her back like a tango dancer, and gives her a passionate kiss. She is about a foot off the ground. I could see my entire future career in Heinz going up in flames. I pick her up. She was known as Auntie Vira. I say, "I'm terribly sorry about that, Auntie Vira". "Oh", she says excitedly, "Don't worry about that, I just don't get enough of it nowadays". Far from subtracting from my career, Tom gave it an enormous boost.

I suppose the vision I aspired to in life is somebody akin to that of C.B. Fry, the great all-rounder. That derives from the Jesuit notion of *moderatio in omnibus rebus* (nothing is so great that you should commit yourself to it absolutely). Everything in this world is temporal. You should be a person who can achieve a certain amount of distinction in academic, sporting, musical, commercial or artistic activities – or simply the distinction of being a good parent of a family, or helping your friends in charitable activities, or creating something that affects a lot of people for the good, like those who help the Ireland Fund. I have an *à la carte* notion of goals, without being specific about them but being able to create a broad picture in my mind, impelled by my Jesuit education – that of moderation in all things, of the all-rounder, and hopefully done with grace and dignity and style and compassion.

My father gave me Kipling's poem, *If*, when I was six or seven. I had it hanging over my bed when I was a child. My children got Raymond Gillespie, a noted sculptor, to make a glorious winding set of stairs with each step carrying a line from the poem. The sculpture stands outside my study in Castlemartin:

If you can keep your head when all about you
Are losing theirs and blaming it on you;
If you can trust yourself when all men doubt you,
But make allowance for their doubting too;
If you can wait and not be tired by waiting,
Or being lied about, don't deal in lies,
Or being hated, don't give way to hating,
And yet don't look too good, nor talk too wise;

If you can dream – and not make dreams your master,
If you can think – and not make thoughts your aim;
If you can meet with Triumph and Disaster
And treat those two impostors just the same;
If you can bear to hear the truth you've spoken
Twisted by knaves to make a trap for fools,
Or watch the things you gave your life to, broken,
And stoop and build 'em up with worn-out tools:

If you can make one heap of all your winnings
And risk it all on one turn of pitch-and-toss,
And lose, and start again at your beginnings
And never breathe a word about your loss;
If you can force your heart and nerve and sinew
To serve your turn long after they are gone,
And so hold on when there is nothing in you
Except the Will which says to them: "Hold on!"

If you can talk with crowds and keep your virtue,
Or walk with kings – nor lose the common touch,
If neither foes nor loving friends can hurt you;
If all men count with you, but none too much,
If you can fill the unforgiving minute
With sixty seconds' worth of distance run,
Yours is the Earth and everything that's in it,
And – which is more – you'll be a Man, my son!

Although there's nothing about God in it, nothing of the spiritual, it's a terrific humanist view of the world. It says live your life like that and you won't go far wrong.

That, I suppose, is an example of all our lives. You try very hard. You win some but you don't win them all – but you must try to the very end.

Appendix: Extract from a Letter to Shareholders August 27, 1973

COLUMBIA

Columbia is an Irish investment holding company controlled by Mr. AJF O'Reilly, whose successful career is well known. Mr. O'Reilly has wide professional experience in many fields and has extensive contacts in international business.

Mr. O'Reilly has joined the Board of the Company and it is the intention of the Board to avail of this association with Columbia to develop the Company into an international communications group, based in Ireland. It is anticipated that this development will be achieved both by internal growth and by selective acquisition. The new operations being examined include, in addition to newspapers, expansion into the fields of advertising, publicity and commercial radio and television. Such expansion will not be limited to Ireland.

13

TOM ROCHE

CRH

I have always had an intense interest and a concentration of effort in whatever I take up. Whatever you're doing, you've got to concentrate and do it better than anybody.

TOM ROCHE was born in Limerick on April 4, 1916, the fourth child in a family of five of Thomas Roche, a civil servant, and Kathleen O'Halloran, of peasant stock.

He was educated at The Star of the Sea National School in Sandymount, at the Christian Brothers' School in Westland Row and at Blackrock College.

He was married to Florence McAvoy of Belfast, who was a school secretary. Their children are Maura, Eleanor, Tom and Claire.

He was self-employed from the age of 16. He tried sitting on various boards but was never easy at board meetings.

He was managing director, in chronological order, of:

- Roche Brothers
- Castle Sand
- Roadstone Limited
- CRH plc.

He was a recipient of the President's Award of the Association of Consulting Engineers of Ireland.

He died on July 8 1999.

*T*his book could not have been written leaving out Tom Roche. He was one of our greatest visionary entrepreneurs, founder of our leading industrial company, CRH. I have plundered an earlier book, Out On Their Own (1991). An old friend, Tony Barry, former CEO and then Chairman of CRH, has written for us a contemporary introduction.

Even Tom's biographical note shows his free spirit.

He gladly agreed to participate in the earlier book. When I sent him the first draft, I got no reply. Some weeks later, there was a knock on my office door, an unusual occurrence because all visitors first pass by Gillian Acton's office. I looked up in surprise and there was Tom, in a long dark de Valera overcoat, standing with an envelope in his hand. He said softly, "No, Ivor". (Tom had been through the horrors, not of his making, of the Bula Mines tragedy, the longest court case in Irish legal history. He had lost all his money but, irrepressibly, had built the East and West Link Bridges over the Liffey.) I said, "Why, Tom?". "Because there are too many bits in it that would hurt people." I said I would take them out. It would still be a great story. He still said "No".

However, I did take them out and sent him a revised manuscript. Next thing, I got a call to have lunch with him in Milltown Golf Club on March 14, 1990. No mention of the book.

We had a pleasant lunch, joined a little to my surprise by a friend of Tom's. Still no mention of the book.

I walked out with Tom to his shark-like Citroen, the one that sits down on its hunkers when you park it. I said, "The book, Tom?". He said, "Oh that'll be all right" and was off. That was the last time I saw him.

The original conversation was recorded in 1989 in Tom Roche's house on Cross Avenue, Blackrock, Co. Dublin.

Tom Roche's biography is in *Out On Their Own* (1991).

A Word from Tony Barry,[39] former Chairman, 1994-2000, and Chief Executive, 1988-1994, of CRH

A few incidents stand out in my memory of Tom Roche. They happened early in our relationship, which dates back to the mid-'60s. He was impressed when I arranged a talk/demonstration on flexibly-jointed concrete pipes for potential customers in Dublin. At the time, I worked with the newly-acquired Cork subsidiary, John A. Wood Limited. What he really liked was that I was able to joint the pipes myself – not rocket science! Doing rather than talking appealed to Tom. However, when some years later, I became MD of John A. Wood Limited, he was not too pleased when I departed from Group policy in buying the fresh-to-the-market robust Hino Japanese trucks as opposed to the less robust and more expensive Fords. I was awarded a kick up the transom in a humorous hand-written note of reproof. However, he had the good grace and generosity to admit subsequently that the decision was right. It also showed, at a very early stage, the willingness to delegate in a business that demands a significant degree of local autonomy to succeed. It has been a hallmark of the way CRH does its business. In another way, the incident epitomised what attracted people to Tom – his generosity of spirit and the admirable acceptance of independence.

When Roadstone and Irish Cement merged in 1970, it brought together from both sides some key people whose foresight and trust in the next generation was the genesis of the CRH plc of today. Tom's brother, Donal, Gunnar Larsen, Anker Lund and Bill Murray were of like mind but it was Tom as leader who made it happen.

They all retired from the day-to-day running of the business and were mostly under 60 at the time. In those days, others would have indulged in a long lap of honour.

It was visionary and sensible and their continuing role as non-executives serving on the Board meant no opting out of decisions. The result was a hugely motivated team of young, able and energetic executives encouraged to take on the world. The retirees, led by Tom,

---

[39] *Management Journal* (1990).

right through to their retirement from the Board, were always constructive and supportive, while challenging. It might not accord with best corporate governance today, but it worked. For us executives, the relationship at Board resulted in lasting friendships – unusual to this degree in the business world.

Jim Culliton succeeded Tom in 1974 and developed and led the team which made CRH what it is today. I succeeded Jim in 1988 and Don Godson took over at the end of 1994. Liam O'Mahony, the current CEO, took over in 2000. All of us were in place at the outset in the early '70s as executives at the coalface. Tom never lost interest and, even after he retired from the Board in the late '80s, would delight in meeting over lunch at regular intervals to hear how the business was going. The scale of success delighted him. His advice and comments were shrewd and valuable and never forced on the listener. Real success on the scale of CRH can be achieved only by a motivated team working together, but it needs to be kick-started by a man of stature, ability, vision and generosity. That was Tom Roche.

TOM ROCHE

I was ambitious, even as a youngster. I wanted to build something, no matter what. The trigger for all that was a small business for which my mother paid £250. It consisted of a yard where we stored coal and a machine with which we made concrete blocks. My brother, Donal, who joined me in the business, left school even earlier than I, at age 15. He's been the steadying influence when I strayed too far from the sensible path.

We had lived first in Sandymount, but when we moved to Inchicore, which was an industrial district, I got to know working people well.

1932 was the year we started, with a truck that carried a ton-and-a-half. By the year the war came, we had four trucks, each of which carried six tons. Donal did more of the bookkeeping and general administration. I was more on the practical side. I kept the trucks going and made bodies for them. I was blessed with the people who were working with me. Of course, I had some unhappy experiences with men, which I now regret, as I should not have been so hard or, at times, so indifferent or callous. It's only when you look back that you realise that.

You could put it this way: one day I was at school, and the next I had a shovel in my hand and I was delighted. My mother set an example. I think that may be common in Irish mothers. My father really died too soon to have influence. But Mother was not strict. She was the opposite.

We used to get clinker or breeze from the railway and make lightweight blocks as well as sand and cement blocks with one of these old hand machines. It was our introduction to the building side. Later, we dropped the coal because an accountant told us we were not making any money. Before that, we'd go down to the docks with a little truck, load it up, put the coal in bags and go round selling it to friends of my father who wanted to help us. I came in touch with the dockers of Dublin. They were a tough lot. That was one of the ways I got to know workmen. I enjoyed the freedom of physical work.

The fact that I went to Blackrock College has always been a great sheet-anchor or point of achievement. I'd often use it when I was young – when I'd meet people on building sites. I'd casually mention that I went to Blackrock. Ah, it was great to have gone there, although at times I was not very happy. I was bright enough, but I was a bad pupil. I did not take to learning. I left after the Inter Cert. The priests of the older régime in Blackrock were tough, but then I was not a very good student. And I got a surfeit of religion. Now that I'm over 70, I really think a lot about the mystery of why we're here. Undoubtedly, there has been some extraordinary Creator – you only have to look at the complexity of living things.

What I look to in times of trial is a depth of inner strength that I can call on. I think it originated in my mother. Fortunately, I can call on mental reserves. I don't need alcohol or pills. I think it also had its origin in the fact that I was grubbing for pennies when I was young. When you start from such a low base, it must condition you afterwards. As you know, we've had rough times financially in this Bula Mines thing so I've had to accept the worst that can happen and learn to live with it.

Bula Mines was a mistake. I was tempted by the piratical aspect and the romance of it. There were a few times when I could have got out, but I hadn't the final say. All the assets I had were sucked into it.

Position for position's sake never seemed to register with me.

No, I don't miss CRH. I look back in a kind of wonderment sometimes that I was head of it and built it up. I have no regrets. It was a marvellous life. In fact, it was unique, because I had absolute freedom in the business, something that's given to very few.

In a way, it's like setting out for a walk. The first step is the hardest. Then you take a second step and a third and it becomes easier. The hardest thing of all was to establish the base of the business. And my mother, God bless her, provided the base in that first tiny little business. I learned an awful lot from the three workmen who came with the business. They were nice people. They showed me the ropes. You have five or six days in the week, you do a little every day and try to build on what was done the previous day. I think it goes back to temperament. You just go on building and building.

Before the war, with our four trucks, we used to carry sand and gravel – and bricks and tiles – for people called Concrete Products, who are now Chadwicks. They were very good to us. In that way, I got to know the building side of things very well.

During the war, we had plenty of time to think what we would do after it. I was always interested in trucks, the bigger the better. It was natural to get in on this washed gravel business. There was practically no washed gravel in Dublin, but there were two good plants in Cork. I went down to have a look and was very taken with them. When you're making concrete blocks, you get to know the best kind of gravel. We formed a little company. My older brother was friendly with Joe Kidney, an architect. Joe's father was an accountant and they were mixed up in Jury's Hotel and were quite well-to-do. I was introduced to the Kidney family and I explained to them that I would like to put up a gravel-washing plant after the war and to buy some more trucks. They were very helpful.

Also, during the war, we got into the demolition business. We made more money pulling things down than putting them up. We knocked down things like jails and workhouses. You then sold the material by auction. It was quite profitable and we accumulated enough capital to go into the Castle Sand business with the Kidneys. It took off. It was very timely. One of our first jobs was Dublin Airport with TJ Moran & Co. This was followed by the Leixlip Hydroelectric Scheme, then the Bus Station in Dublin and a few others. We put up our first plant at Kill, near Naas, a part of the country where there was a lot of gravel.

In or about that time, I met John Wood from Cork. He owned one of the washing plants down there. He was a remarkably far-seeing man. He was going to put up a quarry at the Hill of Allen, about 30 miles from Dublin. We thought this would interfere with our business and suggested that we get together, but he was not forthcoming. We decided to go ahead anyway and put a quarry up in the Dublin mountains. When he saw this, he agreed to come in with us and so Roadstone was founded. We merged Castle Sand with Roadstone and formed a public company.

Dr. Beddy of the Industrial Credit Company helped us. The issue would be called a flop now because the Industrial Credit Company were left with a lot of the shares. That was about 1948 and few people had any faith in the stone or gravel business. Dr. Beddy was one of the most perceptive characters I've met in my life. He could say more with fewer words than any man I've ever met. To the day he retired, he was always supportive.

My way of going for the next 10 years was to spend too much money and then we would have to go to the public for more. My unfortunate brother, Donal, had to worry about it. The business was centred around John Wood's site at the Hill of Allen, a beautiful site, a perfect hill of basalt in the middle of a bog.

In 1949, I went to the States to see what they were doing there. That trip was worth three years at university. When I saw the scale of their operations and their approach to quarrying, I knew exactly what we wanted. We put up this whopping plant – it was one of the biggest in the British Isles at that time. Stone comes out in big lumps and the bigger the first crusher is, the more economic everything else is. We put up a crusher which was five feet wide and three-and-a-half feet the other way. Previously, the little crushers had been maybe two feet wide and one foot the other way. That quarry was quite successful and, being the restless kind, I looked around for number two. I got a set of geological maps and I used to look for lumps of basalt. One of them that stood out was at Slane. The Marquis of Conyngham of Slane Castle owned it. We bought a couple of hundred acres from him for £10,000. One of the high points was having lunch with him in his castle to celebrate. The butler stood behind my chair and I was very impressed. He was talking about his salmon and he used an expression I had never heard before. He said the salmon "ate very well".

That quarry was also successful and it led to our first export venture. About two years after it started in 1955, a chap called Van Neerbos arrived from Holland. He wanted tons and tons of a particular kind of basalt which was about the size of wheat. We put up a set of export bins on the quayside in Drogheda. When a ship came in, we could load it quickly. We then looked to England, which was a hell of a lot nearer than Holland. In Liverpool, they were already importing stone by ship from Wales, but I got a very frosty reception from the Docks Board. I met the whole board, all 15 of them. When they said "No", I said, "Thank you very much, gentlemen" and walked out. However, we got around that by buying a little business there that was importing tin ore for smelting. It gave us a quayside. We bought the Forticrete Company and started to make concrete blocks on American

Besser machines. Eventually, it developed into quite a good business and spread to other places, Somerset, Leicester and Buxton.

Meanwhile, back home, we had taken over Clondalkin Concrete. It did well and then we looked for a quarry near Limerick. We put one up near Bunratty where there was very hard limestone. It only broke even for a while, but eventually became profitable because it was near Shannon Airport and there was a good deal of road activity. After that we went to Castlebar, Castleblaney and Kilkenny. Eventually, John Wood sold out to us for shares. That was very successful because John Wood was a great businessman and had good reserves of gravel. Somehow, we always seemed to be able to raise the money. Dr. Beddy was a calm, resourceful man in this. He was succeeded by Frank Casey, who was equally nice.

We also put up a machine shop in Inchicore, where we would design and make a lot of our own plants. That was one of the things I'm glad about because, years after they might have left us, workmen would come back to me and say, "You know, we got a great training in your place." I didn't realise it at the time but we were acquiring a lot of know-how. I thought this was great for Irish people – we were so behind in these things. We became less and less dependent on English suppliers. I was always very conscious of the fact that the Irish were so low in the industrial scene. We first bought our plant from Goodwin Barsby. The people who came over from them were very superior, very English. I went out to see one of them who was staying at Ross's Hotel. He was at breakfast and asked me, "Who are these Walsh brothers?". I told him the name was Roche and that I was one of them. He didn't suggest coffee. Later on, they could not have been more helpful.

Behind a lot of what I've done was to show that the Irish can do it – and we now know that they can.

I'm an engineer at heart, a builder at heart. I was very interested in houses and built six very nice ones at Woodlands Park. I'd say a builder would define the kind of person I happen to be.

Anyway, the business was expanding and I was managing it in a very personal way, down in the workshops, interested in everything. I would ask the quarry managers what their biggest problem was. We'd start at the biggest one and work back. I would note everything and I would always see that it was done. Donal was getting a bit worried that the business was becoming too big for my style of management and it was he, around 1965, who got in Bill Murray as a consultant. Bill had a profound influence. He set up an organisation and it was no longer a personal business. He said we were selling material too cheaply. Regretfully, when we put our prices up in later years, it brought in a lot of competition. The most valuable thing that Bill Murray did was to recognise the kind of people who would be needed to succeed me. He brought in young men like Henry Lund, Don Godson and Jack Hayes. Jack Hayes is now the number two in the outfit and Don Godson pioneered all the work in America. For six months after they came, I didn't know what to do with them.

Don Godson came up to my office one day and sat down. He's very quiet. He said, "I've been here six months and you won't let me in on what you're doing". I said, "I don't see the necessity, Don". He said, "The trouble with you is that nobody ever told you to fuck off". That was a small remark, but it had a big consequence. As you know, Don grew – he's a remarkable fellow and a great personal friend. It was an organisation now. I also thought that, at the age of 50, which coincided with that time, I had passed my peak. Maybe it was all the influence of these new-style managers.

The next big event was the long cement strike, which meant we were nearly out of business. Then there was the attempted take-over of Cement Ltd, which resulted in the merger. That had a fair amount of difficulty because of personalities. There was a very strong character in Cement, Anker Lund. I got on well with him and with Gunnar Larsen, the chairman, but they did not really want to be taken over, or merge, or have anything to do with us. They had an absolutely beautiful monopoly business going. Let me give you an example. John Wood was doing business with them from the time they started in 1930. Once, a cheque of his got lost in the post. They immediately stopped supplying him with cement. He had to go down to the Post Office and send off a series of £40 drafts – you could not send more than £40 at a time – until his account was cleared. A few days later, he got a letter saying that they had found his cheque in their office, that it had been mislaid, but there was no apology.

The merger would never have succeeded except that, in the middle of the negotiations, Readymix tried to take us over. Cement decided that they would be better to tie up with us, people they knew, than allow Readymix to assume a dominant position in Ireland. The negotiations were difficult and it meant a complete change of style for them. Even still at that time, I was accustomed to running the place as a boss. Once the merger was in place, it became a corporation and had to be run on formal lines and that did not suit me at all. We didn't think much of some of the things they were doing, and I suppose they didn't think much of some of the things we were doing. The two companies continued to be run separately but, in time, Anker Lund and I became joint managing directors of both companies. Funnily enough, we got on very well and he's still a good friend. When Anker retired, I became sole managing director. It didn't suit my style and I stayed only nine months. I was succeeded by Jim Culliton. Jim started out in Bray with us when he was 18, selling gravel to builders. He was one of those fellows who, when an opportunity came, would say, "I think I can do that." One of the things he did was to go to Clondalkin Concrete and make it more efficient. He was a natural successor. Jimmy was the best thing that ever happened to that merger because his personality is so calm and he's so steady and so clever. And he knew the business very well. He was the correct man at the correct time. Things settled down once he came in.

Jimmy Culliton and I were talking one day about who might fill the bill as his number two and I had met Tony Barry in Cork. He seemed to me a very solid, efficient man. I suggested to Jimmy that he bring him up from Cork. He has since proved himself. He is all the things I thought he was at the time: solid and reliable and clever. Thank goodness that worked out very well.

Looking back, it was great fun building Roadstone. I think the merger had one virtue that I used to harp on. Cement sat on their monopoly and did nothing about going abroad. They made little use of the money they generated. They had a very strong link with Denmark which, of course, I resented, being so Irish. With the financial strength of both companies, we could really go abroad and do things. That's the way the British Empire was built. We took over Van Neerbos, expanded in England and, of course, in America, under Don Godson. You see, Cement was a very respected company and we were slightly piratical. I don't think I was well regarded by the establishment. Bobby Kidney was much more acceptable. So, the merger was a good thing in that it enabled us to expand abroad.

When Jimmy became MD, I stayed on for a while, I'm not sure in what capacity. It did not work because you're inclined to give advice, and Jimmy had to say a few times, "We'll have to decide who's running this place". Finally, I thought it would be better to leave.

I have always had an intense interest and a concentration of effort in whatever I take up. I try to do well whatever I'm doing. One of the reasons we were so successful at exporting stone was that we met the needs of very discriminating German customers. I went to an immense amount of trouble to produce for them cubical stone instead of slivers. Whatever you're doing you've got to concentrate on it and do it better than anybody. As a nation, we're inclined to be a bit slipshod: "Ah, sure it'll do". The Americans have that ability to become intensely concentrated on a single small facet: who would think you could build an empire on chickens or Coca-Cola? I suppose one of the things I could tell managers would be to concentrate, not to get distracted, and to do things by *international* standards. I used to have Irishmen coming in selling me machinery. They would have a leaflet with them and they could not get beyond that. If an American were to come to sell you crushing machinery, by God, he knew about crushing. He knew his job. Think of the sort of experiences you have here getting your car serviced. If you go into a garage in France, it's spotless. One of our failings here is simple cleanliness and good housekeeping. We tend to put in three-quarters of the effort and we end up with three-quarters of everything, not 95 per cent.

I have been very fortunate that I was able to express the kind of person that I was.

JAMES SHEEHAN

BLACKROCK, GALWAY & HERMITAGE CLINICS

Since the State has largely taken over the hospitals and now controls the system, it has to be publicly accountable. Public accountability in Ireland is to be able to show how you wasted your money. It does not matter how much you waste, so long as you can show that nobody put it in their back pocket.

JAMES MICHAEL SHEEHAN, an orthopaedic surgeon, is the founder and developer of the Blackrock Clinic, Dublin (1981 to 1985), of the Galway Clinic (2004) and of the Hermitage Clinic, Dublin (2005).

He was born in Tralee, Co. Kerry on July 14, 1939. His father was James Joseph Sheehan, who worked in the Dublin Port & Docks Board. His mother was Frances Mangan. He was second in a family of three girls and two boys.

He is married to Rosemary Sheehan (same maiden name), a banker. They have four children: Kathy, Irenie, Michael and Mark.

He was educated at St. Mary's College, Rathmines, Dublin. In 1963, he took his primary medical degree at University College Dublin, together with a BSc in anatomy and anthropology. In 1966, he was awarded his final Fellowship in Surgery by the Royal College of Surgeons in Ireland. In 1970, he obtained an MSc in bioengineering, University of Surrey, Guilford; and in 1982, he received a PhD in mechanical engineering, University of Surrey.

His first appointment was Resident in St. Vincent's Hospital, Dublin (1963-64); Resident in Orthopaedics, St. Mary's Orthopaedic Hospital, Cappagh (1964-65); Resident, St. Vincent's Hospital (1965-66); Resident, Glasgow Royal Infirmary, Accident & Emergency Unit and Travelling Scholarship from the French Orthopaedic Association (1966-67); Resident, Royal National Orthopaedic Hospital, Stanmore, England (1967-68); Resident, Centre for Hip Surgery, Wrightington Hospital, Lancashire (1968-69); Consultant Orthopaedic Surgeon, St. Vincent's Hospital, Dublin and St. Mary's Orthopaedic Hospital, Cappagh (1970-86); Consultant Orthopaedic Surgeon, Blackrock Clinic (1986 to date). He is also director of Irish Healthcare, a health screening unit in conjunction with the Irish Management Institute.

He has been awarded the following medals: McArdle gold medal in Surgery, UCD; Feeney gold medal in Obstetrics, Coombe Hospital; Bellingham gold medal in Medicine, St. Vincent's Hospital; O'Ferrall gold medal in Surgery, St. Vincent's Hospital.

*T*o meet Jimmy Sheehan is to meet a kindly and soft-spoken gentleman, never mind his legendary care for his patients and his skill as a pioneering orthopaedic surgeon.

However, this is an angry chapter. While Jimmy freely acknowledges that the public health service will never satisfy public aspirations, because of lengthening life-spans, growing affluence and knowledge and almost explosive advances in medicine, nevertheless much of the blockages are caused by incompetence, inefficiency and the reluctance of governments to take on powerful vested interests. For example, public hospitals take 10 years to build, by which time the original plans are obsolete. Jimmy Sheehan's independent hospitals take 15 months.

Twenty years ago, when things were very dark, I wrote: "Nothing is going to alter the proclivity of government to accumulate a stock of errors, nurse them to the point of infection, and waste time defending itself against deserved criticism. People will be near the limits of impatience with its disabilities . . . Paradoxically, despite a healthy cynicism about the purposes and performance of government, the public will go on demanding that it do more and more".[40]

Plus ça change . . .

However, one change was noted by John Monks of Britain's Trade Union Congress: "Trade unions are like gorillas in the forest, suffering from a shrinking habitat". Faced with the inexorable onslaught of competition in the private sector, trade unions have retreated to the high ground of the State sector: monopoly public utilities and health or education. There they strike, not against the employers, but against the public, in the certain knowledge that no Irish government will take them on, at least not for long, and certainly not with an election in the offing.

---

[40] *Government & Enterprise in Ireland* (1984), pp. 34-35.

Jimmy Sheehan showed me a photograph he had taken quietly in a public hospital which shall be nameless. It was of a half-open battered green door, with boxes piled inside. On the door was a sign: You are now Entering a Sterile Area.

He talks passionately about the causes of the awesome problems faced by our present health service.

The conversation was recorded at Jimmy Sheehan's home in Dublin, on January 26, 2005.

His biography is in *Leaders* (2001).

JAMES SHEEHAN

I returned to Ireland in 1970. I am now in my 48th year in medicine. I have seen a great deal of change. A half-century is a long time in the evolution of medical technology.

When I came back to Ireland, I was involved in accident and emergency work in St. Vincent's Hospital, and in elective surgery – surgery done on a planned basis – at Cappagh Orthopaedic Hospital. My particular interest was joint replacement.

In the 1970s, the religious orders were active in providing medical services. Hospitals were still largely staffed by them. The first hospital in Ireland was Jervis Street, founded in the early 18th century. It was run by religious up to the time of its closure. This was the same for nearly all the hospitals and that is why they were known as voluntary hospitals. Without the religious, we would never have had this heritage of hospitals. I feel that, with all the bad press they got in recent years, our gratitude to them for all they've done in both health and education has been lost.

If I were asked what was the greatest single fault in our present health system, I would say it is the lack of the commitment that we got in the past from the religious orders. The nuns who worked in the hospital were not on any designated shift – they were there day and night. There was continuity of care – this is one of the most serious changes in the last 30 years. A lot of nurses now do their week's work in three 12-hour days. Then you have a gap of four days before they're back to the same patient.

Why has there been so much change over that time? Up until the 1970s, there was a limited amount of money put into research and development. Since then, particularly in the United States, there has been a very large research and development budget. For example, in the National Cancer Institute in Washington DC, their budget for one year is the same as our entire health budget. They have approximately 5,000 clinical trials running at one time. Out of these, beneficial effects are identified in, for example, new drug therapy or new medical devices. The difficulty is to apply these benefits worldwide. If you take cardiology, in the last five years, there's been a change from invasive surgery to non-invasive procedures such as coronary stenting. Adjusting to that change means adapting to new technology and the training of physicians and technicians. We just failed in this country to wind up the system rapidly enough to adapt to these changes.

No country in the western world can afford the rapid introduction of these new technologies, because most of them are enhancing the *quality* of life. They are not necessarily life-saving. For example, surgery in my own area of joint replacement is enhancing the quality of, but does not necessarily prolong, your life. The longer people are living, the more they require reconstructive surgery, i.e. eye surgery for the removal of cataracts, treatment of blocked vessels such as coronary arteries or aortas, joint degeneration, all due to the ageing process. Since the 1970s, the average life expectancy of males and females has increased by 10 years. By the middle of this century, the average life expectancy will be close to 100, if it increases at its present rate.

Apart from medical planning, the planning of our general infrastructure, such as our roads, leaves a great deal to be desired. We planned part of a motorway system in Ireland in the 1970s as a ring road around Dublin. Now, 35 years later, we've completed the last section. We know what jetlag is – I call this public lag. There's a 20-year lag between the identification of what needs to be done and the introduction of the necessary change, by which time the need itself has changed.

Let me give you an example of the extent of change in medical care. In the 1970s, we only had X-rays for diagnosis. Since then, you have scans of all types – bone scans, CT scans, nuclear medicine scans and ultrasound scans. When I look back to when I started practice in 1966, there is now not a single operation that was applicable then. When people talk about continuing education, they are actually talking about continual advancement. If you don't change with the times, you are obsolete within your own lifetime of practice. There's huge obsolescence in medicine. People don't understand why doctors have to go to meetings and spend time out for continuing training.

As the religious orders in hospitals have taken a minor role, the State has stepped in to fill the gap. The result is that the problems in our present healthcare system are obvious to all.

However, I still believe the standard of healthcare in Ireland is high. The professionals involved, the nursing staff and the paramedicals, are well qualified and give a superb service. What we're missing in Ireland is the *quantity* of service, not the quality. It's important to differentiate between the two. It's been obvious since the early '80s that we do not have adequate facilities. In the '80s, the Government reduced the total acute bed-stock in Ireland by about 6,000 from a total of 18,000. A number of those beds were in the east of the country. This coincided with an increased migration of people towards Dublin. As a result, the greatest demand for beds is on the east coast.

Government never over-estimate the number of beds needed, but even their own figures suggest we now urgently need 3,000 more acute beds, beds they have not been able to provide.

How do you tackle this problem? Do you wait for the Government to provide the services or should alternative providers get involved?

As our country matures, people feel that it's the State's duty to look after the health of the individual. I believe it's the responsibility of individuals to look after their own health.

It's the responsibility of the State to look after the poorer sections of our community. In the days of the voluntary hospitals, that's what happened. The poorer people were looked after free of charge but those who had resources were expected to pay. No country in the world could provide an unlimited healthcare service free for all. Somebody has to pay. Having the taxpayer pay is not the most efficient system.

The alternative is to introduce private investment. The advantage is that you introduce competition – any efficient system is dependent on competition. Take our airlines. When we had a national carrier with a monopoly, we were overcharged, they were overstaffed and we got a poor service. With the introduction of competition, the prices were significantly reduced, the staff in Aer Lingus were reduced by about 50% and the company went from losses to profit.

If you have private investment in healthcare, this unfortunately gets labelled as providing a service for the privileged, encouraging a two-tier system with people who can afford it getting preferential care over those who can't.

Full credit, therefore, to the PD members of the Government, for introducing the Treatment Purchase Fund, where people who have been waiting for treatment for a designated period can now get private healthcare. The waiting time is now down to three months and allows patients to apply for private care after that time. Once these people enter a private hospital, nobody knows who's paying the bill – they are treated in exactly the same way as those who have private insurance. For the first time now, we have a one-tier level of service applicable to all.

We are getting a little closer to the French, rated as number one in the world. They have both an independent and a public system. People have universal health insurance – they can go anywhere they like with the equivalent of their Visa card and the bill is picked up by the State. The two systems contend with each other. Those who are employed in the public system are exclusively employed there. It works well. The competition between the two sectors gives the customer a choice, something we sadly lack in this country.

I don't like the terms commonly used – public and private. There's nothing private about a private hospital – the term suggests privilege. It's much better to use the term independent. The only difference is that the independent hospitals are funded independently of State funding – they are not paid for by the taxpayer.

A further problem with our health service is that we have never qualified adequate numbers of professionals. When you look back 40 or 50 years, most of our graduates were not employed in Ireland – they had to emigrate. When I qualified in 1966, nearly all my class emigrated and very few have come back. Now it's the opposite – any qualified person who wants to stay in Ireland, can stay. Or else go abroad for part of their training and come back, which is good because they return with new ideas. Because technology has become more sophisticated, we need more doctors and paramedics. Half the entrants to our medical schools are foreigners. The universities are dependent on them to subsidise the Irish students. Of the 50% Irish, 60% are females. This is a result of the points system. It may be fair in some people's eyes, but it is not a suitable system to select entrants for professions such as medicine. You end up with a lot more female than male graduates and, because of child-bearing years and family responsibilities, many of the women graduates do not have the time or motivation to undertake a 10-year post-graduate training programme. When you question female graduates nowadays, many tell you that they have regretted going into medicine. The result is that we now have far too few people graduating who are interested in committing themselves to a long post-graduate programme.

The intake for all the ancillary services is also inadequate. For example, we have not adapted to the need for radiographers in disciplines such as magnetic resonance imaging, CT scanning and ultrasound. The intake has remained at a level that coped with standard X-ray examinations but not with the numbers required to cope with the new modalities. If it were not for the fact that people can train in England and abroad and return home, the service would be totally inadequate. This shortage of trained personnel gives rise to cost increases. Some of these professionals have negotiated significant deals with the Department of Health and are holding the system to ransom. Radiographers now, after 5 o'clock, and on Saturday and Sunday, are paid on a fee per item of service. A qualified radiographer can make up to €800 in an evening on piece-work, undertaking CT scans in a busy department.

We're facing this problem also in other service areas in Ireland, where we are pricing ourselves out of the market. Our costs in medicine now are among the highest in Europe.

In healthcare, we have an accumulation of awesome problems. Any solution to our healthcare problem is going to be very slow. There is the issue of shortage of consultants – there is no quick fix as the training period for a consultant is about 16 years. You can't change that situation overnight and double our consultant numbers as is frequently suggested.

The only way we could rapidly address this problem is by bringing in foreign graduates. There is supposedly free access for graduates from the European Union, but several impediments are put in their way. If an Irish person or an American graduate wanted to come to Ireland, and if they did not do their undergraduate training here, they are not allowed practise even though they are well qualified. The only way they would be licensed in Ireland would be to become a resident for a two-year period by "training" with a suitably qualified practitioner in Ireland. Senior people would have to go back and serve an apprenticeship. The Medical Council run a closed shop. We tried to appoint an experienced hand surgeon from the United States. He had married an Irish girl and wanted to relocate to the west of Ireland.

Unfortunately, he did his undergraduate training in America. He would have been a fantastic asset to the west of Ireland, where there is no hand surgeon. But the Medical Council would not let him practise unless he came back and served his apprenticeship with an Irish surgeon for two years. Then his application would be reconsidered!

The same applies in the paramedical areas where we have shortages. In Spain, they have an excess of radiographers. The result is that they produce their X-rays at a cost significantly lower than here. The average cost of a magnetic scan in Spain is €100. Here, the cheapest scan is in the region of €450. The medical fee alone is greater than the total cost of the scan in Spain. All of this is due to competition. In Spain, they also have an excess of medical graduates all contending to interpret the scans, thus driving the cost down. Back to competition again.

As for hospitals, they have the possibility of increasing their bed capacity but they don't have the services to back up those beds. If, tomorrow, you were to bring back more doctors, you would end up with more doctors doing less work per person. Some newly appointed consultants don't even have a place to see their patients. This is worse for surgeons whose primary need is access to an operating room. A hospital like St. Vincent's has 12 operating rooms for 500 beds. If you increase the efficiency of throughput of patients, you are short of operating time. If you increase the efficiency, you have to increase the technology available at every level and the lead-in time for this is significant.

Since the State has largely taken over the hospitals and now controls the system, it has to be publicly accountable. Public accountability in Ireland is to be able to show how you wasted your money. It does not matter how much you waste so long as you can show that nobody put it in their back pocket.

To respond to our current bed shortages is difficult. The Department of Health has a seven-stage programme for the development of a new hospital. It was 13 stages in the past. With the best will in the world, you can't accelerate these stages and, as a result, the construction of any new hospital takes up to 10 years.

St. Vincent's took 30 years to develop because the War intervened and there were stops and starts. On the other hand, the actual construction in Tallaght was five years after the initial planning process. On completion of construction, you've got a commissioning process. Public construction means you have to tender throughout Europe. That is a lengthy process. The initial contract cost bears no relation to the finished price. This is where independent hospitals can score considerably. They reduce the construction period and they work on a fixed-price contract. Every public hospital built in Ireland greatly exceeded the contract price. The design teams benefit because they are paid a percentage of the total cost. The more the end result, the greater the fees for the design team. I don't know of any other aspect of life where people are paid in proportion to their incompetence. In other words, the more they can drive up the cost, the more they benefit from it. In a rational system, like the independent hospitals, you work on a fixed price and fixed design fees. If anybody wants to spend an extra 10 years fiddling around with the building, they don't get any money for it.

Another problem with public hospital projects is that all contracts are in two phases – a construction contract and an equipping contract. When the hospital is built, the equipment has not been chosen. Often, as in Tallaght, they have to partly rebuild the hospital to accommodate the equipment as the equipment has not been tendered until the construction is complete. They then redesign the building and rebuild it to accommodate the equipment. The commissioning process itself can take between one and four years.

We are starting a new independent hospital in Liffey Valley. The construction and commissioning process will be in the region of 16 months. All the equipment is identified before the construction starts. There is no alteration within the construction period. When we commissioned the hospital in Galway, the commissioning period was 20 days. That was from the day the hospital was handed over by the builder until the first surgery took place. All the equipment was in place, the loose equipment specified and ordered and all delivered within that 20-day period and the staff suitably instructed.

The "new" James Connolly Hospital in Blanchardstown is due to open shortly. The new extension has been locked up for two years. Could you imagine any business in the world building a new factory and not opening it for two years? The Regional Hospital in Tralee was the first hospital in the world where the authorities had to undertake a study to find out what to do with an empty hospital. It was locked up because the Department of Health didn't have the money to commission and equip it. How would you keep the bugs at bay in the period when the hospital was locked up without staff? Beaumont in Dublin was five years from the time it was built until it opened. So long as the Comptroller and Auditor General can see where the money was wasted, rather than going astray, everything is all right – provided no one shouts!

Similar inefficiencies exist in our planning process. We got planning permission for the new hospital in Liffey Valley two-and-a-half years ago. One of the conditions was that we would hand over six acres of land on the banks of the Liffey for use as a public park. We willingly agreed because we had 30 acres and we didn't need those six acres. But it took an awfully long time for their legal department to agree to accept the gift, with the result that the builders had to cool their heels until they could move on-site: frustrating and wasteful.

At an operational level, the cost of the independent hospital is fully transparent. We don't know the cost of public hospitals, as no one can tell you the cost of a procedure. Even if we did work out the costs of the procedure, the capital and equipment costs are not included. There's no depreciation and there's no business appraisal.

Why have we not seen the development of independent hospital facilities over the past 20 years? The blockage rests with our private insurance company. Private insurance was largely synonymous with the VHI, which was founded in the 1950s under the Voluntary Health Insurance Act. They were the sole provider, owned by the State with the Minister for Health as the shareholder. The more private beds in the country, the more the VHI have to pay out in claims. They always realised that there was a shortage of beds and that every bed that was built would be occupied. Some years ago, when they were under pressure from people like myself requesting to develop new hospitals, the VHI commissioned a report. The report suggested that there was no need for any new hospital beds in Ireland up to the year 2004. The report was never released – only a summary and it was unintelligible. For example, it said that, in Limerick, there was no need at all for any private beds. Now there are no private beds in Limerick yet 50% of the population of Limerick carry private insurance. VHI used the report so people like myself were told that they would not sanction any more private beds.

This situation continued until I decided to challenge the VHI by building a new hospital. The reason for building a new hospital in the west of Ireland was because there was not a single new bed added there for half a century. There was a small private hospital run initially by nuns, sold on to a group of private investors and more recently to the Bon Secours nuns who now own it. It had 63 beds – they were the only significant private beds from Donegal down to Cork. And, again, 50% of the population now carry private insurance. That's grown from 30% in the 1980s. Every second person is now privately insured – they are no longer a minority. The waiting lists are incredible. In some disciplines, the waiting list – not even for hospitalisation, but to be seen by a consultant – for example in rheumatology – is six years. In Roscommon, a routine appointment with a dermatologist is currently nine years. Imagine having a skin problem and being told that there was a nine-year waiting list. The cancer facilities in the west were particularly poor. Those needing radiotherapy had to travel to St. Luke's Hospital in Dublin. With radiotherapy, patients have a very short spell of treatment each day, often for 30 consecutive days. Their daily treatment takes 10 minutes. Not only do these patients have to travel, but the waiting time for St. Luke's is 10 weeks. When I first looked at the services in the west, one of the areas most in need was the cancer care service. I decided we would concentrate on this area, as well as on the need for cardiac surgery. There was no cardiac surgery west of the Shannon. Also, people were waiting for many years for joint replacements for arthritic problems. All of this coincided with the advent of the Treatment Purchase Fund. We felt we could cope with a large number of people who were being paid for by State insurance. We could have a mix of both public and private patients under the one roof. This led to the Galway Clinic.

The Galway Clinic is the first example of a community hospital, a hospital where the whole community can benefit, both the people carrying private insurance and those funded by the State. The Clinic opened in June 2004, completed on time and on budget. The total investment is in the region of €100m.

The Clinic introduced radiotherapy to the west of Ireland. Now, 40 patients a day are treated. It also introduced cardiac surgery. It has provided an environment in keeping with the era we live in. We got used to the fact that hospitals were antiquated buildings – for example, in the west of Ireland, the newest building was 50 years old. Compare the hospitals with the rest of the infrastructure in the west. There are now two five-star hotels in Galway. There are new shopping centres. The whole infrastructure has moved years ahead of healthcare. The new Galway Clinic is an effort to bring healthcare into the present era.

The introduction of radiotherapy to the west of Ireland is a good example of efficiency. When we announced that we were undertaking provision of a radiotherapy facility, which is a very sophisticated development, the public system decided they would accelerate their programme which was in train for many years. They insisted that their linear accelerator was delivered from the United States on the same flight as ours. We had two senior people lined up to install, programme and commission the machine. Unfortunately, there was a delay because a part in the machine had to be replaced. We had hoped to become operational in July but were not able to treat patients until September 6, 2004. In the public system, they had 24 people in the department between physicists and therapists available to commission the machine. They hope to start treating patients by April or May 2005, some seven months after our programme commenced.

The importance of competition cannot be minimised. Nobody knew how long it would take to commission a radiotherapy department. It is a complex area. The senior physicist we employed, a very competent man, came from England, worked seven days a week, was basically locked into the radiotherapy bunker until the commissioning was complete. The same process, spread between a number of physicists in the public system has gone on for an indefinite period. There was no yardstick until it was provided by the independent sector.

I would not like to say that independent medicine can replace the State system. There are aspects of our healthcare, like mental health, where a significant input is required from the State. But a great deal of our system could be privatised for the sake of efficiency. As a significant taxpayer, I get very annoyed when I see the wastage of our public funds and yet the difficulty of trying to provide facilities and being blocked by semi-State companies like the VHI.

When I approached them over five years ago to approve a facility in the west, they refused. The hardest thing I've ever done in life was to raise €100m without any backing from the insurance company and no guarantee that the hospital would be used. They finally approved the hospital six weeks before it opened. The alternative insurance company, BUPA, sanctioned it two weeks after we opened.

Having broken the insurer's monopoly with Galway, I think the doors have been eased open. People now realise there is a huge demand for acute hospital beds. Recently, the Department of Health announced that, when counting the number of beds being provided, they're going to include the independent sector. Up until now, it was taken as irrelevant.

In the report on the acute health services, commissioned by Micheál Martin, there were 54 people involved and only one from independent healthcare. That representative was in the pharmaceutical business. No one represented any independent hospital. In a lengthy report, just one page made reference to the independent sector. Now that beds are coming on stream from the independent sector, they are anxious to include them because they themselves have provided a minimal increase in bed stock.

So far as I know, there are only two new independent hospitals in the course of construction, one is the Beacon Clinic in Sandyford and the other is our hospital in Liffey Valley. Apart from that, people are talking about hospitals in Wexford, Newry, Limerick and Cork – in all parts of the country. Making them happen is very different from talking about them, particularly without any comfort from the insurers. The first thing a bank wants to know is who is the insurer.

The same applies to the Treatment Purchase Fund – they will not pre-sanction a hospital. They get annual budgets in line with the general budget. They can't tell you from year to year whether they will have any money the following year. They can't give you any comfort a year in advance. Their attitude is that they will inspect your hospital when it is complete and then decide whether to use it.

We opened our doors in Galway in June 2004. With the best will in the world, we operated on only 250 patients referred from the Treatment Purchase Fund in the first six months. The great majority of these were day-patients. Instead of 250 operations, we could have done 2,500 in that time, but the work was not made available to us. It's an indication of how poorly Public Private Partnerships work. There's a lot of talk about PPPs in road construction. In healthcare, they are a non-event. The lowest common denominator determines what happens. If you're in partnership with the State, it just doesn't work.

In Ireland, we are frequently criticised for our two-tier level of service. In France, there is no such thing as private beds in public hospitals as there is here. We have always held the view in this country that 20% of the beds in public hospitals should be allocated to private patients. It does not work because people are constantly jumping the queue. If people carry insurance, they tend to see a doctor privately and then jump the public queue. This gives rise, and rightly so, to a lot of criticism of our system being inequitable – that if you can afford to pay, you get looked after. I believe you should not be allowed to bring private patients into a public hospital. The doctors are on a contract for which they should be fully committed to the public hospital. It's a controversial area in Ireland because hospitals have always worked on a mixture of public and private patients. If there were an adequate supply of independent beds, then those who could afford them should go there and not displace people in the public hospitals. Or, at the very least, there should be a common waiting list so that people who wish to avail of a public hospital and carry private insurance, should go in the same queue. The consultants should not admit patients out of turn.

In Ireland, we also have a tradition of providing private facilities attached to public hospitals. Good examples are St. Vincent's Private and the Mater Private Hospitals. Most consultants are contracted for a 33-hour week but they often work twice or three times that amount. Once they have fulfilled their public work, there is nothing wrong with them looking after people in a private hospital. That is not displacing people in the public hospital. By and large, such private hospitals are independent but there is an overlap of some facilities. In an ideal world, they should not use any of the public facilities. For example, the Mater Private is very much an independent hospital. St. Vincent's would be more dependent on the public facilities – they don't have their own laboratories and there are limited imaging facilities. On the other hand, the private hospitals have radiotherapy, which allow them treat people from the public hospitals and thus they are helping the public system. In the future, I would like to see the two systems separated. There is a move in the Department of Health to encourage the building of private hospitals adjacent to the public hospitals. This is a mistake. I would much rather see the doctors employed in the public system having better facilities there and spending more of their time working in the public hospital and not to encourage them into a two-tier level of service on the same site. That would be retrograde.

There are two politicians that I admire and who have been helpful to the health services. One is Charlie McCreevy. He was one of the few politicians who was deaf to public opinion. He introduced a Finance Bill to encourage investment in private hospitals. He did this with a good deal of opposition. That has made it easier to raise money for private hospitals and has indicated a degree of Government approval. The disadvantage is that every developer and every farmer who owns a field feels there should be a hospital on it. The increase in land value after rezoning is a significant problem. People are getting such a mark-up in the value of land that it's quite inequitable. You end up with young couples having to get a huge mortgage to pay for the additional cost of the site. They are paying for all their lifetime. You have a very small number of people making enormous amounts of money. This has happened particularly in the west of Ireland where every area that's rezoned, the owners become multi-millionaires. I believe the Government is looking at ways of keeping down the added value following rezoning, but nothing has been done so far. The tax-breaks for areas such as car parks in the inner city are petering out. Private developers see private hospitals as an opportunity and that is absolutely the wrong motivation to build a hospital. They are not looking at the true needs of where the hospitals should be positioned but simply how they can use the tax-break.

The other politician I admire is Mary Harney, who has taken on the Department of Health portfolio. No matter what a politician does with the Health portfolio, it will never satisfy the people. The demand is unsatisfiable. She was brave to take it on. She's decisive. The problem is that she has a very short timeframe. It's difficult, if not impossible, to get any real change in a two-year period. I do hope, however, that she will set the tone for a much better health service in the future, something she won't see in her present term of office, unless she's back in that portfolio for a five-year period.

The reforms with the new Health Service Executive do not sound great. They have undertaken to re-employ all the people who were already in the service. It's very hard to reform a service if you take everybody back in with jobs for life. It's only a rearrangement of the deckchairs. I fear that some aspects of the reform will be very disappointing. Apart from those two politicians, everybody else is paying lip service to patients languishing on hospital trolleys, but not much action.

I do not believe in writing reports but in positive action. I feel I have been in a very privileged position to be able to make a few things happen. The few things that I have made happen are miniscule in relation to the shortcomings in our health service. I have helped develop 300 beds – a drop in the ocean. I believe, however, they are the start of providing modern, up-to-date hospital beds. When Blackrock opened, it was labelled an exclusive hospital for the rich. All it was was an up-to-date hospital. In this day and age, there's nothing fancy in having a bath off your bedroom. In a hospital, it's the basic minimum for hygiene. The Galway Clinic and the Liffey Valley Hospital are simply what we should expect in the 21st century.

One person I have to mention, particularly in relation to Blackrock, is my colleague, George Duffy. He is a physician I have worked closely with for 35 years. Our development in Blackrock was a joint venture with him. He is a superb physician. He introduced nuclear medicine to Ireland. In the last few years, he introduced PET scanning, which is particularly useful for cancer diagnosis. The only two PET scanners in the country are in Blackrock. That's another indication of the way the independent sector can provide what's necessary. The same happened with magnetic scanning. The first magnetic scanner was in the Mater Private and, shortly after that, in the Blackrock Clinic. They were the only two scanners in Ireland for six or seven years. It was 10 years later when the first public scanner became available. The Galway Clinic has provided radiotherapy and cardiac survey and this will be a fantastic boon to the west of Ireland. The same happened with Blackrock some years ago, when it too introduced new technologies. It was regarded as a benchmark and led to improvements in the public services.

Having a benchmark where, hitherto, there was none, does make a difference. People accepted a very poor standard in hospitals, because they knew no better. By laying down benchmarks, it makes them look critically at graffiti in lifts, dirty hospitals and inadequate facilities. In a number of our hospitals, the standard of hygiene, even down to hand-washing, has not been adequate. These areas are now under scrutiny because the public are becoming better educated. They're connecting to the Internet and seeing what should be available. They are now going into the doctor and asking why he can't do a certain procedure for them.

If I achieve nothing else but getting these three hospitals functioning as prototypes, I will be satisfied. They will be good examples of community hospitals that can be reproduced in other parts of the country.

What I'd really like to turn my attention to is our paediatric services. Two-and-a-half years ago, I was asked to join the board of Crumlin Hospital to look at its redevelopment. Crumlin was built in 1956 and was funded by the Archdiocese of Dublin by John Charles McQuaid. At that time, it was a leading-edge hospital. To an extent, it was fashioned on Great Ormond Street in London. It has proved itself a superb children's hospital – its name is synonymous with a high level of care. However, the care is not matched by the premises. Over the last half-century, there was very little investment. In the past few years, they have opened a new theatre block, which is the first major investment by the State in Crumlin. It now needs a long-overdue redevelopment. It is still owned by the Church but is fully funded by the Health Board. There were two other children's hospitals in Dublin, in Temple Street on the northside and in Harcourt Street on the southside. Harcourt Street has since located to Tallaght Hospital. If you look at international practice, we need one major children's hospital for a population of five million. Ireland lends itself ideally to one first-class paediatric hospital to cover the entire country. There's a great opportunity to have a new children's hospital that serves the north and the south of the country, strategically located on the east coast.

When you're looking at a dedicated children's hospital, you're talking about tertiary or complex care. Children who get sore throats and run-of-the-mill conditions are treated in their local hospital in a children's ward. When we are considering the more sophisticated problems – children who need cardiac surgery, children with leukaemia, who need bone marrow transplants and other complex conditions – all should be located together in a sophisticated hospital. We should now amalgamate the tertiary care of the three children's hospitals into one hospital and include Northern Ireland. What better way of unifying our country than starting with the children of the next generation? We already have a model in the Veterinary Campus in UCD. My ambition would be to work on this development over the next few years. There is no reason why we could not have one of the finest children's hospitals in the world, because the staff that are available in Crumlin are second-to-none. If they were matched by a level of facility in keeping with their expertise, we would have one of the finest paediatric services in the world.

Please God, over the next few years, I'd like to turn my attention to this development. I'd like to see it developed as a foundation, independent of the State and not run by the Government for the reasons I have spoken about. The model is there with hospitals like the Mayo Clinic or the Cleveland Clinic in the United States. They are set up as independent foundations. The Government can fund the individual patients. With an independent foundation, it can set its own standards, its quality of care and appointment of personnel. It also takes the workforce employed by the hospital off the State books. There are approximately 100,000 employed by the public service in healthcare. With a new Crumlin, we would have the seeds sown for a more progressive healthcare service which the citizens of this country deserve. What better ambition could one have for the future?

15

MICHAEL SMURFIT

JEFFERSON SMURFIT GROUP

*I must, I can and I will. I never look over my
shoulder and ask what if.*

MICHAEL SMURFIT is Chairman of Jefferson Smurfit Group.

He was born in St. Helen's, Lancashire on August 7, 1936, first in a family of seven.

He was educated at Clongowes Wood College and had management training in the USA with the Continental Can Corporation. He has four sons and two daughters.

He joined his father's company, Jefferson Smurfit & Sons Ltd, in 1955. Some 12 years later, he was appointed Joint Managing Director of Jefferson Smurfit Group Ltd, before becoming Deputy Chairman in 1969. In 1977, he was appointed Chairman and Chief Executive, Jefferson Smurfit Group. He held both positions until his retirement as CEO in November 2002 and, today, he holds the position of Chairman.

Initial expansion in Ireland in the 1960s and early 1970s was followed by a series of acquisitions in the United Kingdom, United States, Latin America, and, over the last 10 years, in continental Europe. In 1994, JSG more than doubled its sales base in Europe, with the acquisition of paper and packaging operations in the French company, Saint-Gobain.

In 1998, the Group effected the largest-ever merger in the paper-packaging sector with its US associate, Jefferson Smurfit Corporation, and Stone Container Corporation, to form the Smurfit Stone Container Corporation, an organisation of unprecedented size in the sector, with 70,000 employees and 500 facilities covering 30 countries.

The acquisition and subsequent privatisation of the Group by Madison Dearborn Partners in November 2002 was another shift in strategy. The Group's core focus is now in the South American and European markets.

Michael Smurfit is a Fellow of the International Academy of Management, with honorary doctorates in law from Trinity College Dublin, the National University of Ireland, University College Galway, the University of Scranton, Pennsylvania and Babson College, Boston. He is the honorary Irish consul to Monaco and has been honoured by the Governments of France (*Légion d'Honneur*), Italy, Venezuela and Colombia, and most recently by the UK, his country of birth, when he was appointed a Knight Commander of the British Empire (KBE).

I first met Michael Smurfit years ago, when he brought me to dinner in the Russell Hotel on Stephen's Green, long since gone. He arrived in a great black square Mercedes, designed, I think, for heads of state. Two things I remember about that dinner: first was Michael's boundless energy and curiosity and second that the Russell gave you little wooden mushrooms that you were to plunge up and down in the champagne to get rid of the bubbles. The monk in Epernay who discovered champagne and announced to his startled brethren that he was "drinking stars" would have been upset.

When I left the IMI, I was invited in 1983 to become independent chairman of the Smurfit Paribas Bank, a banque d'affaires, whose office was a stone's throw from where the Russell Hotel used be. We had a distinguished board, half-Paribas, half Smurfit. A highlight was a phone call from the then Governor of Bank of Ireland, Louden Ryan,[41] one of my oldest friends. He was seeking my permission to approach Howard Kilroy, Michael's right-hand man and a member of the Smurfit Paribas Board, to invite him to become Governor. I graciously gave permission. Toujours la politesse.

I made enduring friendships working on three major consultancies for the Smurfit Group: 96/97, 97/98 and 01/02.

When, on January 12, 1987, nearly two decades ago, I spoke with Michael for the first book, In Good Company, he had tears in his eyes when he remembered his father. His love for his father, rather than lessening, increased his relentless competitiveness. He started on his own in England, partly because he did not want to work in his "father's back yard" in Dublin.

---

[41]   *In Good Company* (1987).

In that earlier book, Michael Smurfit said, "If you don't go on the field determined to win, you are not going to win. A guy who starts off believing he's going to fail, is going to fail. Nobody remembers who was second in the Grand National. You have to be totally dedicated to making a thing a success. If you enter a horse for the Derby and think you are in for the run, then don't enter the horse . . .

"There was never any particular time when I decided what I wanted to be. The heavens never opened for the spirit to descend on me. What I do remember vividly, however, is the time when I suddenly realised I was going to hold the ultimate responsibility. My father stood up at an AGM and said, without any warning, 'My sons are better qualified by their background, education and training than I am to run this business and I hereby resign'. The next day he packed his bags and went on a world cruise with Mum".

The conversation was recorded at the K Club, Straffan, Co. Kildare, on December 27, 2004.

Michael Smurfit's biography is in *In Good Company* (1987).

MICHAEL SMURFIT

I started work at 16. My father always said that you buy brains and make business people. All of us, my brothers and I, started work at 16 – no university education – from ground zero, in the business from the bottom up. I learned how the machines worked, how the business delivered goods to customers, how we collected cheques.

I secretly tried to leave my father and found out, through a required medical exam, that I had tuberculosis. Instead of going to Canada, I ended up in a sanatorium – the boat sailed the day I walked in. No, that did not affect me deeply – I was young. What did affect me was holding people's hands while they died. I became a sort of altar boy and looked after people. That religious revival, if you will, affected me for a period of years. I was very shy when I was young. I was even shier when I came out of the sanatorium. I was fat, having been fit all my life. You lie for months on the flat of your back and get jabs of needles up your rear end. You bloat. I worked on it to get back trim again.

I then got my Dad to send me to America where I learned an awful lot. Just two years ago, I went back to the Connecticut plant in which I started my career. The manager who was there when I was a young fellow came back to meet me. It was an emotional few days.

I got my initial enthusiasm for business while in America. I had grown up in a business where my father had made the equipment himself. It worked after a fashion – some days it did and some days it didn't. But we got a good living out of it. What I saw in America was the modern way of doing things. I quickly decided that was the way to go. I wanted to bring those new ideas into Smurfits but Dad would have none of it. He knew his way of working, it worked well and he didn't want to change. This frustrated me.

As well as that, I was concerned about the future of the country, but we were doing pretty well because, at that time, corrugated was replacing wood. This was 1963/1965.

When Norma and I decided to marry, Dad did not approve of her because she wasn't Catholic. He was a convert and a true believer, probably greater than if he had been born into the faith.

I decided to start my own business in England. Dad encouraged me and helped me financially. I got a chance there to put into practice on my own what I had learned. I chose England, partly not to be working in my father's back yard, but largely because we had an established market there. We were, in fact, shipping stuff from Ireland to England, not very much but enough to give us an insight into that market. My brother, Alan, came back from France to work with me. Jeff looked after my father. Jeff was very good at sales and marketing, which were never my forte. We had in England a local partner who guaranteed us a lot of business, Phil Jacobs, a Jewish gentleman who had a great entrée to Marks & Spencer. That worked out well.

I got married, settled in England and, very quickly, Jefferson Smurfit Packaging, as it was then called, was as big as our business in Dublin. After three years, we were very successful. We called the business after Dad – he was a huge factor in my life, a real character, one of the boys.

England took off. I found that my competitors there were not so much dozy, as working through a club system. It was all cartels – price-fixing was the norm. I got in under that umbrella and still undercut them, even though my quality was probably poorer than theirs because my equipment was not what I wanted.

Meantime, Dad had gone public in Ireland, against my advice, at eight shillings a share. They opened at 12 shillings and never looked back. Big fortunes were made in our stock – at the family's expense.

Dad never had any money in his life. There was never a time when he wasn't stretched. He wanted some security and came over to see me in England. I had just, after three years, moved to a house in Forest Grove. He wanted me to come back and run the parent company. He was impressed with what I had done. I said I'd come back only on the basis that I would have a free hand. My way and his way of doing business were radically different, but he was quite happy to retire. He said he would sell me *Tyne Villa* in Stilorgan, the house we grew up in. This was on a Friday and I asked him when he wanted me to start. He said, "Monday morning". I said I'd be there.

I went home and told my two young boys, Tony and Michael. My first two sons were born in England, my first two daughters in Ireland. The family stayed on in England a little while longer while I got things arranged in Ireland.

IBI, Richard Hooper, worked for the Group, and Martin Rafferty, AIB, for me, to put the two companies together, because it just wouldn't work for me to have the Smurfit name in England. I could not run a public company and have a private business with the same name. The negotiations were tortuous.

I came up with the idea that I would take no dividends for 15 years, a very low salary, and I would be the largest stockholder in the company. The dividend stream on a 15-year basis was growing at 10% per annum. I got what were known as B shares. I got a salary of £7,000 at the time. Far more important, I negotiated that myself and my brother, Jeff, had 10% of the pre-tax profits only when the profits reached a quarter-of-a-million. If they doubled, we would still have 10%, which is where my huge salary eventually came from. In time, that got changed from pre-tax profits to earnings per share because there was a perception by the bank 10 years later that I was essentially buying profits. It was not intended to be like that, but that's the way it turned out. Then Jeff died and his 5% disappeared. Eventually the bonus got so big that, without pressure, I reduced my 5% to 2½%. I refused to go beneath that, because in the process, we had created billions for shareholders.

When I came back to Ireland, I saw that the industry was totally fragmented, an absolute mess. I joined the then Confederation of Irish Industry and took an active role in projecting myself into Irish business. I did not like the Anglo-Irish Free Trade Agreement. It was going to cause enormous problems for Smurfit. I decided the only way out for us was to rationalise the Irish industry. This meant taking them over, and then to have a solid base from which to move into the UK so that, under the Trade Agreement, when England started to attack us, particularly from Northern Ireland where Reed's had, and still have, a very big plant, we would be in a position to fight them with some reasonable strength. It was basically fear that motivated my rationalisation.

I might as well have talked to the wall. They were old Ascendancy-type companies. Alan Nolan, Brown & Nolan, was probably the only

Catholic in the business, but he was very hoity-toity. The Protestant companies, Hely Group, Gibson Guy & Smalldridge, Eagle of Cork, Temple Press – any of them I talked to treated us as upstarts. I began a series of manoeuvres that finally resulted in the whole industry getting rationalised. Hely's, Brown & Nolan's and Temple Press joined Smurfit as did Eagle of Cork. Gibson Guy & Smalldridge joined the Clondalkin Group. That was the Irish industry totally rationalised. Then there was just us and Clondalkin, with a couple of small players like Dakota who are still around.

I decided to move into the UK. Very quickly, we bought WJ Noble and Temple Press. We called that project "Virgin" and that was the time I had my first real scare in a takeover. Nobles was owned by a woman, Mrs. Verity who, every month, wrote her stock up. It was a big lesson for me of the need to do a thorough due diligence. We then took over the Alliance Box Company. That gave us a base.

What we found when we took over those companies, in Ireland and in England, was that we were good at managing things. I was always good at hiring the right people. I knew my own limitations – I was not a good accountant or a salesman. But I knew I was a good detailed person at controlling the business, with the quarterly accounts and reviews, strategic reviews, annual budgets – I knew my strengths and I knew my weaknesses. We took on Alan Jeffers, Kevin McGoran, Robert Holmes, Howard Kilroy, Jim Malloy, my brother Jeff, Brendan Carolan, David Austin – all had the strengths to make up for my weaknesses. I built a team and moulded a system that was quite unique in the paper business. For the first 15, maybe 20 years in the business, I knew where every penny was.

Then it got too big to do that. Now we have the numbers every month. So, despite the fact that, at one stage, we were running a business of $22 billion in total managed sales with 70,000 people, we still knew where more or less every penny in the company was. From time to time, we made a few mistakes but we operated a simple system called the Moat System – every time we bought a company, we charged them for what the company cost us. We were doing leveraged buy-outs – why would you buy a business if it couldn't pay the interest on the money it cost? It has to bring its own debt down. Would you be buying it just for ego? Or do you want to be big just for the sake of being big? So we charged the true cost of capital into the business and called it senior debt. The first question at a review meeting was, "How's your senior debt?". How much debt you've got down tells you how the business is doing. If it's profitable and cash-generative, it's paying down debt. If it's still in the process of growing, that's OK too. But, sooner or later, the business must repay the debt. Did we succeed? We succeeded 90% of the time. We failed 10%. This was the first step in the growth that took us to being the largest paper and packaging company in the world. That was never an objective. It was just the way it turned out. Each time we did something, we saw a further opportunity, more things to do, more new doors to open. At one time, we had a very strong African policy – 25% of our profits came from Nigeria. It was worrying, because the profits were not sustainable. It was a boom country. We started two new companies in Nigeria on top of what we had acquired.

It wasn't just buying things, we were building as well. We built a new factory in Walkinstown and one in Northern Ireland.

It became clear to me that the next step after the UK was continental Europe. I started a Paris office, had a manager working full-time over there, was back and forth regularly myself, visited competitors and other people but found quickly I couldn't do anything at that particular time. I decided to go to America. I got into America through a total accident. A company called Hanson Scales had just started an operation here in Ireland. We were supplying them with boxes. I found that this guy from Chicago, Don Hindman, was setting up a factory to supply boxes to them. He controlled a company, Time Industries, and I did not take kindly to an interloper coming into my territory. I got to know him very well. Eventually, I bought Time Industries, which stopped them coming into Ireland! They had a drug company together with a paper mill – boxes, laminating and coating, both of which we still have today. I bought in with 40% initially and that was my base in America. 100 Wacker Drive in Chicago was my first office there. I got to know Roger Stone, one of my competitors, whose company eventually became part of Smurfits. He was the biggest producer of corrugated in the US. He offered me 25% of his business. I said, "Roger, you and I could not work together". That turned out to be true and was still true years later when we took over his whole business and he left.

Once I was in America, I was able to spread my tentacles and quickly bought several other companies which made us the largest paper and packaging company in the world. We are not today the largest because Smurfit Group is now a totally separate entity from Smurfit Stone. The only connection between the two companies is the name and the fact that I'm Chairman Emeritus of Smurfit Stone with no executive role.

It's all about shareholder value – creating value, dividends, capital appreciation. You can't be emotional in business, you have to look at it clinically, find what's the right thing to do and do it, even if it costs you mentally some problems.

Going private was not an easy decision for me but it was the right decision. Every day that goes by, it proves to be more and more the right decision financially. Whether it was the right decision emotionally and for any other reason, I'm not so sure. It certainly wasn't an ego decision. I don't feel I have an ego, though other people may perceive that I have. I don't let ego get into the decision-making process, a process that's made me what I am, which is, "I must, I can and I will" and don't look back. I never look over my shoulder and ask "What if?".

I was shooting recently with the Duke of Abercorn, whose wife incidentally is a Pushkin, a very nice man and a very nice lady. Paul Smithwick, a friend of mine, was at the shoot. At dinner that evening, he got up to make a speech. He sang my praises, that I was in front of my time and all that. Paul did not know me that well! He said, "Your Grace, you may not know that he was responsible for the school where my sons went, St. Gerard's in Bray. Back in the early '70s, the school was in deep trouble and Michael gave us some money and bought some land for us. The other day we sold the land for €13m!". I told him that he had ruined my weekend shooting – I had given them £100,000!

I owned 50% of the Setanta Centre in the middle of town near the old Confederation of Irish Industry building. I partnered first with Larry Goodman and then with Pat Doherty and Harry Dobson. I was not a property guy, so I sold my share to Green Properties. Green Properties gave me shares. They promptly doubled and I sold them. I doubled my money twice and thought I did very well until I found out that Green Properties sold it the other day for €170m or something – ginormous.

You can't buy loyalty. You can't buy respect. You can buy people and have them in fear of you. What makes a true leader in my view is a person who gets utter respect and commitment and that, of course, is both ways. You get respect if you give it back. I have had failures and disappointments with people. But, on the other hand, take Howard Kilroy, my closest associate for many decades. He is still thriving. I can't tell you the number of times he resigned from the company. I would say something that would offend him and immediately I would get a riposte, a letter of resignation. I'd go back to his office and tear it up.

I have also made friends with my executives. They worked *with* me, not *for* me. I have been able to share the financial success with them – all my key executives became multi-millionaires working for the company. Money isn't the main motivator – it is one of the key ingredients in the jigsaw puzzle that makes up why people stay in a company. They don't work primarily for money, but they don't work either without it. Part of the attraction of Smurfits in the '70s, '80s and '90s, when we were growing rapidly, was that it was an *exciting* place to work. You were getting very well rewarded and, as part of a winning team, you were going to share in the glory and the avalanches of wealth. When we went private, we cashed in our options at a record high price.

The fact that the managers had a personal stake in the company was a key motivator. I think we were the first company in Ireland to introduce stock options. I don't think options will necessarily disappear now when they have to be expensed. You can skin a cat in many ways. We used have what were called "phantom" stock options. You don't actually hold the option. Instead, there is a legally-binding phantom scheme that is linked to how the share price does. If you were, say, 10 years with the company, there could be a payout for that time. You then don't actually have to expense them. You get the money but not the shares but it's directly linked to the performance of the shares.

In the '70s, I used criticise the Government something terrible, when I was down in the Confederation of Irish Industry. On one occasion, amongst several, when I was a keynote speaker, I slammed the Government. We were spending way beyond our means, through politicians buying votes. When I was asked to sort out either the Post

Office or the telephone system, I decided on the telephone system. It took 30 years to fix but we fixed it. I call that my national service. I gave my salary to charity and didn't take expenses. I had the smallest office in the building – why should I have a big office when I was firing thousands of people to streamline the organisation? I was also on the Racing Board at the same time.

I survived the Staines air crash.[42] I was in Berlin at the time. Noel Griffin, chief executive of Waterford Glass, could not make it. We were the only two left standing.

When I see the Ireland of today, with the wealth that has been generated and the success of the country on a wide range of fronts, it gives me immense satisfaction. Ireland has got rid of its 600 years of domination by a very powerful economy next door. Now the Irish are wealthier than the average English person. It's a fantastic achievement. Yes, we have problems with growing pains. The infrastructure is inadequate, but I'd rather that than empty roads. I'd rather the problems we have today than the problems we had yesterday. The problems we have today are a hangover from the good times. The problems we had yesterday were a hangover from the bad times.

Ireland was impoverished – I was the first person to give any real money to a university to form the Smurfit School of Business because I felt education was the way forward. In the bad old days, two-thirds of the students we were producing were emigrating. We were not keeping the best and brightest at home – we were keeping the less enterprising. The taxation policy has helped. I used pester minister after minister and government after government to introduce a benign policy of taxation rather than where we were. 10% of something is better than 100% of nothing. Get the companies in here. They'll create

---

[42] On Sunday June 18, 1972, 12 Irish business leaders were on their way to Brussels to discuss issues connected with Ireland's entry into the EEC. After a short stopover in London, they took off in a British Airways Trident. 19 seconds later, the aircraft crashed at Staines, killing everyone on board. At a stroke, the CII lost its president, Con Smith, its immediate past-president, Guy Jackson, the director general, Ned Grey, the business policy expert, Michael Sweetman, the economics and trade officer, Fergus Mooney and Michael Rigby-Jones who was a Council member and a former chairman and president of the IMI, together with representatives of the Dublin Chamber of Commerce and the Employers' Confederation. The shock reverberated throughout Irish business.

VAT, they'll create income for the companies that supply them, they'll create services, Aer Lingus will do better and so on.

My father once told me that he paid 101% of his income in tax in one year. We were driving the best and brightest abroad. We have today net immigration with 35,000 a year. Everything multiplies – houses, land, VAT, shops are doing better – the effect is like a stone thrown in the water, the benign effect ripples right through the economy. The alternative we had was like a whirlpool, sucking things down. I was sad to see Charlie McCreevy go – his was a steady hand. I'm scared that governments will slip back into their bad old ways and there are real, serious, fundamental flawed problems in America that could drag us down. It certainly won't do us any good.

I always kept a pen and paper beside my bed because I'd get ideas during the night. There have been occasions – the last one was the Smurfit Stone deal – when the market turned against us and we were on the hook for the biggest single acquisition of our lives. In the old days, I could always beat the market because I was small enough. But now, as by far the biggest, I was going from 8% to 20% market share worldwide. That scared me – I wondered if I was betting the business. I was in my early 60s. It was not something I could just turn off and start again. I had never before bet the business and I hoped I was never going to. Fortunately, Smurfit Stone, while it was within the Smurfit Corporation, was a separate legal entity – we were going to be a minority partner. That had, to some extent, isolated and reduced the risk. Maybe half-a-dozen times in my life I have been scared to death about what I was doing.

I have bet the Smurfit company twice in my life. The Hely Group was first. If I got it wrong, we were toast. I was highly aware of this because I had read quite extensively, particularly when I was in hospital, about mergers and takeovers – more mergers and takeovers went wrong than ever went right, by a factor of five or six. So I had to ask myself what do I have that is absolutely unique, that will allow me to turn this thing around. The Hely Group had a big scandal at the time: a man called Martin Prescott had taken them to the cleaners. I was the only one prepared to walk through their front door. I thought it could not be all bad – there were plenty of good assets. They had shops in Henry Street and Grafton Street, great properties, a trust company, Standard Trust. They produced Bush television sets and

Kilroy Brothers, which they owned, was a great company, distributing toys. Yes, I have had more than one sleepless night.

I'm on the Board of the European Roundtable – 40 top European industrialists. I meet a lot of people with powerful positions, Krups, Daimler-Benz, Volkswagen, Saab. I have learned a lot from these people but none of them knows their business like I knew mine.

How many chief executives do you know that were members of the Irish Transport & General Workers' Union? I was. How many chief executives do you know who went to union meetings? I was for the workers against the boss and the boss was my father! How many people started at 16 and worked on every machine on shift-work – that's how I got tuberculosis. When I walked into a factory, I knew immediately what was right with it and what was wrong with it. I did not even have to talk to the manager – I could sense it, because I knew it. That broadened out into an instinctiveness about business, what was good and what was bad, what was right and what was wrong, what we could do and what we could not do. It was that early grounding that gave me tremendous confidence that nobody could tell me about my business, because I knew it better than they did. I'd been there, I'd done it. They would tell me a machine could not do 10,000 an hour. I would tell them it could do 12,000, because I'd worked it.

16

BRODY SWEENEY

O'Briens Irish Sandwich Bars

*My vision was not my little chain in Dublin or even in the
UK – I wanted 1,000 stores and world domination.*

BRODY SWEENEY is Chief Executive of O'Briens Irish Sandwich Bars Limited, which he founded.

He was born in January 1951.

He is married to Lulu O'Sullivan. They have four children: Frank (16), Hannah (14), Jack (11), and Rory (6).

He was educated at Blackrock College, Dublin and at Rockwell College. He went to NIHE Dublin (now DCU), but dropped out in second year.

He founded O'Briens Irish Sandwich Bars in 1988. The company specialises in made-to-order sandwiches and gourmet coffee, in a contemporary Irish setting. It is one of Ireland's successful export brands.

O'Briens now has 300 outlets in Ireland, UK, Spain, South Africa, Denmark, Australia and Asia (India, Singapore, Taiwan, Malaysia, Thailand, Indonesia and Saudi Arabia). The UK is the largest market with 140 stores. It is the largest gourmet sandwich and coffee chain in the UK and Ireland and one of the fastest-growing restaurant chains in Europe. It plans to grow to 1,000 stores over the next five years.

O'Briens was one of the six main sponsors of one of Ireland's most successful national events, the Special Olympics World Summer Games in 2003.

Brody Sweeney owns a 100-year-old Galway Hooker and has a passion for sea-fishing.

He is a director of Paddy Power Bookmakers plc and, in 2005, he announced that he is to seek a nomination to run in the next general election in the Dublin North-East constituency.

He has just published (2005) his book, *Making Bread*.

I *had never met Brody Sweeney until I had this conversation with him. It took me a while to find his modest office at 23 South Frederick Street. Being an unreconstructed culchie, after 50 years I'm still uncertain about the less-familiar streets of Dublin.*

There was nowhere in the office to have a quiet conversation. Brody brought me to a nearby café, not yet open for morning business. The proprietor, decent man, gave us a room upstairs and brought us coffee.

If ever there was a classic entrepreneur's tale, this is it. As a child, Brody wanted "to become rich and famous as quickly as possible".

His picture of an Irish sandwich in the '80s will bring back memories: "two skinny slices of bread and a slice of ham you could see through".

I learned from him what the living dead is: "a retail operation that is not so bad you should close it down but is not so good that it makes any money". He says that to call a halt was harder than to carry on because, in a cash business you can delay the inevitable.

This is at times an hilarious story, but Brody Sweeney knew also the dark night of the soul. With total honesty he says, "I almost gave up. I didn't know what to do".

The business pages are hirsute with self-aggrandising annual reports and press releases. Brody says, "I was reading a report on a business recently. They hadn't had a good year and they were laying the blame on many factors. What they did not report was that they, the management, had made a dog's dinner of the business".

His first successful sandwich bar was a miniature 203 square feet in the St. Stephen's Green Centre. The day he was talking to me he had just opened his 100th store in Ireland, with 125 in the UK and with another 30 spread around the world.

The conversation was recorded in a café near Brody Sweeney's office in South Frederick Street, Dublin, on February 17, 2005.

BRODY SWEENEY

I was born in Monkstown in Dublin, a nice sleepy suburb. My Dad was a lawyer. I am one of seven kids – I come number five in line. My Mum was married twice – her first husband was an engineer with the colonial service in Britain. When the first two children were born, he went to Kenya. The day before she was to join him, he died of malaria. She had worked in Aer Lingus as an air hostess, but had to retire when she got married. When she was widowed, she went back to Aer Lingus and moved out to a flat in Sandycove with her two kids. The flat was rented by my great-aunt, as it happened. She then met my Dad, who had polio as a child and walked with a limp. They fell in love and got married and produced five more children. When I was about 12, we moved to Killiney. I'd say I had an idyllic upbringing – good parents who loved each other.

I was not great at school. I went to Blackrock. I had a very serious authority problem. In my fifth year, the Dean said that either he or I had to go. I finished up in another Holy Ghost school, Rockwell, boarding, which I enjoyed thoroughly. I then went to the NIHE in Glasnevin which had just opened – now DCU. I did business studies and dropped out in second year. Last year, DCU approached me to ask if I would become a trustee. On the website, the trustees have all their handball medals displayed. Diplomatically it says, "Brody Sweeney attended DCU".

I was always looking to make money – I set up my own business when I was 15, cutting down trees in Killiney. I got business cards printed and we employed my older brother – it was great money at the time. It all went well until we knocked a tree down, which fell across the Vico Road. The fire brigade had to be called. The lady who employed us realised she'd made a bit of a mistake, that we were only children. We were despatched back to our parents post haste.

My motivation, growing up, was to become rich and famous as quickly as possible. That was what drove me. Even when I was at school, I was looking for ways to get out and make money. In college, I was the same – I couldn't stand it. In my second year in NIHE, my father bought the master franchise for Prontaprint in Ireland. I begged him to let me come out of college and run it for him. I was 21 at the time and not getting anywhere in NIHE. I ran Prontaprint for eight years. It never made any money but it was a good, hard school of business. Because it never made any money, I had no airs and graces about me. The franchise touched on all the business disciplines – purchasing, marketing, accounting and finance, and motivating people. I was helping other people set up as franchisees around Ireland. It was a great lesson for me to see how other people approached the same business model. The lesson I learned was that, while the business was the same, the way people approached it was different. Some people were fantastic at it, great at knocking on doors, very organised. Others were scared to death to go knocking on a door. The good guys were really good business people in their own right and made money – the franchise was only a tool to help them. The bad guys were no good whatever they did and could not see the benefit of it. It was great training but it was a horrible, painful time not making any money. When I started O'Briens, it was not so much that I knew *how* to do it, it was that I knew *how not* to do it.

I was only a young fella with little experience when I did Prontaprint and I thought all business was like that. My Dad died in 1988 – about eight years after I started. I realised I was going nowhere, that the Prontaprint business model did not work as a master franchise in a small country like Ireland. I had 16 shops at the time. I needed about 40 and there were never going to be 40 in Ireland. I sold it back to the parent company and looked around for another franchise to start. I had no particular leaning to food – I just wanted to start another franchise.

Like lots of young fellows, I went to see some businesses in America with a view to buying a master franchise and bringing it back to Ireland. One of the companies I saw was Subway, making submarine sandwiches in 700 outlets. I didn't think they were very good. Subway have gone from 700 in 1988 to 23,000 now. I have developed a healthy respect for them but, at the time, I thought I could do much better.

I also discovered that these American companies wanted a lot of money for a master franchise. I had no money at all. A master franchise involves buying, first, the brand, then training, and then you pay a royalty. A master franchise usually applies to a country.

I came back realising I could not afford to buy a master franchise. I liked the Subway model – it was very simple. There was no cooking involved and it was relatively easy to train people. When I researched the fast-food business in Ireland, I found that sandwiches were biggest by far, bigger than all the others together, yet it was the only sector without a dominant brand. When you think of fast-foods, you think of hamburgers, pizzas – Burger King and McDonald's, Pizza Hut and Domino's, KFC. The fact that there was no brand name for sandwiches went off like a light bulb in my head. Here was an opportunity to do something that nobody else had done, to put a brand on a sandwich.

Back in the '80s, an Irish sandwich was two skinny slices of bread, a slice of ham in the middle and, if you could not see through the ham, you didn't sell it – it was not thin enough. They were sold in cling-film, they were awful, and nobody was making any money out of them. My idea was to do much bigger American-style sandwiches, really good quality, at a fair price and then to put a brand around them.

That was the nucleus of the idea. Out of that came the question, what was I going to call it? I knew from the Prontaprint experience that the Irish market was too small for my ambitions. I wanted to go abroad. I wanted an Irish-sounding name. I looked through the phone book for all the O's. O'Brien turned out to be the most common Irish surname – that's where that came from. The name O'Briens Irish Sandwich Bar would give it a theme you could hang your hat on, particularly if it was in a UK high street. At that time, Irish culture was popular – U2 were doing well, *My Left Foot* was out in the cinemas, *Riverdance* came a little while after that. The culture was sexy and Irish brands were attractive.

We had to come up with a USP on the product side. Having tried some bigger bakers, we went to a small one. Sliced pan is cut with a saw. I got them to take every second tooth out of the saw so that we got thick slices. If you put my chicken sandwich beside one from Dunnes Stores or Marks & Spencer, my sandwich is twice the size – it's a thick bread sandwich. I invented that! It gave us a point of difference. In the early days, some people would say to me that my sandwiches were 50p dearer than Dunnes Stores and I would reply, "Yes. But look at the size of it. This is a serious sandwich – it's a meal".

I always liked the planning process. I wrote my business plan and found the first location in George's Street in Dublin.

I came up against my first insurmountable barrier as a businessman – no money. I did something that I am told is illegal now. The first shop was going to cost about £50,000. I went to three different finance houses on the same day – the sort of people who lend you money for cars. I told them I had just bought a flat and would they lend me £7,000 to buy some new furniture for it. Because I went to the three on the same day, they were not able to do cross-referencing. The three of them lent me the money. Armed with my business plan and my £21,000, I went into Bank of Ireland in College Green. I told them I was trying to start a new sandwich-bar business and that I had saved £21,000 of my own and could they lend me the balance. They did. That was my £50,000 seed capital to get the business off the ground, which was not so smart because I had no capital base in the business. We opened the bar in George's Street on June 1, 1988. It turned out to be the living dead. The living dead is a retail operation that is not so bad that you should close it down but is not so good that it makes any money. You keep on and on at it, but it's just a waste of time. After three years, I gave up on it. If it's really bad, you just shut it down. If it's really good, you make money. The living dead are the worst type.

The second one I opened was in the brand new Stephen's Green Centre, a tiny little shop, 203 square feet. When I applied to the Health Board, they pointed out that it was a food business and I would need a staff toilet and male and female toilets for customers. Toilets take up about 300 square feet. However, we got away with it as it was in a shopping centre and we could use the public toilets. It was tiny but made huge money. It kept the whole business going for the next number of years.

I did a third one in Mary Street on the north-side. I was learning a bit but I had also lost the run of myself – the one in Mary Street was a disaster. I had come from the wealthy south-side of the city. I knew by now you needed loads of people walking past. There were loads of people walking past the shop in Mary Street but I did not understand the type of people you needed. We were selling a sandwich for, say, two quid a time. The people in Mary Street were looking for three sandwiches for a pound. There was no common ground in the middle. I put the shop on the market five days after I opened it. It took me a year to sell it. Every week I had it open, it lost a fortune. I had had no money to open it and it cost about £100,000 to build. I was confident the cash-flow would pay for the builder. The cash-flow could not pay for the builder and he was threatening me. I was under serious pressure. I was way behind on the mortgage. It was another horrible time – the pressure was unbelievable.

In the middle of that, I lost faith in myself – I thought I was not cut out for it at all. I almost gave up.

Bewley's advertised for a manager to run their cafés in Dublin. I talked it over with Lulu at home. I said to her that we were in deep shit and, if I got the job, I'd take it and we'd close down the business. Overall, the business was a disaster, even with the one candle burning in the Stephen's Green Centre.

I went for the job, didn't get the interview and went home to Lulu that night and told her that I was a complete failure. The business was going down the tubes. Nobody would give me a job – I was unemployable. I didn't know what to do.

I persevered because I could not get out of it. To call a halt was much harder than to carry on. One of the things about a cash business is that the cash comes in every day and you can delay the inevitable for longer than you would in a normal business. It was nothing noble or brave, great depths of character – bollix – I just wanted to get out of it. The least worst alternative was to carry on because, if I got out of it, my credit rating was shot and I had no money – we could have been out of the house and everything. I have just sold my house and realised that it was mortgaged seven times, to keep re-investing in the business to keep it going.

We bought our house for £45,000. I borrowed £40,000 from the bank and got a loan of £5,000 from somebody else for the deposit. I tried to explain to the kids the other day that, when you get a mortgage, you pay it off over 20 years. We were 16 years into our mortgage and I owed €270,000.

I had a graph in the office always going up. People thought it was sales and profits. It was the losses. Every year for the first six years, I lost more money than the previous year – that was the upward graph.

After six years, I ran out of mistakes to make. I mostly never made the same mistake twice. Eventually, things started going right. After those six years, I had three shops. I had another living dead in the

Powerscourt Centre – I set it up to be a franchise but I was determined not to try a franchise until I was satisfied I had it reasonably right.

Before I opened my first shop, I'd been writing my franchise manuals. The shop in Stephen's Green had a newsagents attached to it in which I had no interest. I decided to sell it to cash me up to open a shop in the UK. I was beginning to get a bit of confidence and the Celtic Tiger was starting. It all coincided. Those six years, however, were a struggle, living from hand-to-mouth, driving a second-hand van, somehow keeping the show on the road. It wasn't great fun – I would not look back on it with any fondness.

I still had in my mind the picture of franchising the business. While the shop in Stephen's Green was great, it was not enough to pay for all the other cock-ups I was making. But I felt I was not flogging a dead horse. If I'd had the choice I would have gone, but there now seemed to be some light at the end of the tunnel.

When I sold the shop in Stephen's Green, the value in it was in the newsagents. I sold it to a Mayo man, Tom Cunningham, an accountant. I told him I was trying to start a franchise and I would like to leave the O'Brien's name over the door, but if I couldn't sell three franchises, he didn't have to pay me any money. He had to pay me a royalty only on the sandwich bit, not on the newsagents. The margins were very thin in the newsagents but quite generous in the sandwich bar. He agreed and that was great. It was easier to sell a shop that was up and running and had a profit than an idea.

The whole trick with franchises is to get the right people in at the beginning and then the franchises will follow. If you get the wrong people in, it doesn't matter what your agreement says or how hard you police them, you're wasting your time. We supported the shop and marketed it with the other three stores I had at the time.

1994, we sold another couple of franchises in Dublin. What really convinced me that I was onto something and that there was a future was when Tom Cunningham came back to me and said he'd like to do a second one. That was the most significant moment for me. He would not have come back to me unless he felt there was a future in it. That was my first big milestone. Here was somebody who had experience of a franchise, not someone who naïvely bought it, even though he first had his eye on the newsagents. That was definitive proof to me that the idea had legs.

The thing began to snowball – I used the money Tom gave me to open a shop in Crawley, Sussex. I deliberately went to a non-Irish area – I did not want to go to Kilburn or somewhere like that. I wanted to prove that the brand could stand on its own two feet. That shop went OK.

Back in Ireland, there was now more spending money. After I got six shops in Dublin, we began to see the inklings of a brand.

A brand is so valuable in terms of sales – we now have 60 shops in Dublin. We found, when we had opened the first 15 of them or so, not only did the new one do well, but it lifted the sales in the other shops by 2% or 3% each time. We were not cannibalising the business. The brand was becoming bigger and more popular.

When we opened the shops in Dublin in the mid-1990s, they were doing £3,000 a week. Now many are doing €15,000 plus a week. That was the start of it.

The original motivation, as I told you, as a young fellow, was to be rich and famous. I wanted to be like a movie star, a rock singer or a Richard Branson. They were my role models. I did not want a job in the civil service or a job that was making a living. I wanted the jets and the Jags – that's what I thought was important to me. That's not important to me now but, at the time, it was what spurred me on. When I was setting up O'Briens, that was about my fourth or fifth written business plan. I wanted to have a big O'Briens – that was my clear vision back in the '80s. There was no question about that. My vision was not my little chain in Dublin or even in the UK – I wanted 1,000 stores and world domination. That's still the vision for the business. My first thought was that we could do it in five years. Now it's a rolling five-year plan. Now we have about 280 stores. We're putting 20% a year onto the target. It's beginning to ramp up a little so we might put on 60 stores this year. We've just opened our 100th in Ireland and 125 in the UK. We've another 30 spread around the world. We have six different Asian countries where we have a flag flying – Indonesia, India, Singapore, Taiwan, Malaysia and Thailand. We're open in Spain, the Netherlands and South Africa. We'll open soon in Saudi Arabia and China. We're in Australia. All the stuff outside Ireland and the UK came from people asking me if they could do it – we never tried to sell ourselves at all. We have a great guy in Singapore who has developed the Asian countries – we have 12 shops in Singapore and we've just opened our sixth in Kuala Lumpur. There's the guts of a decent chain there. We'd be optimistic about our fledgling chain in Jakarta, Indonesia.

We discovered early on that our customer-base is the same wherever we go. A typical O'Briens customer is young, white-collar, female. She is health- and diet- conscious. She wears designer jeans and listens to U2. She's got a high disposable income. She's drinking coffee with bread-type products. So it's not all that strange that we're opening in Singapore. In the centre of Singapore, there are KPMGs, PriceWaterhouseCoopers and Western companies employing these young females who have an hour's lunch-break. That's exactly the same in the centre of Kuala Lumpur, Chicago, Cork, Edinburgh or Manchester. It's 62% female. We've discovered that it's cool for women to walk around with an O'Briens sandwich bag. It's uncool to walk around with a McDonald's bag. A McDonald's bag implies you're less health-conscious. An O'Briens bag is considered healthy – and that's OK. You could have a sandwich in an O'Briens bag that had twice the calorie-count of a McDonald's Big Mac and chips.

People ask me how we could go to Taiwan and sell sandwiches. The answer is that, in any big city, you have this group of people – the young, white-collar females. The world is a small place. You're not re-inventing the wheel. We discovered a gas thing in Taiwan, where they're eating our sandwiches with a knife and fork. It's exactly the reverse of our going into a Chinese restaurant in Dublin where we use chopsticks. They think it's highly sophisticated to have a lash with a knife and fork.

100 stores in Ireland with a population of four million – the same penetration in the UK would be nearly 2,000 stores. That's the prize we're after. It's nice to have all these stores around the world but really it doesn't take up too much time – we let them have what we have developed here.

There are lies, damn lies and statistics but, if you were to define the business under food-led coffee offers, we'd be number five in the European market. If you defined us under any other heading, we're not on the Richter Scale. We need four or five hundred shops to become a national brand in the UK – that's our primary objective.

When we opened a shop in Enniscorthy recently, the brand awareness was 70% or 80% for our first shop in that town. Next week, we're opening Southend in England and we shall have no brand awareness there. Brand awareness makes a huge difference about how quickly you get off the ground. In Southend, it depends totally on the location and the strength of the owner-operator. Stores are much slower to take off in the UK – it's a business much more painful to develop than our Irish business. When I first went into the UK, I was arrogant. I thought the shops, food and so on were the same as here. I did not take account of the strength of the brand we enjoyed here at home. We have more than 40 shops in Scotland – and that's a brand with a population of five million people.

We're making steady progress, nothing spectacular. We made a little money in England last year, after seven years. We didn't make much, but that will get better and better. I keep emphasising to all the people around me that we must love our franchisees and take great care of them.

If you ask anybody in the office what our objectives are, they'll tell you. To describe the brand: we're Irish and proud of it. We're trying to be the fast-food chain that sells food that's good for you. We have an ethical element. We look after the Christina Noble Children's Foundation as their principal sponsors. We raise a quarter-of-a-million every year for them – we're contracted for three years. We have other ethical elements in that we do Fair Trade Coffee – a cappuccino in O'Briens is made with organic milk. Coffee is a terrible business. What we pay three quid for, the guy who grew the beans is getting about a cent. It's immoral and outrageous. The result is that we have decided to pay a higher price for our beans.

We are in the middle of re-launching the business this year – new food, new brand, new logo, new interiors for the stores, retraining all the people in the business – but it's mainly around the new food. I invented a Shambo myself – it's like ciabatta bread but I got it punched out in the shape of a shamrock. It's unique and totally Irish. In the new shops, we have hand-carved organic roast beef and roast pork. Another point of difference. If you want a nice salad, you go to Dunnes or Marks & Spencer. You'll get a nice salad, but it was made the day before. We'll toss the salad in front of you with exactly the type of dressing you like. We're trying to build an image around our brand, which is Irish, fun, friendly, a little bit quirky, a bit odd, that sells really good food. That gives us an edge over the McDonalds and the KFCs who have dumbed everything down to the lowest possible common denominator. Deep fried chips are not particularly healthy for you. It's a great place for us to be, where we're appealing to the top 10% of sandwich consumers who care about what they eat. They know where the food came from, they see it made in front of them, they know it's fresh, they don't see it as coming from a factory where someone was picking their nose, all under a friendly, warm Irish banner with a bit of personality. One of the things that attracts our franchisees into the business is that they feel like people, not just a number. We talk to them, we put our arm around them, we call them by their names, we work really hard on the relationships. That's a natural Irish resource – we have an ability to build relationships with people that a lot of other races do not have. The English, in particular, love us for that. They love the fact that there are real people involved. With some of the other franchises in the UK, they are literally a number with little warmth or sense of fun.

In the UK, it's a great combination. The Brits are much better at business practices than we are. I'll give you an example. We get our shops to do a report every week – every shop has to do it and work out the P&L. The ones from the UK come in on time 95% and are correct. The Irish ones come in at 70% and often don't add up. Irish and English are all trained in exactly the same way and it's exactly the same business, no difference, but the innate characteristic of the British people is to get it right. What we bring to the business is a bit of personality, flair and humour. When you put the two together it's a great combination.

When I first went to the UK, I was dead scared, what with IRA bombs and Canary Wharf. I thought we might be getting bricks through windows. What I found was that the average Brit is well disposed towards the average Irish person. We are married to them – we're interbreeding. The bit they like about us is what they call the *craic*, probably spelt "crack". They found that, with us, there was a fun element and that business did not always have to be boring, serious and rigid.

I'm proud of a picture of Bertie Ahern sitting at a table with 14 Chinese colleagues in Singapore, all franchisees. These are people whose customers have never heard of Ireland and wouldn't know where it was. But to me, as a marketeer, it's like a blank piece of paper on which you can build a picture. We built a picture of green grass or Atlantic waves, of great food and drink, or we bring a few Irish dancers down. We have a fellow called Big Rory, whom I found in England, who goes round opening shops for us on stilts. He's originally from Scotland, but we call him Irish now.

Whether a business succeeds or fails, it's down to the people you do business with. I believe we have not yet worked out in the States who the right people are – it's not a question of not being able to make it work in the States. You often hear managers blaming things as distinct from people. I was reading a report on a business recently. They hadn't had a good year and they were laying the blame on many factors. What they did not report was that *they*, the management, had made a dog's dinner of the business. It didn't work out for us in Germany, simply because it did not work out with the people we were with. It's not a failure of O'Briens or of the concept. It's a failure of me not choosing the right people to partner with. Where a shop is not successful, and you change the driver around, it comes right very quickly. It's always a people issue – not the concept. I'm very strong on people taking responsibility.

When we invite new people in for training, I take the first session with them and I always find it a bit of a downer. We've got them there with our glossy brochure and they've been to see our shops. They seem to like us and I bring them right down to earth by talking to them about their setting up this new, small business whose success or failure is entirely down to them. Whether or not it's going to be a good or bad shop is not down to O'Briens – it's them. The best shops we have and the people who make the most money are true business people in their own right. They use the franchise as a tool to make them successful. The franchises that are not good are run by people who may well be good at something else but can't cut it in the business. We have people starting up businesses and their track record is absolutely irrelevant, as are their academic qualifications. Some of our best franchise partners were never in business before – they had it intuitively, they had it in the head. They were able to grasp the concept and to use the tools we gave them. We have people with track records as long as your arm and they have turned out to be disastrous. We got a few of McDonald's franchisees – we were so excited and proud, somebody from McDonald's looking at a little franchise like ours. A number of them were disastrous. I copped on pretty quickly that people don't leave McDonald's, they're fecked out and we were picking them up. Age doesn't matter. We have 19-year-old franchisees who are terribly successful. We have some fellows of 50, with 20 years of management experience, and they're a waste of space.

We've just opened another shop in Cork in the new Mahon Point Centre. It's five weeks old and became our busiest shop straight away. It's the 10th shop owned by the same franchisees in Cork, two brothers, Bill and Leonard Lynch, who don't appear to do a tap of work but they have about the 10 best shops in the chain. I went to another shop yesterday, one guy, couldn't spend five minutes with me he was so busy, 16 hours a day, chasing his tail and going absolutely nowhere. He's in a tiny little shop making no money. He can't get out of his own way. We say he can't get his head out of a coleslaw bucket, can't see the wood for the trees.

In theory, it's a very simple thing to sell sandwiches and coffee. In fact, it's very complex. Some people, like our guys in Cork, are able to stand back, see the bigger picture and manage the business well. They are making good money, I love it. If you get the people bit right, everything else will follow. Before we even begin to train people, we ask them to spend two days in a shop. The people we lose are the ones who cannot get on with staff, are rude to customers or, point blank, refuse to stand behind the counter because it is below them. It's great to catch them before they get in to open your shop. We could probably have expanded much quicker had we been less choosy about our franchisees. Now we have good guys making good money.

That was the invaluable bit that came with the pain of the first business. It's not perfect, but now, by and large, we have good people. That's where the strength of the thing is.

17

ED WALSH

UNIVERSITY OF LIMERICK

*You go for scale. You go for quality. You associate with
people who have a track record of achievement and a
commitment to excellence.*

ED WALSH was born on December 3, 1939 in Cork.

He is married to Stephanie Barrett. They have three sons and one daughter: Michael, Stephen, Eoghan and Elizabeth-Jane and live in Co. Tipperary. He is the only living Irishman to have founded from scratch a thriving university, the University of Limerick. He was its first President (1989-1998), having previously set up the National Institute for Higher Education Limerick from which UL sprang. He served as President of the NIHE from its origin in 1970 to 1989.

A chartered engineer, he took his PhD in Iowa State University in 1964. He has received honorary doctorates from the University of Dublin, Queen's University Belfast, the University of Ulster and the NUI. He is a fellow of the World Innovation Foundation, the Irish Academy of Engineering, the Institution of Engineers of Ireland, the Institution of Electrical Engineers, London, the Royal Society of the Arts, London and a member of the New York Academy of Science, the Royal Irish Academy, the Royal Hibernian Academy of Arts, and the National College of Art & Design.

He is, *inter alia*, Chairman of the Irish Council for Science, Technology & Innovation and Deputy Chairman of the Irish Chamber Orchestra. *Inter alia* hardly covers the organisations he has been involved in, over 40 at last count.

He is a sailor, a registered silversmith, plays violin and piano and is a frequent speaker on the issues of the day.

*E*ven *in universities, which are awash with committees composed of indentured individualists, it still takes one determined person to get things done. It took the determination of Michael Tierney, President of UCD, 1947-64, to push through in 1951 the historic move from Earlsfort Terrace to the greenfield Belfield campus.*

Determination and unremitting focus are the characteristics of the three academics in this book.

Ed Walsh gives a picture of his first days in Limerick: "I had no authorisation to paint that one room allotted to me in a dreadful tenement, totally dilapidated. I got a painter to come in at night and paid him myself". He gave to an itinerant his contract to move his few possessions. He had no telephone. He searched the building. "There were abandoned telephones lying on the floor amid litter. I lifted each one of them to see if they functioned. Right up at the top, there was one that did. I brought the lead from it down to my office and I was in contact with the world".

He said that one of his great strengths was a lack of understanding of how the Irish public sector worked. He called the Secretary of the Department of Education in his home at 7.30 in the morning. This lese-majesty must have been close to lighting your cigar from the sanctuary lamp.

Despite formidable opposition from the NUI, in particular, University College, Cork – "I was naïve and unaware of the viciousness of academic politics" – he prevailed and retained his indomitable optimism until he achieved the now-thriving University of Limerick.

He was a formidable fund-raiser: "Interfacing with business people in the US probably stood to me better than my academic work". His watchword came from Ezra Cornell, who began as a carpenter and who co-founded Cornell University: "Undertake no small projects: they are so difficult to accomplish".

The conversation was recorded at Citywest Business Park, Dublin 24, on December 8, 2004.

ED WALSH

The University of Limerick concept was someone else's – it was the people of Limerick. In 1845, the Queen's Colleges were established in Belfast and Cork and there was to be a third in either Limerick or Galway. Galway was chosen. That was a major problem for the people of Limerick. So the campaign really started in 1845! Donogh O'Malley, a Limerick TD, was Minister for Education in the 1960s. He brought about major investment in education. Obviously, Limerick was on his mind. Lemass's new ideas about the Irish economy were beginning to flourish and the universities were not exactly cooperative. They did not give much priority to the needs of enterprise: indeed one university president was strongly opposed to the idea of teaching business studies in any form. If some of their graduates proved useful to business – fine, but they were not going to prostitute themselves. The Government, however, was not going to reproduce in Limerick a college like the ones in Galway and Cork, and spoke of something better, something that would be more responsive to the needs of the community.

I was in the States in the '60s. The backdrop was that there would be an institute of higher education in Limerick. It would not be a copy of any of the Irish universities. There was an awareness that new technological universities were being established on the continent. In the States, there was something called MIT – to the people of Limerick, it did not sound like a university, but for some in Government, it seemed to be hugely important to the American companies that were being recruited into Ireland.

I had spent nine years in the States, at two Land Grant universities. They had emerged in the 1850s. At that time, the States were in a formative mode and developing agriculture was a priority. Washington allocated to each of the States 30,000 to 50,000 acres of land as the asset for the creation of a new college. These colleges were given the traditional missions of research and teaching but, unlike their European counterparts, they were asked also to serve the community. I spent my time in Iowa State University and Virginia

Tech. In Iowa, where I got my PhD, I was doing postgraduate work in nuclear engineering, designing nuclear reactors. Ireland was then in the process of constructing a nuclear reactor. As the only Irish person with a degree in nuclear engineering, I was hoping to come back to a leadership position.

The space race was on and research was focused on getting small nuclear reactors into satellites as power supplies. There was a US Atomic Energy Commission Laboratory located in Iowa – it had done pioneering work in the Manhattan project on the design of the moderator material for the atomic bomb. The Korean war had finished, Vietnam was starting, the arms race was on. There were a lot of US military people on campus. Admiral Rickover had his major submarine programme. He led the team that successfully adapted nuclear reactors as a means of ship propulsion. The first vessel so equipped was the USS *Nautilus*, the world's first nuclear submarine, launched in 1954. That was the kind of environment I was in.

I then went to Virginia Tech. Even though it was a Land Grant university, it was focused on science and engineering. With my doctorate, I was appointed an Assistant Professor at 24: the youngest in the university. I was fortunate to be pursued at this stage by several universities. I had a phone call from Virginia. I told them that I was really more interested in MIT. They said, "Never mind. Come down for the weekend". I met the President, Marshall Hahn. At 35, he was reputed to be the youngest university president in the US. (He went on to be chairman of Georgia-Pacific.) He said, "We are anxious to recruit young people like yourself. I have considerable freedom on remuneration. The only salary that is controlled in the university is mine". He told me what it was and I thought it was enormous. He said, "I can pay you that and I can pay you more if you're worth it". So I got a fine job offer and went to Virginia against my career instincts. Virginia Tech, while it was known, did not have anything like MIT's reputation, but Hahn had created an environment in which the able and energetic young people he had recruited could flourish. You could try to do almost anything you wished.

My first year there, I proposed that I would attempt to fund-raise for research with the utilities on the East coast. They could not get graduates because all the young people wanted to be in space research. Anyway, we did a deal that we would interest the undergraduates in energy research. I got a very small percentage of the utilities' earnings each year – I had more funding than we could absorb. This gave me an opportunity not only to be working in American academia but to be in and out of the offices of major corporate leaders. I empathised with them – I knew that they needed something and I needed something, so we put deals together. Interfacing with people in enterprise in the US probably stood to me better than my academic work. However, for family reasons, I decided I was coming back to Ireland. I applied for anything that would seem to fit my work, including the Limerick project. At the time, I believed that, if Ireland needed another university, it should probably be put somewhere like Kilkenny. It would be a marvellous university town I thought, serving a large hinterland. I applied to UCD and was offered a lectureship in electrical engineering, which I accepted. I withdrew from Limerick. I went back to the States and got a telegram saying, "Notwithstanding the fact that you have withdrawn your application, would you consider reactivating it?". My wife said, "If they have done that, they must be very interested in you". I rang up Morrissey, the professor of engineering in UCD, and told him that, having just accepted the position with him, I could not go for the Limerick interview without his permission. He said, "This is a bit of a pain in the neck, but go, go, do the interview". So I flew back, was interviewed for an hour-and-a-half by the Higher Education Authority, whose chairman was Tarlach Ó Raifeartaigh, former Secretary of the Department. He, with Paul Quigley of Shannon Development and Ian Howie of Trinity, were the core members of the selection committee. I left my new book on energy conversion on the table (I had got married on an advance of royalties for the book). I flew back to the States and there was a telegram offering me Limerick.

The salary did not compare with what I was paid in America. It was £4,000 a year in 1970, but it was sufficiently large for headlines in Limerick. I was happy to come back – it seemed exciting. I did not close my US bank account because the position in Limerick was highly speculative. On January 1, 1970, my wife got off at Shannon and I went on to Dublin to meet Pádraig Faulkner, the Minister for Education. Seán MacGearailt was then Secretary of the Department. Seán was reading the *Irish Press* in front of a turf fire. We had a cup of tea and he brought me in to the Minister. At that time, there was no base for the project in Limerick. I was hired as chairman of the planning board to create an institute of higher education and then to be its director. The Department of Education was the paymaster and, when I asked what funding was available, the Secretary told me they had £5,000 from the Minister's subhead.

The guidelines were simple: (1) the institute was going to be outside the university system; (2) it was going to relate to the emerging needs of the country, particularly in science, engineering and business, and (3) there was really no money for it. While the absence of funding appeared as a profound problem, the absence of many guidelines made the project most attractive. Were I coming back to a job in, say, the UK, there would have been a limiting framework: here in Ireland, it was more or less a blank sheet.

Limerick was very hostile to what was being offered. It was not what they wanted. There was a huge campaign in the 1960s. Judge Cearbhall Ó Dálaigh (later President of Ireland) was chairing a commission that led to the seminal report, *Investment in Education*, published in 1966. Paddy Lynch, professor of economics at UCD, was the driving force behind that report.[43]

The Ó Dálaigh Commission operated out of the Four Courts. Dermot Kinlen SC represented Limerick. Limerick wanted a university in the UCC, UCG mould with faculties of law, medicine, arts and so on. Engineering and business would not be terribly important.

Donogh O'Malley died during the 1966 election campaign.

He had brought in the World Bank to fund new comprehensive schools and regional technical colleges. Your close colleague in the IMI, Noel Mulcahy, subsequently Vice President in UL, was involved with Donogh O'Malley. Partly as a tribute to Donogh, the Government decided to do something significant in Limerick. Mention was made of the technological universities on the continent and MIT, which was described as "better than a university". As this was explained to the good people of Limerick, they were appalled: law and medicine would not be taught. Engineering and business would be and, as a sop, a significant element of the arts.

There were two parallel projects: Limerick and Ballymun, the latter emerging ultimately as DCU. I was given a slender document

---

[43]   See **Chapter 9**.

recommending "the provision of third-level educational facilities at Limerick".

I spent a week in the Department, met immediately with the Minister – there was not only little money but also very few plans. Galway had then about 1,500 students and was hoping for a new library and science building. Cork was somewhat larger. The Department felt that 500 places in Limerick would meet the immediate needs of the community. But the short-term objective was perhaps to meet the political needs of those who had made the original decision. I was greatly disillusioned at the fact that there was no significant funding. Who should I talk to? The Department were not quite sure but thought maybe the Office of Public Works. The scenario was bleak.

Based in the Department of Education in Marlborough Street for the first week, I was told I should go and meet some significant people. I went out to Tierney, President of UCD, again in front of a turf fire, at that time in Earlsfort Terrace. He conveyed to me that it was all very interesting but not of much relevance to him. I went to Donal McCarthy, President of UCC, who made it clear, in body language and otherwise, that he was not going to be helpful. Cork, since its foundation in 1845, had been pressed to be helpful to Limerick. McCarthy immediately rushed to the rescue by introducing a Higher Diploma in Education based in Mary Immaculate College in Limerick. He would announce it quickly and this would be a consolation prize.

I landed in Limerick from the train in the first week of January and took up residence in Hanratty's Hotel. We had nothing, no land, and I did not have even an office. I borrowed my mother's car and initially lived and worked from it and the hotel.

The Department warned me to be careful because, in Limerick, not only was there the University Project Committee but a militant youth group. Not so long before that, students had made their point with cobblestones in Paris riots. That was the spirit of the time.

I learned that Limerick County Council had moved to new offices and had abandoned an old building in O'Connell Street. They agreed that I could take a room in it. It was a dreadful tenement, totally dilapidated. When I arrived in Limerick I received a message from a lady saying that I needed a secretary and she would like to do the job: Ann Sadlier. I phoned Dublin and was told I could employ her on a kind of weekly contract.

I had no authorisation to paint that one room allotted to me in the tenement. I got a painter to come in at night and paid him myself. I wanted to move my few possessions: a typewriter, books and office furniture. Outside the offices, there were some itinerants begging. I gave my next contract, ten shillings, to one of the itinerants to do the move. My new office had no telephone. I searched the building. There were abandoned telephones lying on the floors amid litter. I lifted each one of them to see if any functioned. Right up at the top, there was one that did. I brought the lead from it down to my office and I was in contact with the world.

I attempted to identify people with whom I could work. Brendan O'Regan[44] and Paul Quigley were making exciting things happen in the Industrial Free Zone at Shannon, and Joe McHugh, who later went on to become an excellent City Manager in Cork, headed up a regional development organisation. With their assistance, we looked at six possible campus locations. I zeroed in on a dilapidated estate, magnificently perched on the Shannon at Plassey with enormous potential and, despite the fact that the local authorities would have preferred if I went closer to the cement factory in Limerick, I opted for the beautiful site. It lacked roads or infrastructure.

One of my great strengths in those early days was a lack of understanding of how the Irish public sector worked. In frustration, because I had not received approval to purchase the campus site within four weeks of making the recommendation to the Department of Education, I found myself calling the Secretary of the Department at home at 7.30 in the morning and demanding to know what in heaven's name was holding things up. This rather unorthodox approach to the Irish public service seemed to have an impact. Six weeks after my arrival in Ireland, we had approval from both the Department of Education and the Department of Finance for the purchase of the campus. There was to be a Planning Board to design the new initiative. It was to be composed of six members and I was to serve both as chairman and chief executive. I also had an opportunity to influence the choice of membership and, as a result, we were able to move with reasonable coherence and at lightning speed compared to the rest of the Irish academic community.

---

[44]   *In Good Company* (1987).

Without any approval from the Department of Education, I took the whole planning board on a whistle-stop tour of technological universities in Europe. After five days, we knew what we wanted to do – to create an institution of university-standing rather similar to that of the technological university in Eindhoven in the Netherlands. We took their advice – get going with a pilot group. We convinced the Department that we would admit 100 students with a small core of staff in September 1972 using the existing old manor house and stables.

I identified two people in the Department of Education who made all the difference. An Assistant Secretary, Sean O'Connor, who had worked with Donogh O'Malley, and Noel Lindsay, the head of the Building Unit. I told Sean O'Connor I needed a minute of his time each day. He agreed to a 30-minute meeting each month and there, in the heart of the Department, I conspired with a man who was impatient to bring about change and rock the boats of the traditional Irish universities. But we had no money. However, the World Bank was in Ireland considering investing in the proposed new comprehensive school system. Having run an international competition and produced plans for an 8,000-student campus that caused gasps of annoyance or pleasure, I interested the World Bank team in the concept. This led to the emergence of a strong partnership with a team led by the Dean of Engineering in Carnegie Mellon University. Once World Bank agreement to finance the new campus was obtained, I had the leverage I needed within the Department of Education. The Bank team were happy to threaten that, unless our wish-lists for laboratories and equipment were included in the plan, they would refuse to fund the project.

To the annoyance of key people in Dublin, I went outside the country to the largest firm in Europe, BDP in London, for the 20-year plan for the campus. A special partnership was created with an excellent young Irish architect, Patrick Whelan, who addressed the detailed implementation. As a result of this, in a very short time, we had plans for a world-class campus, funding through the World Bank for a complex of laboratories, and equipment that outranked by orders of magnitude anything available in the country, and a hand-picked core of students and faculty members driving the pilot phase forward. Jack Lynch, the Taoiseach, performed the opening ceremony in a tent

in September 1972 on the hard-core foundations for the new World
Bank buildings.

We lost no opportunity to declare what amazing things we were
doing and how superior these were to anything under way in the
established universities. We imported the North American module-
credit academic system, and the philosophy that was then building
some of the world's great universities. We went for faculty members
who could combine theory and practice and further infuriated those in
the existing universities by failing to short-list many of them because
they lacked practical experience. Meanwhile, Sean O'Connor was
happily starving the established universities of funds, in the belief that
they would be more responsive to the wishes of the State if they
realised there were other options. Limerick was the spearhead of his
strategy.

All of this collapsed around us when the Government changed. The
Cosgrave Fine Gael/Labour coalition had three distinguished
academics in the Cabinet. A Cabinet Committee, including Garret
FitzGerald, Conor Cruise-O'Brien and Justin Keating, recommended
that Limerick should not operate outside the established university
system and should become a Recognised College of the NUI. As a
result, UCC was given the statutory function of assessing our
programmes and recommending any changes to NUI. That was not a
good experience. It lasted for three years, before we managed to escape
from the clutches of the NUI and secure our own independent
legislation. We had been thrust upon the NUI by government decision.
It was like Coke being thrust upon Pepsi for assessment. We were very
seriously damaged. The NUI then consisted of UCD, UCC and UCG,
with Maynooth as a "Recognised College". When I learned that we
were to be made a Recognised College, I was not as disturbed as I
should have been – Maynooth seemed to be moving ahead without
major difficulties. We, on the other hand, had greatly antagonised
Galway and Cork. We lost no opportunity to point out their
deficiencies and the superiority of the new US modular-credit system
and the educational philosophy we were introducing. More frustrating
for Cork and Galway was the money being pumped into Limerick and
the world-class facilities being constructed and equipped. A
Recognised College serves a kind of apprenticeship to one of the
constituent colleges.

Our first students were to graduate in the summer of 1976. The teams from UCC were visiting us at the beginning of the year. A report prepared by UCC was leaked to the press. It horrified us: UCC had proclaimed our courses seriously deficient and in need of major modification before they would be considered acceptable.

We knew they were wrong. We were confident our programmes were what was required for the emerging new Ireland. The World Bank told us so, enterprise agreed and there was a procession of people from abroad admiring what we were doing. Ray Stata from Analog Devices came into my office. He told me he was looking at Europe as a location for a new manufacturing facility – in fact a design, manufacturing and marketing facility for silicon chip manufacture. Even though he had been advised against considering Ireland because of its lack of development, he was attracted by what he had heard of our initiative in Limerick. I told him, "If you are successful in locating in Ireland and we are associated with you, we too are going to be successful. We will do anything we can to help".

The second time he came, he brought two text books and, even though at that stage our first students were in the middle of their programme, we changed the content of two degree courses to meet his needs. A large number of our graduates were recruited by Analog Devices. The company turned out to be a huge success and astonished everyone, proving that they could design and manufacture high quality chips in Limerick as successfully as in Boston. Analog Devices are still prospering. Their arrival was the herald of things to come. Other hi-tech companies, the Intels, the Hewlett Packards and the IBMs were aware of their success in Ireland.

On the academic front, we had approaches from Columbia and Fordham Universities in New York. Volpe, Columbia's Dean of Business, flew in. He had heard that we were putting in place a US-type curriculum with which they could relate. He volunteered an exchange programme with his faculty and students.

So here we had Columbia University approaching us to consider linkages, we had a leading hi-tech corporation singing our praises, we had people from business organisations phoning us up to say that the NUI BComm was totally hopeless and that they understood something better was going to happen in Limerick. The World Bank told us that what was happening in Limerick was being used as a point of reference in other developing countries. We *knew* what we were doing was better than what was happening in the NUI. But I was naïve and innocent and unaware of the viciousness of academic politics – we confidently expected that what would emerge from the UCC exercise was an endorsement.

The press headlines came as a bolt out of the blue: "Deficiencies in Mathematics, Deficiencies in Languages", you name it. We had substandard degrees. Honours would not be awarded. If our students hoped to graduate with honours through the NUI, then they would have to take a remedial programme after completing their four-year course.

We were brought to our knees, absolutely humbled. We had no statutory standing, no means of defending ourselves and nowhere to go. In frustration, the students refused to fill out NUI Matriculation forms and instead marched in Dublin and burned the forms outside the NUI offices along with an effigy of the Minister for Education, Dick Burke. Fortunately, Ken Whitaker[45] was NUI Chancellor and he represented the fair and honourable face of NUI. There were several special meetings of the NUI Senate. Dick Burke chaired a meeting at NUI offices. Paul Quigley was Chairman of our Governing Body and provided fine leadership. Meanwhile, the students and their parents were in a state of turmoil. It was Easter and the students were due to graduate in June. We were over a barrel, but so was Burke whose attitude was remote and somewhat dictatorial. The Governing Body was not prepared to accept the terms offered by NUI and the students would not apply to NUI for Matriculation. We were, in fact, refusing to do what the Minister was directing.

He sent down his Assistant Secretary, Micheál Ó hÓdhráin, who sat in my office with a letter for the removal of the Governing Body if we continued to refuse to do what the Government directed.

We had a day-long meeting. We were surrounded by a student blockade. Even requests for water were denied, unless we agreed to reject the Government's decision and refuse to be a college of the NUI.

Late in the evening, we ended up in negotiations with the students. Governing Body strategy was to yield a little and outlast the Government. It wasn't going to help us at all if the Governing Body

---

[45]   **Chapter 18.**

was removed and we had somebody from the Department of Education directing our affairs. The students thought we were not very heroic.

After protracted negotiations with NUI, significant concessions were won and, at the very last moment, the students signed up for Matriculation and so Limerick's first degrees were awarded by the NUI.

The Government fell and the incoming Fianna Fáil Government approved our wish to break the link with the NUI. John Wilson was Minister for Education and, shortly afterwards, our departure from the NUI was announced and our freedom to innovate was restored. Legislation gave us, for the first time, the protection of a statutory base. Confidence and growth blossomed again. We were able again to pursue our vision. The National Council for Educational Awards awarded our degrees in the 1980s.

We needed to award our own degrees and have an unambiguous university title. There was another change of Government, with Garret FitzGerald as Taoiseach. Gemma Hussey was Minister for Education and asked me to chair the Curriculum & Examinations Board. I had a good relationship with her. We managed to convince the Government to bring in international assessors. The assessors recommended positively, but the Government fell, and I had to take the message into a Fianna Fáil Government. I made fine progress with the Minister for Education, Mary O'Rourke. Albert Reynolds, then Minister for Industry & Commerce, was giving a talk with us. His main message was that branding your product was of enormous importance. As I walked to the car-park with him, I said, "Albert, we have a dreadful brand. You are absolutely right. We need the 'university' word rather than this NIHE thing. We would like to have the legislation amended so that we can award our own degrees". He said he would mention it at Cabinet. With a lot of behind-the-scenes effort, we managed in 1989 to get legislation through for a University of Limerick. We were now an independent autonomous University with power to award our own degrees, unlike Cork and Galway, which remained as colleges of the NUI.

All sorts of doors started opening.

I had refused to fund-raise with the bad brand of NIHE, but focused on extracting as much money from the State as we could. The

World Bank pulled out of Ireland and then I approached the European Investment Bank. Noel Whelan, who I subsequently recruited as Vice-President of the University, was Vice-President of the Bank. I worked with him and we were the first university in Europe to receive EIB funding.

When the proposal first went to the Bank's Board, the Commissioner vetoed it saying that he knew of no university that was a stimulant to economic development. This was precisely our platform. We persisted and eventually got EIB approval. That took us on another trajectory. In the '80s, Japan was at its peak. I had heard of their investment in universities in North America and elsewhere. I went off to Japan, spoke of what we were doing and proposed a joint venture with Asahi. Yumakura was President of Asahi. They had a big plant in Killala in Mayo. They did their assessment. I was backwards and forwards to Tokyo. In Japan, it takes forever and a day to get decisions. Jim Cashman, who was the IDA representative in Tokyo, told me I must be careful not to rush the Japanese. That was not the way I did business – I had a crunch meeting with Yumakura on a Tuesday in Tokyo. I told him that I knew that in Japan, they took a long time to make decisions but that, in Europe, we did not: "I'm going to Kyoto and, by five o'clock on Friday, I want a decision from you, 'Yes' or 'No'". I got a "Yes"! I went up to Tokyo and he told me that they had decided on something that was different from what I had proposed. "We like what you're doing in Limerick, but we would prefer to build a new campus in Nobeoka. The plan is that the city of Nobeoka will provide you with a campus site. Asahi will build the campus and you, of course, will run it at a profit." I came back and there was great excitement. The Government and the IDA were delighted. The only other European university with a similar offer in Japan was Oxford. We did our due diligence and found that there were 17, mostly American, operations in Japan and they were struggling. If a student failed to get into any of the 500 Japanese universities, from the best to the worst, then you applied to one of these foreign places. We decided not to accept, despite considerable pressure from Ireland to do so. We then proposed a Masters Programme 50/50 Irish-Japanese. We believed this would attract potential leadership from the major Japanese corporations and we would get outstanding students. A modified version of that worked.

Noel Whelan, fresh from the European Investment Bank, headed up the Japanese initiative.

As soon as we got the university title, I went back to repeating what I had been doing in the 1970s, knocking on corporate doors in the US. With the generous support of a remarkable entrepreneur, Chuck Feeney, things started to happen. Money started to flow but, as important, I was able to put together a group of outstanding leaders of enterprise. I went to the States a week every month. This served to move the University of Limerick to a new plateau. We then had a group of some 20 US and Irish corporate leaders as members of a new Foundation. With Chuck Feeney as Chairman, we commenced major building work on campus, including a concert hall, library and student residences.

Ezra Cornell, the co-founder of Cornell University, said, "Undertake no small projects: they are so difficult to accomplish". That thought lay behind the idea of an 8,000-student campus, even though it was considered ridiculously ambitious in the early '70s. But then it was so significant that senior people in Government had either to reject it or endorse it. We had a magnificent model of the 8,000-student campus produced. The announcement was of such national significance that the Minister of the day, Richard Burke, agreed to unveil the plans in the heart of Dublin.

That guideline of 'undertaking no small projects' has proved useful: first of all in the university concept, then in planning for the National Technological Park, and, after I stepped down from Limerick, in proposing to Tánaiste Mary Harney that billions rather than millions should be allocated to Ireland's research effort.

On a rainy November's day, I was invited to lunch by Lord Ross in Birr, where the famous telescope needed repair. He wondered how he could raise £60,000. Over lunch, we made it into an £8m project in two phases! For the first phase, we got onto the Chairman of the OPW and convinced him this was a matter of world heritage. We asked him for some of his people to help develop the first £4m phase of restoration. Birr Castle complex would become an Irish science heritage centre. The OPW produced a magnificent plan, which took us into Albert Reynolds' office, Taoiseach at the time, for major public sector support, and subsequently, when John Bruton was Taoiseach, we secured support for a £250,000 telescope mirror. If the project had remained at

£60,000, you certainly would not be in the Taoiseach's office talking about it, nor having Tony O'Reilly's[46] agreement to chair the Birr Foundation and give the major lead gift. The £4m Phase 1 project was completed and I stepped down and handed over.

The Ezra Cornell dictum has proved itself over and over again. You go for scale. You go for quality. You associate with people who have a track record of achievement and a commitment to excellence.

---

[46]   **Chapter 12.**

18

KEN WHITAKER

*Experience has strengthened my belief in the power of
simple ideas such as that of St. Francis: it is in giving
we receive.*

KEN WHITAKER was born in Rostrevor, Co. Down, on December 8, 1916, the only son in a family of two.

His father was Edward Whitaker, a departmental manager in a textile factory. His mother was Jane O'Connor, a nurse.

He was educated at the Christian Brothers' School, Drogheda and later obtained an MSc(Econ) by private study from London University.

In 1941, he married Nora Fogarty, who was a civil servant. They had five sons and one daughter: Kenneth, Gerald, Raymond, David, Catherine and Brian. Nora, Gerald and Catherine have died.

He has held the following positions:

♦ Secretary, Department of Finance, 1956-1969.

♦ Governor, Central Bank of Ireland, 1969-1976.

♦ Chancellor of the National University of Ireland, 1976-1996.

♦ Senator, Irish Parliament, 1977-1982.

♦ Joint Chairman, Anglo-Irish Encounter.

♦ President, Royal Irish Academy, 1985-1987.

♦ Chairman of the Council of the Dublin Institute for Advanced Studies, 1980-1995.

♦ Chairman, National Industrial Economic Council, 1963-1971.

♦ President, Economic & Social Research Institute, 1974-1987.

♦ Chairman, Bord na Gaeilge, 1975-1978.

♦ Chairman, Agency for Personal Service Overseas, 1974-1978.

♦ Chairman, Committee of Inquiry into the Penal System, 1983-1985.

♦ Chairman, Constitution Review Group, 1995-1996.

♦ Chairman, Salmon Research Trust of Ireland, 1981-1994.

♦ Director, Bank of Ireland, 1976-1985.

♦ Director, Guinness plc, 1976-1984.

His honours include:

♦ DEconSc, National University of Ireland (1952).

♦ LLD, University of Dublin (1976) and Queen's University, Belfast (1980).

- DSc, New University of Ulster (1984).
- PhD, Dublin City University (1995).
- Life Fellow, Irish Management Institute.
- *Commandeur de la Légion d'Honneur* (1976).
- Fellow of the International Academy of Management.
- Freeman of Drogheda.

His publications include:
- *Financing by Credit Creation* (1946)
- *Interests* (1983)
- *Economic Development* (1958)(co-authored).

*I*n Ken Whitaker's biographical note, he omits mentioning that he was voted The Greatest Living Irishman of the Twentieth Century and that he was awarded the Millennium Gold Medal by the Irish Management Institute, the only medal of its kind (at least until the next Millennium).

He was born in the epochal year of 1916. He is older than the State he served peerlessly. It would be beyond trite to say he has witnessed many changes. It is not trite to say he was a promoter of several transformative changes, one of which was away from the irredentist claim of sovereignty over our six sundered counties to the belief that Irish unity would be attained only by the consent of a majority of the people of Northern Ireland.

His love for, and fluency in, the Irish language comes through. It is hard to believe now that Government policy, which he helped to change, was meant to replace English by Irish as our vernacular.

However, his more public accolade is primarily for our conversion from a stagnant protectionism to free trade and inward foreign investment, the sources of our present startling affluence.

When I invited Ken to participate in the first book in this series, he refused outright because he "associated the leadership concept with the Führerprinzip of the dictatorships which clouded so much of our adult experience". He never stands on his dignity and, to my delight, he eventually agreed.

He is a joy to work with. He twice meticulously edited the script, not to change the sense, but to correct my French and the Donegal Irish.

When the tape was turned off, we chatted about the length of his perspective and the fact that he could remember people who could remember the Famine. As I left his home on the Stilorgan carriageway on a sunny morning, and saw all the Mercedes whizzing by, and recalled the television pictures of present famines in Africa, it was hard to grasp that we were not that far away from famine ourselves.

The conversation was recorded in Ken Whitaker's home in Dublin 4, on November 29, 2004.

His biography is in *In Good Company* (1987).

KEN WHITAKER

I found myself in the Department of Finance in 1938 after doing some exams. I had never heard of economics until it was a subject for the Assistant Inspector of Taxes examination. I had already been working towards a BA degree in London University in Maths, Latin and Celtic but then switched to a BSc(Econ), followed later by an MSc. From the vantage point of the Department of Finance, I was observing the Irish economy. There were official inquiries in progress into emigration and other problems. We were greatly interested in what was happening in Britain towards the end of the war: the Beveridge Report was a comprehensive scheme of social insurance, covering the whole community without income limit. Published at the height of the war, it was a remarkable testimony to Britain's hopes for the future and has since formed the basis of much social legislation. There were discussions at the Statistical & Social Inquiry Society, in which the late Paddy Lynch[47] was also involved. We discussed the implications of Keynes for monetary and employment policy. The Chairman of the Emigration Commission, Jim Beddy, was a good friend of mine – we fished together on Lough Inagh. Unkind people suggested that the Emigration Commission itself had emigrated. The situation got worse in the 1950s: we had difficulty with the balance of payments and, in 1952, a harsh budget – "cruel, unjust and unnecessary" was Mr. Costello's description. There was a palpable degree of despondency as I described in the first chapter of *Economic Development*. Parents were asking themselves whether there was any future for their children. Politicians were puzzled as to how they could turn failure into success, how it was that we had lost our way. The old Sinn Féin ideals of self-sufficiency in food and the protection for new industries seemed to have failed. Political independence, won in 1922, seemed to have wasted away in our hands. We had not turned it into economic or social progress.

---

[47]   See **Chapter 8**.

I was appointed Secretary of the Department of Finance at an early age – 39. With my colleagues – people of a similar age, like Charlie Murray – we felt we owed something to the society that had brought us that far, one of the early cadres of well-educated young people in the public service. Most of us felt a duty to help bring us out of that Slough of Despond. In the autumn of 1957, I was urged on by a cartoon in *Dublin Opinion*. The picture was one of Ireland, a rather bedraggled but still handsome lady, consulting a fortune-teller, a crystal ball between them. Ireland was asking pathetically, "Have I a future?".

We had set up in Finance the Capital Investment Advisory Committee. I had written a paper for the Statistical & Social Inquiry Society, which emphasised the need for more productive capital investment to try to bring us into an economic upswing. It became clear to me that it wasn't just capital investment that needed to be reviewed but the whole of our economic policy, particularly the basic question whether we were to continue trying to raise ourselves by our own bootstraps or whether we were going to embrace free trade and welcome foreign investment. I saw the latter policy as the only way forward.

Mr. Lemass had been Minister for Supplies during the War and saw how little the protected industries could contribute. He had come to realise that protectionism was outmoded. In 1947, he sponsored legislation to introduce the stick alongside the carrot – to push industries towards efficiency by reducing their protection. That legislation was never passed because the Inter-Party Government came in in 1948. Nevertheless, it showed the slant of Mr. Lemass's mind.

We wrote in *Economic Development* in favour of the abandonment of protection and competitive participation in world trade. Lemass's mind was already tuned in to that change. I have often thought that nobody was better equipped to achieve it than Lemass, the arch-protectionist himself. He could dismantle protection more easily than anybody else. It was like de Gaulle and North Africa. The great patriot was the only one who could easily disengage from Algeria. No taint of defeatism could attach to him.

That was our main contribution then – that basic change, a complete reversal of Fianna Fáil policy.

Mr. de Valera, Dr. Jim Ryan and Mr. Lemass, expert politicians, saw they could reverse policy more easily by attributing the change to the advice of independent civil servants. The whole business got through without even a debate in the Dáil. The Opposition either missed their chance or were so delighted with it that they let it pass.

The problem then was how to dismantle tariffs without suffering unduly. At the time, there were free trade movements in Europe. Obviously, it would be to our advantage to join something which would give us some advantage in return for reducing our own tariffs. A general European free trade area was mooted but it did not have any agricultural support content – and we were looking for 25 years of a transition! That free trade area idea faded away.

The European Economic Community was founded in 1958 with six members. It would have been much more attractive for us to join that. We couldn't dare join it until Britain joined it too. By joining it without Britain, we would lose all our preferential access to the British market.

We looked at the alternative to the EEC, which was EFTA: the European Free Trade Area, comprising Britain, the Nordic countries and Portugal. Again, it had no agricultural content. Indeed, the watering-down of our industrial preferences for British goods might result in our losing the only agricultural support we had, which was through our live cattle participating in the British support scheme.

We went on to 1959 in a state of inanition – no welcoming free trade door was open. There was a real risk that the Department of Industry & Commerce would revert to protectionism. Towards the end of 1959, there was a forceful exchange of semi-official correspondence between the Secretaries of the four economic departments: Industry & Commerce, Agriculture, Foreign Affairs and Finance, all intended for the eyes of Lemass and other ministers. In Finance, we were trying to sustain the faith in free trade but Industry & Commerce seemed to be clouded in doubt.

In the course of that correspondence, I remember saying to J.C.B. McCarthy, then Secretary of the Department of Industry & Commerce that, like many Irish Catholics, he was in danger of becoming more Catholic than the Pope. The Federation of Irish Industry had already asserted in public their acceptance in principle of free trade.

It took a long time, from 1959 to 1973, before we actually entered the European Union.

General de Gaulle never regarded Britain as part of traditional Europe. He wrote a book after the War called *Mémoires de Guerre*. Con Cremin, Secretary of Foreign Affairs, and I bought the book to see what his views were. His *politique d'après guerre* was to *"amener à se grouper, aux points de vue politique, économique, stratégique, les Etats qui touchent au Rhin, aux Alpes et aux Pyrénées"*. Anybody with any sense of geography knew that did not include Britain or Ireland. His objective was to form *"une troisième puissance planétaire"*, which might one day be the arbiter *"entre les deux camps soviétique et anglo-saxon."* We were obviously outside the range of his *"vaste plan"*. In 1963, he vetoed Britain's entry application and we had to go to the sidelines too.

Meanwhile, we decided we had to do something to dismantle protection and promote industrial efficiency. We decided to have a free trade area with Britain, to lower progressively our tariffs against them. That was a good discipline, and, at the same time, various teams were working with Irish industries to see what they needed to do to modernise, what grants might be given to help – Charlie Murray and Louden Ryan[48] were involved in that process. Up to 60% of our exports were going to the UK at that time.

It was at the end of 1965 that the UK Free Trade Area Agreement was signed. We were still looking longingly towards the European continent. In 1970, that door was opened and there began a year or two of negotiations. Then we had the Referendum in 1973, which overwhelmingly sanctioned our entry to the Community. It was not only wealthy but had an agricultural support system.

Negotiations always had their lighter side. I remember the late Denis Maher, who was a great admirer of O'Casey, coming in from some session that was, to say the least, unfruitful. He and his colleagues were sitting around glumly, waiting for a drink, and Denis looked at them and said, "Yous are all rightly Shanghaied now". Denis had a prominent role in our negotiations for accession to the EEC and wrote the authoritative account, *The Tortuous Path*.

One of my stories from that time relates to de Gaulle. I was going around the various EEC capitals in 1967, in attendance on Jack Lynch as Taoiseach and Charles Haughey as Minister for Finance, after the British had reactivated their application for membership of the EEC.

---

[48]   *In Good Company* (1987).

The British application was meeting with frostiness from de Gaulle. We were still trying to achieve membership. We put the Elysée last on our list. De Gaulle had Jack in for a tête-à-tête before lunch, in which he explained how Britain's application to be a member of the European Economic Community posed serious problems. He thought that, in the circumstances, Ireland should seek merely association, not membership. Jack came out, crestfallen, before lunch, and told us that de Gaulle thought association was good enough for us. During the lunch, I was sitting beside Pompidou, who was Prime Minister at the time, trying to explain to him in French the difference between the rules of rugby and Gaelic football. Charles Haughey was on the left side of de Gaulle. As well as arguing our case, he was trying to be bright and cheerful and improve the shining hour. He referred to the difficulty of ruling a country that had 300 varieties of cheese. De Gaulle turned majestically to correct him: *"Trois cents quatre-vingts dix!"*. That finished the conversation. After lunch, word came to us unexpectedly that the President wanted to see each member of our little delegation separately. This was something we had never experienced before. I was first to be called and, realising the situation was desperate, I decided I had better speak in French, rather than use an interpreter. De Gaulle received me very graciously and took me down carefully though the list of difficulties he had about Britain joining the Common Market. He told me why he thought Ireland should seek associate membership and then more or less said, "Over to you!". I drew a deep breath and said, in French, in my best accent, that the Irish had for centuries been trying to – I really meant to say detach ourselves from Britain, but I could not think of the simple word *détacher*. So I said, *"Depuis des centaines d'années, nous essayons nous arracher à l'Angleterre"*. *"Bon! Bon!"*, said de Gaulle. This strong phrase, "tearing ourselves away" from England had favourably impressed him. After that, I was on the pig's back. He listened very carefully to all I said about our economic development needs. I shall always remember this happy mistake, this *felix culpa*.

That's the story of protection being eventually replaced by free trade. The policy change was promoted by Finance and was argued strongly – but there were doubters elsewhere whose stance persisted till the end. We did not get much support from other Departments. There were setbacks but you just have to sharpen your sword. I hope some semi-official correspondence at that time will be published, because it shows civil service argumentation at its best: forceful, cogent and clear. In all that time, I never sensed any kind of despair, because I felt that Lemass was always with me. When other Deparments were against us and Lemass was Taoiseach, I got his support. He realised that we had the better part of the argument. It was a remarkable turn-around from *The Control of Manufactures Act (1933)* to an amending Act called *Encouragement of External Investment Act (1958).* That change of titles indicated a fundamental change of attitude and policy. Now, with inward investment, people are employed here who might have had to work for the same enterprises abroad. It was all given impetus by the EEC. That was the ideal context in which to rid ourselves of protectionism. That was where we'd get the most value for dismantling our tariffs completely over a period. An immediate advantage was agricultural support on a wide scale. We were also an attractive base for Americans, Japanese and others seeking access to the Community for their products.

One result of all this, which I believe is underrated, was the change in national psychology, the move from despondency to confidence. It was very powerful in raising the rate of progress – the annual increment of national produce – from under 1% to 4% a year. There was an environment of buoyancy in world trade and also a widespread uplift of spirit. It was the Kennedy era. It was quite remarkable that, in Ireland, the ending of despair and the growth of optimism originated in that most unlikely source, the Department of Finance, whose reputation was the opposite of Micawberism, always waiting for something to turn down! From then on, nobody was heard arguing for a return to the old protectionism.

No matter how well you do, there are always begrudgers and revisionists. The latest revision is that our economic progress has been a cancer in the system, evident in such malignancies as alcohol and drug abuse, moral laxity, etc., etc. Everyone has his or her own ideals – from de Valera's Ireland of a people satisfied with frugal comfort and devoting their leisure to things of the spirit, an Ireland of athletic youths and the laughter of comely maidens, to one of being in the van of "progress" in every way. There is always an opportunity for criticism.

While I'm not happy about some developments, I am happy that most people are so much better off. I noticed one sign of that recently, when looking through statistics on housing. Even up to 1960, *most* of the dwellings in Ireland did not have running water. Now they all have. What that has meant for hygiene and health must be very significant. In my lifetime, the lifespan of men has been extended by 15 years and of women by a few years longer. That's a wonderful change. I remember as a boy staying in my grandmother's house in County Clare, a typical, thatched farmhouse, long, pink-dashed walls with eglantine growing on them, but without running water. When the oil lamp was lit in the evening, the *Grace for Light* was said: "The light of Heaven to our souls", I remember in Drogheda the loud hiss the gas mantle made and the welcome silence that descended when electricity came.

There were two other memorable chapters in my public service story. Let's take first, the Irish language. My interest was aroused by a wonderful lay teacher in the Christian Brothers' school in Drogheda, Peadar McCann. He taught Irish in the secondary school. He was a little man, dark, rather like his own description of Robespierre, eyes well set back in his head. He taught not only Irish, but also history. He could teach anything he turned his mind to. He was from Newry and had learned Irish first in Omeath, therefore it was East Ulster – Oriel – Irish. For example, the word *ann* (there), was pronounced "oun" in Munster, "on" in Connaught, "un" in Ulster, but for him it was "ann", as in a woman's name. Irish was ebbing out of Omeath in the 1920s. Father Larry Murray moved his college from Omeath to Rannafast in Donegal. From Munster Irish, which the Christian Brothers usually taught, we were brought into contact with Ulster Irish. In 1931, at the age of 15, I got a scholarship to Rannafast and was enchanted by the place. I met there not only Father Murray but Paddy Weldon (Pádraig Ó hUallacháin), father of the well-known singer, Pádraigín. I remember the thrill, having acquired some fluency in Irish, of being in Omeath in 1933 at the open-air Stations of the Cross, a great occasion on August 15. I was listening to a band of women who had come down from the hills and were speaking Irish and I was able to join in with my smattering of Donegal Irish. As I sat in 1931 on the wooden seat of the little train from Letterkenny to Crolly, when we came to a place called Tobar an Dúin, a crowd of shawled women came in, a lovely waft of turf smoke from them. They were all speaking Irish, the first time I had ever heard Irish being spoken naturally. I listened carefully. We were passing a big mountain (Muckish) and I thought I'd put in my spoke. I said in my best schoolboy Irish, "Cé'n t-ainm atá ar an sliabh sin, le do thoil?". The lady said to her neighbour, "Goidé tá sé a'ráit?". "Ó, c'ainm atá ar an chnoc adaigh", explained her companion. Then I realised for the first time the difference between Irish as it is spoken, *caint na ndaoine*, and school Irish. But I still treasure the memory of speaking with that little last group of native speakers in the area which runs from County Louth into Armagh, a place from which many poets came.

I really fell in love with the language. I went back to Rannafast many times in the 1930s. Later, when I had three children old enough to be brought to Rannafast, I brought them there for a month. Two of them had been in Ring for a year and had acquired Ring Irish at an early age. On a Sunday, I had them at the pier in Bunbeg. At that time, Gola Island was inhabited and the islanders would come in by boat for Mass and shopping on a Sunday. An elderly woman had got a bit tired and had come back to the boat and was sitting at the stern while my children were playing with the ropes. I would say something to them occasionally in Irish and the older two were talking Irish among themselves. The old woman said, "Tá Gaeilge mhaith ag na tachráin seo ach chan í Gaeilge na háite seo í". The fluency in Irish acquired had stood to me in various civil service exams. Nowadays, it has helped me build a bridge between Donegal Irish and Irish in North Mayo, where I have a converted schoolhouse. There is still some Gaeltacht in Mayo – people of my own age, mostly. Their Irish was influenced by the Cromwellian settlements. Cromwell pushed a lot of people from Tyrone and Fermanagh westwards. That left its mark on the dialect. There are a lot of McNultys (Mac an Ultaigh).

Back to the Department of Finance. There was a Commission in the '60s on the revival of the Irish language. Father Tom Fee (later Cardinal Ó Fiaich) was the chairman. Their report was about to be published and to go to the Government. No Department was saying anything about it. I said, "Damn it all, it's propounding something that is not really sensible. I'll have to get going on this". So I wrote a memorandum, which went to the Government, outlining the limitations of the report. I was contesting the validity of the thesis that

Irish expressed the heart and soul of the Irish community and should be restored to its one-time supremacy. I then wrote another piece on bilingualism. (Both are reproduced in my book *Interests* (IPA 1983). The result was that, when the Government decided to write a White Paper to respond to the report, the drafting was entrusted to the Department of Finance – of all places! Not Education, not Roinn na Gaeltachta. With Séamus Ó Ciosáin, I drafted the White Paper. We knew that, when we had drafted anything, it went off to the Park. Dev was looking at things quietly in the background. None of his ministers trusted themselves sufficiently to have as much respect for Irish as he had. Of course, we were not told that, but we guessed it. The White Paper came down against any notion of ousting English and in favour of embracing bilingualism, not of necessity, but out of love and respect for the language and all that was embodied in it of our heritage. I was happy about that. I had a face-to-face with Father Tom who accepted that there was such a point of view. We were always good friends.

The third and quite different strand of my public service relates to the North and the principle of consent. It's good that the 30 years rule has liberated a lot of documents from that time. On August 15, 1969, Jack Lynch spoke to me on the phone when I was down in Carna. That was a critical time. There had been many outbreaks of violence and we had moved ambulances and so on to the Border. It looked as if we might be preparing to invade Northern Ireland for the protection of the Catholic population. I counselled very strongly against such a move. Jack Lynch asked me for names of some people he could speak to in Northern Ireland. From then on, I was very close to him and tried to bring Fianna Fáil policy away from the old idea of jurisdiction over Northern Ireland, claimed in Article 2 of the Constitution, towards accepting the need for the consent of the majority in Northern Ireland for any peaceful long-term settlement.

It was not easy to wean Fianna Fáil away from belief in our right to take over Northern Ireland. It just would not work in the circumstances of today. I wanted them to accept something much more fundamental, that the people in Northern Ireland had a right to decide in what circumstances they would join the rest of Ireland. The phrases in the Constitution were that Ireland consisted of the island of Ireland and "pending the reintegration of the national territory ...". That implied that Northern Ireland could be taken over by force. There were ministers who believed that that would be justifiable – perhaps not practical, but justifiable in principle. I drafted for Jack Lynch a speech, which became known as "the Tralee Speech", which outlined the principle of consent. I also wrote a memorandum on policy regarding Northern Ireland. There were ministers who did not accept consent as a principle, people like Charles Haughey and, to my surprise, Michael O'Kennedy. And of course Blaney and Boland, who also came to the fore in the 1969 Arms Trial period.

To have played a part, as a behind-the-scenes adviser, in steering that change in fundamental policy on Northern Ireland was a great satisfaction to me. Experience has strengthened my belief in the power of simple ideas such as that of St. Francis: it is in giving we receive.

Envoi: A Lesson Learned?

A Lesson Learned might be a presumptuous title for the concluding note to the five books in the series, even with the question mark as a qualification. There is a line in T.S. Eliot's play, *Murder in the Cathedral*, "Men learn little from others' experience". My working life has been spent with practising managers. They learn little from what they are told, a lot from what they do. The work of the Irish Management Institute is based on "experiential" learning. New knowledge can remain at the somewhat useless level of "interesting" until it is hooked on to and expands or questions what is already inside our heads. They say a test of a good paper is that you should be able to explain it to a New York cab driver between Kennedy and Manhattan, so that he not only understands it, but adds to it.

My day job with companies working on their strategies ends up with two reports:

- The first is diagnosis – what are the barriers?
- The second is the cure – what should be done?

Both the diagnosis and the cure are guided by me but they are written by the managers who carry the can, not by a finger-wagging professor who departs in a cloud of exhaust smoke.

This next sentence might read: "I am, however, optimistic", a phrase beloved of politicians anxious to please, which undoes all their preceding portents. But if you, dear reader, get even one new idea, or if you are led to question a long-held assumption, or even if you get mad and disagree violently, then our journey will not be in vain.

What are leaders?

Leaders are people who have followers. That's it. Without followers, there are no leaders. I have met a few chief executives who spend time talking to themselves. They are tolerated by the organisation. It somehow gets along under its own steam.

Are leaders born or made?

This question is remarkably enduring. Leaders are not born full-blown. Neither are they made like instant coffee. They are slow-brewed in the circumstances of the time. I had one of my own assumptions questioned by Denis Brosnan and Dermot Desmond, when they said in this book that skills are transportable from one business to a different one. I strongly believed that too, until I saw leaders skilled in a particular area come a cropper in another. It depends on the individual. You can't generalise.

Where do leaders come from?

There was an answer in the first book, *In Good Company* (1987). The 15 participants were not a statistical sample, but a common thread was strengthened in the four books that followed, with over 80 participants: They all had loving parents. When they talked at length about their fathers and mothers, they did so with great affection.

How important was their formal education?

Some described themselves as mediocre at school; some rebelled like Tom Roche and Brody Sweeney; some were brilliant, like Michael MacCormac, Jimmy Sheehan, Ken Whitaker, Louden Ryan, getting first at everything. Gay Byrne in *In Good Company* said he had lost any resentment at not going to university because he had "come across so many people with university degrees who were as thick as two planks".

Silver spoon?

Having wealthy parents was by no means a route to subsequent success. Neither was having poor ones. Homes ranged, even in the present affluent era, from wealthy to frugal. Louden Ryan said: "We must have been poor", and adds that, as a child, he could have been suffering from all kinds of afflictions but had no words to describe them, not having studied sociology.

Luck?

Anatole France wrote: "Chance is perhaps the pseudonym of God when He does not want to sign His work". Bishop Casey said in *In Good Company*: "If something crosses your path, it does not do so by accident". The late Niall Crowley summed it up: "I've had a lot of luck. Looking at it another way, I suppose I've always kept a weather eye open for opportunities coming my way". While they all had unremitting focus, they also had very good peripheral vision.

Intelligence?

Yes, they were intelligent. Some were brilliantly intelligent, some not obtrusively so. However, IQ isn't everything. A brilliant academic record cannot ensure success in life or in management. People with a high IQ don't necessarily make good decisions. They often fall into the intelligence trap, skilfully justifying their wrong decisions. They are so talented at arguing with and criticising others that they focus on that rather than arriving at constructive solutions. The men and women in the books were streetwise and aware – aware of their own emotions and of how to manage them.

Tony O'Reilly said in *In Good Company*: "I occasionally flap internally, but I make every effort to conceal it. Sometimes, anger and irritation will show but I have analysed my irritation as a management instrument and found that I am less effective when I am angry and irritated. I am not as eloquent, not as thoughtful, and I'm often wrong".

Were there similarities?

Yes, but, first, as I wrote in *Leaders*, there were different personalities. Some were gregarious, enjoying people and parties, others were solitary, preferring the sanctuary of their families. Some were nice guys, others were affectionately known as right bastards. Some were impulsive and moved too quickly, others took ages to decide. Some were warm and welcoming, others were distant and aloof. Some were vain and sought publicity. For others, publicity was pointless:

Tom Roche would not go to the AGM. Some were austere – a decent suit and a modest car – others were inclined to ostentation. Some liked applause, others would be embarrassed by and suspicious of it. Some were introvert and, having listened to advice, would work things out inside their heads; others were extrovert, thinking out loud and changing their minds as the discussion progressed. The one thing several of them did *not* have was charisma.

I have come to the conclusion that charisma does not matter a damn. If you have it, it can be helpful for getting attention but it can also be overpowering, inhibiting genuine communication.

Back to the question. Here is the similarity: almost 20 years ago, on December 11, 1986, Brendan O'Regan, who created at Shannon the first duty-free airport in the world, said for *In Good Company*: "If you're involved in developing an important idea, you have to let it possess you. If you keep knocking on the door, the door will open. You'll get there, not particularly with your own ability, but with others that you gather around you".

Focus, absolute but shared focus, is where we began and where we end. That, I hope, is the lesson.

Appendix

Participants in previous books/articles:[49]

Baker, Keith	BBC Northern Ireland	*Talking to Ourselves*	1994
Barrington, Tom+	Institute of Public Administration	*In Good Company*	1987
Barry, Tony*	CRH	*Management Journal*	1990
Bowler, Gillian	Budget Travel	*Out on Their Own*	1991
Brady, Conor	The Irish Times	*Talking to Ourselves*	1994
Brophy, Michael	The Star	*Talking to Ourselves*	1994
Brosnan, Denis*	Kerry Group	*In Good Company*	1987
Browne, Vincent	The Sunday Tribune	*Talking to Ourselves*	1994
Burrows, Richard	Pernod Ricard	*Leaders*	2001
Byrne, Gay	RTÉ	*In Good Company*	1987
Carroll, Don+	Carroll Industries	*In Good Company*	1987
Casey, Eamonn	Bishop	*In Good Company*	1987

---

49   * In this book also; + Died since the conversation took place.

Cluskey, Frank+	TD	*Management Journal*	1977
Collins, Tom	The Irish News	*Talking to Ourselves*	1994
Crowley, Laurence	SKC	*Management Journal*	1990
Crowley, Niall+	AIB	*In Good Company*	1987
Cullen, Bill	Renault	*Leaders*	2001
Cunningham, John	Connacht Tribune	*Talking to Ourselves*	1994
Curran, Edmund	Belfast Telegraph	*Talking to Ourselves*	1994
Dand, David+	Gilbeys	*Management Journal*	1990
Dargan, Michael+	CRH	*In Good Company*	1987
Darragh, Austin	Institute of Clinical Pharmacology	*Out on Their Own*	1991
Dempsey, Gerry	Aer Lingus	*Out on Their Own*	1991
Desmond, Dermot*	National City Brokers	*Out on Their Own*	1991
Doyle, Vinnie	Irish Independent	*Talking to Ourselves*	1994
Fanning, Aengus	Sunday Independent	*Talking to Ourselves*	1994
FitzGerald, Mark	Sherry FitzGerald	*Leaders*	2001
Fitzpatrick, Sean*	Anglo Irish Bank	*Leaders*	2001
Freaney, Oliver+	Oliver Freaney & Company	*Out on Their Own*	1991

Gageby, Douglas+	The Irish Times	*In Good Company*	1987
Galvin, Paddy	Waterford Glass	*Management Journal*	1991
Geaney, Donal	Elan	*Leaders*	2001
Hastings, Billy	Hastings Hotels	*Out on Their Own*	1991
Haughey, Eddie*	Norbrook	*Out on Their Own*	1991
Healy, Liam	Independent News & Media	*Management Journal*	1993
Hely-Hutchinson, Mark	Bank of Ireland	*Management Journal*	1990
Horn, Chris*	IONA Technologies	*Leaders*	2001
Jordan, Eddie	Jordan Grand Prix	*Leaders*	2001
Kavanagh, Mark	Hardwicke	*Out on Their Own*	1991
Keane, Michael	The Sunday Press	*Talking to Ourselves*	1994
Kenny, Stewart	Paddy Power	*Leaders*	2001
Kiberd, Damien	The Sunday Business Post	*Talking to Ourselves*	1994
Killeen, Michael+	IDA	*Management Journal*	1981
Kingston, David	Irish Life	*Management Journal*	1990
Lambert, Hugh	Irish Press	*Talking to Ourselves*	1994
Looney, Brian	The Kerryman	*Talking to Ourselves*	1994
Lorimer, Sir Desmond	Lamont Holdings	*Out on Their Own*	1991

Martin, Geoff	The News Letter	*Talking to Ourselves*	1994
McClelland, Colin	Sunday World	*Talking to Ourselves*	1994
McCourt, Kevin+	IDL	Management Journal	1978
McGrath, Paddy+	Waterford Glass	*In Good Company*	1987
McGuckian, Alastair	Masstock	*Out on Their Own*	1991
McGuinness, Gerry	The Sunday World	*Out on Their Own*	1991
McNamara, Bernard	Michael McNamara & Company	*Leaders*	2001
Melia, Kevin	MSL	*Leaders*	2001
Moffett, Carol	Moffett Engineering	*Out on Their Own*	1991
Moran, Joe	IWP	*Out on Their Own*	1991
Mulholland, Joe	RTÉ	*Talking to Ourselves*	1994
Murphy, Michael	Farmer	*Leaders*	2001
Naughton, Martin	Glen Dimplex	*Leaders*	2001
O'Brien, Denis	Communicorp	*Leaders*	2001
O'Callaghan, Fergus	The Cork Examiner	*Talking to Ourselves*	1994
O'Connell, Emmett	Eglinton Exploration	*Out on Their Own*	1991
O'Regan, Brendan	SFADCO	*In Good Company*	1987

O'Reilly, Frank	Ulster Bank	*In Good Company*	1987
O'Reilly, Tony*	Heinz	*In Good Company*	1987
Quinn, Feargal	Superquinn	*Out on Their Own*	1991
Rafferty, Martin	Serial entrepreneur	*Out on Their Own*	1991
Read, Geoff	Ballygowan	*Out on Their Own*	1991
Roche, Tom+*	CRH	*Out on Their Own*	1991
Rooney, Fran	Baltimore	*Leaders*	2001
Ryan, Louden	Bank of Ireland	*In Good Company*	1987
Sheehan, James*	Blackrock Clinic	*Leaders*	2001
Smurfit, Michael*	Jefferson Smurfit Group	*In Good Company*	1987
Sutherland, Peter	European Commission	*Leaders*	2001
Teeling, John	Cooley Distillery	*Out on Their Own*	1991
Walsh, Kieran	The Munster Express	*Talking to Ourselves*	1994
Went, David	Irish Life & Permanent	*Leaders*	2001
Whitaker, Ken*	Chancellor, NUI	*In Good Company*	1987

INDEX

Other books by Ivor Kenny from

FREEDOM & ORDER
Studies in Strategic Leadership
€25 hb : ISBN 1-86076-120-8

> For the past 15 years, Ivor Kenny, Ireland's foremost management
> thinker, has worked closely with some of the top Irish companies
> to help them see clearly the issues they face. This work has
> produced a unique set of insights: how these organisations work,
> what makes them successful, what the stumbling blocks are, and
> where they are headed.

LEADERS
Conversations with Irish Chief Executives
€30 hb : ISBN 1-86076-221-2

> Personal interviews with top Irish CEOs: Richard Burrows, Irish
> Distillers; Bill Cullen, Renault Distributors; Mark FitzGerald,
> Sherry FitzGerald; Sean Fitzpatrick, Anglo Irish Bank; Donal
> Geaney, Elan; Chris Horn, Iona Technologies; Eddie Jordan,
> Jordan Grand Prix; Stewart Kenny, Paddy Power; Kevin Melia,
> MSL; Bernard McNamara, Michael McNamara & Co – Builders;
> Michael Murphy, Dairy Farmer; Martin Naughton, Glen Dimplex;
> Denis O'Brien, ex-Esat; Fran Rooney, ex-Baltimore Technologies;
> Peter Sutherland, Goldman Sachs; David Went, Irish Life &
> Permanent.

CAN YOU MANAGE?
€15 pb : ISBN 1-86076-266-2

> **Can You Manage?** is the latest book by Ireland's leading
> management thinker, Dr Ivor Kenny. It provides fresh ideas and
> inspiration for Irish businesspeople. This is a short book of short
> chapters, written for today's busy practising managers. In this
> book, Dr Kenny has distilled all the lessons learned from his
> experience of over 40 years dealing with Irish and international
> managers.

OAK TREE PRESS
is Ireland's leading business book publisher.

It develops and delivers
information, advice and resources
to entrepreneurs and managers –
and those who educate and support them.

Its print, software and web materials
are in use in Ireland, the UK, Finland,
Greece, Norway and Slovenia.

OAK TREE PRESS
19 Rutland Street
Cork, Ireland
T: + 353 21 4313855
F: + 353 21 4313496
E: info@oaktreepress.com
W: www.oaktreepress.com